The Middlesex Hospital Medical School
Centenary to Sesquicentenary
1935–1985

The Middlesex Hospital Medical School

Centenary to Sesquicentenary 1935–1985

Sir Douglas Ranger MB BS, FRCS

Hutchinson Benham

London Melbourne Sydney Auckland Johannesburg

Dedicated to the Founders of
The Middlesex Hospital Medical School
and to all those who have contributed
to its growth and achievements
over the course of its 150 years

M 8610

3/10/85

Hutchinson Benham Ltd
An imprint of the Hutchinson Publishing Group
17–21 Conway Street, London W1P 6JD
Hutchinson Publishing Group (Australia) Pty Ltd
16–22 Church Street, Hawthorn, Melbourne, Victoria 3122
Hutchinson Group (NZ) Ltd
32–34 View Road, PO Box 40–086, Glenfield, Auckland 10
Hutchinson Group (SA) Pty Ltd
PO Box 337, Bergvlei 2012, South Africa
First published 1985
© Sir Douglas Ranger MB BS FRCS 1985
Set in Linotron Ehrhardt
by Input Typesetting Ltd, London
Printed and bound in Great Britain by Anchor Brendon Ltd,
Tiptree, Essex
British Library Cataloguing in Publication Data

Ranger, Sir Douglas
 The Middlesex Hospital Medical School:
 centenary to sesquicentenary 1935–1985.
 1. Middlesex Hospital Medical School—History
 I. Title   II. Middlesex Hospital, *Medical School*
 610'.7'1142132   R773.M5

ISBN 0 09 160900 3

Contents

Foreword

As with other sciences, there has been a tremendous acceleration in the advance of medicine in the last fifty years and The Middlesex has been in the forefront of this advance. Those years have also seen the trauma of the Second World War and many organisational changes for both the Hospital and the Medical School. The suggestion that one way of marking the sesquicentenary of the School should be to publish a history of the last fifty years as a sequel to Dr Campbell Thomson's history of the first hundred years was therefore quickly adopted and it did not take long to decide that Sir Douglas Ranger should be asked to write it.

Sir Douglas has spent most of the last fifty years at the Middlesex, ending with nine years as Dean, and has been in the thick of the organisational changes as well as making his contribution to the advance of Otolaryngology. In his Preface he thanks those whose memory and interpretation of events have helped him compile the history but a great deal of it comes from his own recollection and from his participation in the events he records.

He does not sufficiently record his own contribution to the direction of change. In 1971 he was the author of what is commonly known as the Ranger Report which recommended the directions in which the Hospital should develop and the specialties which should be emphasised. He was a member of the London Working Group established by the Minister of State for Health in 1970 to recommend how the particular problems of London should be dealt with in the proposed reorganisation of the Health Service. When funds became short following that reorganisation in 1974 he was a member of the Bed Allocation Working Party which determined again where the priorities should lie in The Middlesex. It was next the turn of the University to face cuts and Sir Douglas chaired from 1978–83 the Planning and Resources Committee of the School referred to on p. 164. More important, he was closely involved in all the discussions in the University consequent on the setting up and the report of the Flowers Working Party on Medical and Dental Teaching Resources in the University of London. He was a member of the Joint Medical Advisory Committee and of the Joint Planning Committee of the Court and Senate of the University during the extensive discussions which led to the restructuring of medical education in London with the formation of a joint medical school between The Middlesex, University College and the Institutes of Laryngology and Otology, Orthopaedics and Urology.

Because the events which he records are so recent and because he was himself so closely involved, Sir Douglas rightly makes little attempt to pass judgment on the last fifty years but, when sufficient time has passed for dispassionate judgment to be made, there can be little doubt that Sir Douglas's own influence on events will be seen to have been considerable.

As a lay member of the Medical School Council and of the Board of Governors and its successor Health Authorities, I have been privileged for nearly half the period covered by this book to observe the dedication, the care, the medical and scientific skill, the hard work and, above all, the friendliness and mutual cooperation with which the surgeons, the physicians, the scientists, the teachers – and indeed all the staff of The Middlesex – go about their business, and none more so than Sir Douglas. He rightly lays emphasis in this book on the spirit of friendliness and cooperation which unifies The Middlesex Hospital and its Medical School and which has contributed as much as has the brilliance of the individuals who work there to the great advances in Medicine which they have made. Let us hope that, when the history of the next fifty years comes to be written, that spirit and unity will be seen to have been carried forward into the new single school with University College and the Postgraduate Institutes and its association with the Bloomsbury Health Authority.

David Money-Coutts

Preface

Teaching began in the wards of The Middlesex Hospital shortly after its foundation in 1745 but it was to be another ninety years before a distinct medical school was formally established. In *The Story of The Middlesex Hospital Medical School 1835–1935* Dr H. Campbell Thomson described the decision to form a medical school which was taken by the General Quarterly Court of Governors of the Hospital on 7 May 1835 in response to a submission which had been made the previous month to the Weekly Board by six 'medical officers' of the Hospital: Francis Hawkins, Thomas Watson, Charles Bell, Herbert Mayo, James Arnott and Edward Tuson – the Founders of the Medical School. Campbell Thomson then went on to describe the rapid construction of the School buildings, with the roofing ceremony taking place on 22 July and the formal opening on 1 October the same year, at the start of the session in which thirty-four students were admitted. The book dealt with the developments which took place in the School up to its centenary in 1935 – the year which also saw the formal opening of the rebuilt Hospital on 29 May by the Duke and Duchess of York, who were to become at the end of the following year King George VI and Queen Elizabeth.

Much has happened in the School since then and in preparation for the Sesquicentennial Celebrations in 1985 Council decided that there should be an account of the School during the years 1935 to 1985. It is a great responsibility and honour to have been entrusted with the production of a book to cover the third fifty years of the School's history and I can only hope that, in part at least, it does some justice to the great developments which have taken place during the period and which I have been able to observe in one capacity or another, except for a few years in the Royal Army Medical Corps, since entering the School as a student in 1936.

This book attempts to provide a short history of the Medical School over the course of the last fifty years. The Middlesex Hospital and School are so intimately linked that it would be impossible to deal with one without the other. It is important, however, to keep in mind the primary purpose of the book in order to accept some of the emphasis of the material included in this volume. In 1995 the Hospital will be celebrating its first 250 years and its history will then be brought up to date.

A judgement has had to be made on topics which might prove of greatest general interest, bearing in mind the very wide age range of potential readers and also the extent of their knowledge of The Middlesex. Without drastic rejection of a vast quantity of interesting material, no book short of a multi-volume, multi-author encyclopaedia would have been possible at all. While I have sought the advice of as many people as possible in the time available, I accept full personal responsibility for the choice of content and the manner of its presentation.

At the time of writing, there are 272 members of the academic staff working in the School, 360 medical laboratory and scientific officer staff, ninety administrative and clerical staff and twenty-five ancillary staff. Many more have worked in the School at some time since 1935. They are all important but clearly only a very small number of them can be mentioned individually. The staff of the Hospital is very much larger. I apologise unreservedly to all those who have contributed to the achievements of the School and the Hospital but have been accorded no mention or only a very inadequate one.

A large number of people have not read the book by Dr Campbell Thomson which is now out of print. Accordingly, reference is made in this volume to some items prior to 1935. These serve as a background to many of the developments which have taken place since then and set them in better perspective.

Needless to say, it would have been quite impossible for me to have produced this book without the willing help and advice of a large number of people. Professor Cyril Keele, Emeritus Professor of Pharmacology and Therapeutics, has assisted me assiduously throughout in everything connected with writing the book and has been a constant source of knowledge and wise advice. Without his help the book could not have been produced in its present form. Mr Ralph Winterton, Emeritus Consultant and Archivist of The Middlesex Hospital, has not only made his extensive archives available to me but has provided much additional information from his own wide knowledge of events. My two predecessors in the office of Dean, Professor Sir Brian Windeyer and Professor Eldred Walls, have given me invaluable guidance and encouragement and have contributed greatly to my understanding of recorded events. The Chairman of the School, Mr David Money-Coutts, and the Dean, Mr William Slack, have been a constant source of encouragement and help. I am deeply indebted to Miss Eileen Walton, Secretary of the School from 1949 to 1965, who assisted Dr Campbell Thomson in the preparation of his book fifty years ago and has now assisted me with this one. Mr Peter Wood, Assistant Secretary to the School from 1968 to 1983, had a major responsibility for buildings while in office and has given me invaluable help on that aspect and also on many others. Councillor Miss Jean Crawford, Committee Secretary to the Board of Governors of the Hospital, allowed me access to her personal notes and provided also further valuable information in discussion. The Librarian, Mrs Janet Cropper, and the Assistant Librarian, Miss Diana Mercer, have shown exemplary resource and tolerance in dealing with my many varied requests. I am greatly indebted to Mr Ray Phillips, Chief Medical Photographer and Head of the Department of Medical Illustration and his staff for their untiring assistance and expertise with the photographs and illustrations. Miss Marcia Langdon, Personal Assistant to the Dean during my term of office, gave me invaluable assistance at the difficult stage of starting on the book and made many arrangements of lasting value before taking up another post. Dr Geoffrey Rivett was kind enough to lend me a copy of the manuscript of his book *The Development of the London Hospitals* and has also given me much informal advice and help.

I am greatly indebted to Mr Q. Morris, a member of the Council of the School and Finance Director of BP International, for putting me in touch with Mr Roddy Bloomfield of Hutchinson Benham where he, Miss Emma Hogan and their colleagues have shown me every kindness and courtesy in deploying their expertise to this book so efficiently and effectively in spite of the problems of time and the difficulties of dealing with an inexperienced and exacting author.

To all these and to a whole host of other friends who are far too numerous to list I express my heartfelt thanks for all the help and encouragement they have given me during the daunting task of writing this book.

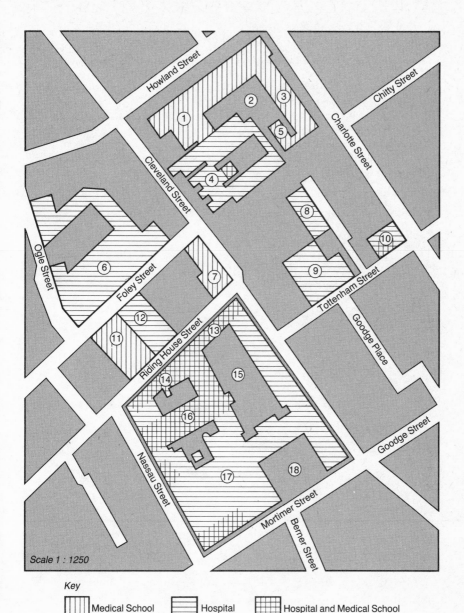

Scale 1 : 1250

Key

| | Medical School | | Hospital | | Hospital and Medical School |

1 The Windeyer Building
2 Astor College Garden
3 Astor College
4 Outpatient Department
5 Examination Hall / Gymnasium
6 John Astor House
7 Courtauld Institute of Biochemistry
8 Tottenham Mews Day Hospital
9 Arthur Stanley House

10 James Pringle House
11 School of Pathology
12 School of Radiography
13 Bland-Sutton Institute of Pathology
14 Wolfson Building
15 Hospital Garden
16 Sir Jules Thorn Institute of Clinical Science
17 The Middlesex Hospital
18 Hospital Forecourt

—1—
The Changing Scene

Everyday life – Travel – Population and demography –
Diseases and their treatment – Hospital arrangements –
The Middlesex Hospital – Retail Price Indices

The fifty years covered in this book have been ones of dramatic and
widespread developments in scientific and technical knowledge and
manufacturing expertise which have produced profound changes in
virtually all aspects of life. Just as students and staff of 1935 could not
have envisaged the great changes which would occur during the course
of the next half century, today's students must have difficulty in appreciating the nature of everyday life in 1935 and also the great limitations,
by present-day standards, that existed in respect of the investigations
and treatment available to patients. In spite of that it is interesting to
note that, even then, criticisms were being made that students were
paying too much attention to technological advances and too little to
the essential need to learn as much as possible by getting to know
their patients, by taking comprehensive histories and by making careful
clinical examinations. They seem to be precisely the same comments
as those heard on several occasions in recent years at meetings of the
Academic Board and the Collegiate Board of Examiners.

Fifty years ago flying was still a special event and airlines throughout
the world carried about three million passengers in the course of a year,
using flying boats to a considerable extent on long-distance routes. Now
it is very much a standard and routine form of travel and over 700
million passengers are transported each year in large commercial aircraft
flying at speeds well in excess of what was the world air-speed record
of 1935. In January 1936 *The Middlesex Hospital Journal* carried an

15

announcement to the effect that 'Mr Gordon-Taylor went by air to Calcutta last month to examine for the Primary F.R.C.S.' Today a similar event would be recorded only if the journey was made by some other means of travel. The standard method at that time was the one described by Sir Alfred Webb-Johnson (later Lord Webb-Johnson) in *The Middlesex Hospital Journal* of 1939 recording a trip to Egypt, India, Australia and New Zealand, all undertaken by sea on the P & O liners *Strathallan* and *Mooltan*, finally returning to England across the Atlantic on the *Aquitania*. Nowadays the liners have disappeared from the regular routes and when Dr J. F. Arthur left the Bland-Sutton Institute in 1969 to take up a professorial post in New Zealand he made the voyage in his twelve-ton auxiliary sloop *Songvaar* which he and his wife sailed across the oceans themselves.

The great developments which have occurred in travel since 1935 have had considerable effects on staff and students and on the ease with which overseas visitors can come to The Middlesex. Now, over three-quarters of Middlesex students spend their elective periods many thousands of miles away in Africa, India, Pakistan, the Far East, the West Indies, the USA, Canada and other places.

Population

Along with the general developments which have taken place, improvements in living standards, together with greatly improved knowledge concerning the prevention and treatment of disease, have led to significant alterations in the size and age structure of the population, and these are still changing. At the 1931 census the population of the United Kingdom was 46,038,000 with 7.7 per cent under the age of five and 11.5 per cent over the age of sixty. At the 1981 census the population of the UK had risen by just over one fifth to 55,773,000 and of this number 6 per cent were under the age of five and 19.7 per cent were over the age of sixty. During the period 1931–81 the deaths of children under the age of one year fell from 67 per 1000 live births to 11.2 and the expectation of life at birth has risen from 58.4 years to 70.2 for males, and from 62.5 years to 76.2 for females.

Diseases

Some diseases which were rampant and serious have been eradicated completely or have become almost insignificant, while others which were unknown at the start of the period or seemed to be relatively uncommon have now assumed serious proportions. Until 1940, when active immunization against diphtheria was introduced in this country, there were about 50,000 cases each year with about 2500 deaths. During the decade 1968 to 1977, notifications in England and Wales averaged nine per annum and there were only six deaths from this disease in the whole of the ten-year period.

Bacterial endocarditis, tuberculous meningitis, generalised (miliary) tuberculosis, osteomyelitis of the frontal bone and other severe infections were invariably fatal. Other infections such as streptococcal septicaemia, meningococcal meningitis, pneumococcal pneumonia and pulmonary tuberculosis had high mortality rates and when recovery occurred it was slow and often complicated. About 55,000 cases of tuberculosis were notified each year and there were approximately 30,000 deaths annually. Now there are about 7000 notifications and 750 deaths each year.

In contrast, during the same period the recorded deaths from carcinoma of the lung have increased six-fold, from under 5000 per year to nearly 30,000. Diseases spread by sexual activity are increasing at a rapid rate and the number of patients seen in clinics for sexually transmitted diseases (now usually known as Departments of Genito-Urinary Medicine) has risen three-fold in the last fifteen years. There are now over half a million new patients seen in such clinics each year in England and Wales.

Treatment

Before 1935 there was no anti-bacterial chemotherapy but in that year Domagk revealed that Prontosil Rubrum could cure animal and human infections caused by haemolytic streptococci and a few other organisms. The active agent was sulphanilamide and subsequent chemical modifications of it were to widen its scope of action. Penicillin had been discovered by Alexander Fleming in 1928 but in 1935 it was only its *in vitro* activity which was used in the laboratory to create conditions in which micro-organisms insensitive to penicillin could be cultured.

17

Its purification and its introduction as a therapeutic breakthrough had to await the inspired work of Florey, Chain and their colleagues in Oxford beginning in 1938. Thus began the antibiotic era.

Heparin was known in 1935 for its *in vitro* anticoagulant properties but was not available in sufficiently pure form to be administered to patients. Its antithrombic activity was soon to be shown in experimental animals. Oral anticoagulants had not been discovered, though the existence of Vitamin K was recognized in 1935. Progesterone was isolated and its chemical structure determined in 1934. Oestradiol and testosterone were both isolated in 1935.

Insulin had been isolated by Banting and Best in 1921 and was introduced for the treatment of diabetes mellitus in 1922. In 1935 regular insulin was in general use, its activity being assessed by biological standardization. There were no long-acting preparations although protamine zinc insulin was introduced in 1936. There were no orally active antidiabetic drugs.

For general anaesthesia, after premedication with morphine and atropine, nitrous oxide was used for induction to be followed by ether or chloroform. Two short-acting barbiturates, Hexobarbitone and Thiopentone, had just been introduced for intravenous administration but at that time were used for very short operations rather than for induction.

The surgical treatment of patients was limited by the lack of chemotherapy; by the range of anaesthetics available; by the fact that plastics and a number of other materials were not known at that time; and by the general state of scientific knowledge. For example, in 1935, apart from surgical sympathectomy which was being performed in attempts to improve blood supply to the limbs, the only treatment for cardiovascular diseases was medical. There were no implantations of pacemakers, no open-heart surgery, no coronary by-pass operations and, of course, no transplants. The subsequent development of those procedures was dependent on advances in all the fields of knowledge already mentioned.

In the field of Orthopaedic Surgery it was not until 1938 that the first total hip replacement was to be undertaken. That was at The Middlesex by Mr Philip Wiles. Although that surgery was soundly based and is widely acclaimed as a breakthrough in this field, prolonged success had to await the development of more suitable prosthetic materials than were then available.

DNA

The electron microscope of 1935 had only just succeeded in providing a resolution greater than that of optical microscopes. Although the basic chemical formula of desoxyribonucleic acid was known it was to be nearly another twenty years before biochemists were able to propose a structure for this long-fibre molecule and recognize its central role in life processes. It was to be a while longer before its acronym DNA was to become a word in everyday use. Genetic engineering and cloning were some years later still.

Hospital Arrangements

During the years there have been progressive advances in hospital practice but there have also been sudden changes in hospital organisation. Prior to the introduction of the National Health Service in 1948 there were two separate hospital systems in the country: the 'municipal hospitals' financed and run by the county councils and the 'voluntary hospitals' financed by donations from individuals or groups of people and also by voluntary contributions of varying amounts from patients using the hospitals.

Within the County of London there were, in 1935, about 6500 beds in the voluntary hospitals with undergraduate medical schools; about another 3000 beds in voluntary general hospitals without undergraduate schools; and about 16,000 beds in acute general hospitals administered by the London County Council. There were also, of course, convalescent hospitals, hospitals for the chronic sick, for infectious diseases and special hospitals.

The municipal hospitals were staffed by salaried medical and surgical officers but the voluntary hospitals attached considerable importance to the principles that the doctors in charge of patients in the wards should not be paid for their work; that the patients should not make any payment for treatment received, but could make contributions if appropriate; and that the state should not be involved in any way with the financing or running of these hospitals. At that time this last principle was strongly endorsed by government and the concept that the state should make no financial contribution to such hospitals had been fostered by successive Chancellors of the Exchequer. Accordingly, the 'honoraries' of that time were the physicians and surgeons appointed to the staff of the voluntary hospitals. They received no remuneration of any kind for their services to the patients in the wards of the hospitals. They received honoraria from the schools for lectures and for some examinations.

To be an honorary of one of the voluntary hospitals was a privilege which was keenly sought and those appointed discharged their responsibilities with great devotion and conscientiousness. To be appointed as an honorary to one of the great teaching hospitals was a special distinction and it was from their ranks that the presidents of the Royal Colleges and other distinguished office holders were likely to come. In his book, Campbell Thomson refers to the year 1906 when members of The Middlesex Hospital honorary staff included the President of the Royal College of Physicians, the President of the Royal College of Surgeons and the Dean of the Faculty of Medicine of the University of London – Sir Richard Douglas Powell, Sir Henry Morris and Sir James Kingston Fowler respectively – commonly referred to as 'The Triumvirate'.

The Middlesex Hospital

As in other voluntary hospitals, at The Middlesex there was a gradation of the honorary staff. The senior members were designated as 'Physicians' or 'Surgeons' while their juniors were appointed as Physicians or Surgeons 'with Charge of Out-Patients' or as 'Assistant Physicians' or 'Assistant Surgeons'. The distinction was not quite as absolute as the titles might suggest, but certainly on the general medical and general surgical firms with two honoraries apiece the physician or surgeon would not hold any regular out-patient clinics and would be in charge of most of the in-patients. Commonly he would have well over thirty of the forty or more beds on a floor unit, except during 'take-in' weeks on the surgical wards when the assistant surgeon would normally be responsible for the emergency admissions. In a number of the specialities other than general medicine and general surgery there was only one honorary but in those departments with two or more there were 'physicians' or 'surgeons' and also 'assistant physicians' and 'assistant surgeons'.

In addition to the honorary staff of the Hospital there were, in 1935–36, a Resident Medical Officer, four medical registrars (including one 'junior medical registrar'), four surgical registrars, one obstetric and gynaecological registrar, one otological registrar, two casualty medical

20

officers, one casualty surgical officer, fourteen house officers (medical and surgical, including general medicine and surgery and specialities), two resident anaesthetists, and one clinical assistant to the Courtauld Wards.

The Resident Medical Officer post was a senior one and Dr H. L. Marriott held that position for nine years before being appointed as an Assistant Physician in 1936. The Hospital regarded the post of RMO as valuable but it did not accord with the staffing pattern established in the Health Service and was abolished in 1974. The Registrars received a salary (£300 p.a. in 1935–36) of which half was contributed from School funds in recognition of their contributions to teaching and research. Such an arrangement clearly demonstrated the very close liaison between Hospital and School and the need to combine patient care, teaching and research in teaching hospitals in order to promote the highest standards of medicine. In the multitudinous discussions taking place today there are many comments on the way in which the trend to divert resources and staff to meet immediate local service needs is jeopardising the long-term future of the Health Service by curtailing research and the teaching which is so dependent on it. It is interesting to speculate whether the long-term future of the Health Service would have been better safeguarded if medical schools had been enabled to continue meeting half the salaries of Registrars (and now Senior Registrars) in teaching hospitals. The house officers of the day were not salaried but they were provided with free board and lodging.

In 1935 The Middlesex Hospital had just been rebuilt and during 1936 the average number of available beds had risen to 587; from 564 in 1935, 533 in 1934 and 433 in 1933. The balconies on the garden sides of the wards on the north ends of the East and West Wings and on the Crosspieces had not then been closed in and this partly explains the fact that the figure for available beds was less than the present figure of 648. In those days, however, patients stayed in more than twice as long as they do now. Also the practice of setting up extra beds in wards, while not necessarily welcomed, was by no means the forbidden exercise it is today. Because of those factors there was a high bed occupancy in all hospitals and The Middlesex had a particularly high figure compared with others. In the five years from 1933 to 1937 it always exceeded 94 per cent and in 1936 was 95.6 per cent, compared with 79.5 per cent in 1983. As a consequence, there were more beds occupied than there are today – 561 in 1936 compared with 512 in

1983. However, because the average length of stay was 20.8 days in 1936 compared with 9.5 days in 1983, only about half the number of in-patients could be treated in the year – 9821 in 1936 compared with 19,786 in 1983.

Here it is interesting to note that in those days the numbers of in-patients were always recorded as 'Admissions' for the year. Under the National Health Service the figures are invariably recorded as 'Deaths and Discharges' for the year. There may have been some reason for making the change but it is certainly not apparent and many patients as well as doctors find the new method curious, and unfortunate, in its terminology.

In 1936 some 21,134 new patients were seen in the Out-Patient Department while there were 34,125 seen in 1983. The difference must be considered in relation to the fact that the 1936 total included only 408 new patients (eight per week) attending the Venereal Diseases Department compared with 8832 new patients (170 per week) attending the Genito-Urinary Medicine Department in 1983. In 1936 the number of new patients in the Casualty Department was 22,922. In 1983 the figure was 33,333.

Whatever differences there may be in the statistics about patient numbers, they pale almost into insignificance in relation to the changes in expenditure. In 1936, with an income (excluding capital-building funds) of £184,298 the Hospital had a working surplus of £5139. The expenditure of £179,159 on running the Hospital for that year compares with an expenditure of £28,893,891 in the year ending 31 March 1983. In 1936 the average cost of an in-patient week was calculated as £5 3s 9d contrasting with £786.80 in 1982–83. The average cost of an out-patient attendance then was 1s 9d contrasted with £30.99 in 1982–83. In other words, while the Retail Price Index rose approximately twenty-fold over the period, hospital costs rose about 160-fold.

The source of the Hospital's income for 1936, set out under very broad headings, was:

Voluntary gifts, legacies, etc.	£69,553
Patients' contributions	£68,184
Fees for services rendered (public and private)	£6,110
Interest on investments	£25,238
'Extraordinary' income	£15,213
Total:	£184,298

In those days, except for emergency admissions made on a very temporary basis, there was a strict upper-income limit for patients who could be admitted to the wards of the Hospital. Nursing homes tended to be expensive and poorly equipped and patients in the middle-income range had difficulty in obtaining proper treatment. The Middlesex had an excellent private-patients' wing in which the charges were modest and the medical fees which could be charged were limited. It had been opened in 1934, having been established as the result of a gift made by Lord Woolavington (James Buchanan) in memory of his wife.

Charges for accommodation in the Woolavington Wing in 1936 varied with the size of the room and its location on either the street or garden side, ranging from £4 4s to a maximum of £12 12s *per week*. The charges imposed from 1 April 1984 are the same for all rooms, whatever their size or location, and amount to £148 *per day* for any single room irrespective of its size or position in the Hospital.

Other Events

During the fifty years covered in this book there has been a Second World War, fortunately with no permanent damage to the fabric of the School or Hospital in spite of bombs scoring direct hits; a National Health Service has been established, with fundamental changes to the great voluntary hospitals; there have been two major reorganizations of the Health Service with substantial effects on the university hospitals and the medical schools; there have been considerable changes in the medical curriculum and examinations; there has been an increase in the number of students, and over 40 per cent of the undergraduate students entering The Middlesex Hospital Medical School are now women, in contrast to the 100 per cent men up to 1947; the School has been almost entirely rebuilt and greatly extended; a Royal Commission on Medical Education proposed a number of changes in medical education and in the size and structure of medical schools in general, and made certain specific recommendations for The Middlesex Hospital Medical School which proved to be impractical and which have since been superseded by different restructuring arrangements; there have been changes in the constitutional and financial arrangements for running the Medical School and in the cost of doing so.

Throughout the period under review there has been an irregular but progressive decline in the value of money so that, overall, the purchasing power of the pound in 1935 was approximately twenty times greater than it is today – or, in other words, a shilling (the coin now designated 5p) of 1935 can be regarded as roughly equivalent to £1 today, as indicated by the relevant Retail Price Indices. The calculations of RPI started only in 1914 but other calculations for periods prior to that suggest that, in the hundred years after the foundation of the School in 1835, the purchasing power of the pound fell by about a half, or one tenth of the fall in the fifty years 1935–85. It means that a sum of £25,000 in 1835 would roughly represent £50,000 in 1935, £250,000 in 1972, £500,000 in 1977, and £1 million in 1985. The costs of medical care and of medical education have increased far beyond the general levels shown by the Retail Price Indices, however, and therefore comparisons, and conversions to modern values of money, can be misleading. For general guidance a few conversions to 1985 values, based on RPI figures, have been included in brackets after the actual amount quoted at a particular date.

—2—
The Start of the Third Fifty Years

The Middlesex Hospital and Medical School a single
institution – Council and committees – Buildings – School
staff – Teaching and the curriculum – Hospital staff –
Student activities – Annual events – Middlesex institutions

In 1935 the School and Hospital were one institution. The School was
managed by the Council but its decisions, or, strictly, recommendations,
needed ratification by the Board of Management of the Hospital and
School. This remained the constitutional position until the changes
brought about by the introduction of the National Health Service in
1948, described in a later chapter.

HRH Prince Arthur of Connaught had been Chairman of the Board
of Management since 1924 and the Chairman of the School Council
in 1935 was Mr Samuel Augustine Courtauld, who became Chairman
in 1930 in succession to Mr S. G. Asher. Campbell Thomson records
the great good fortune which accrued to The Middlesex Hospital
Medical School as an indirect result of the Revocation of the Edict of
Nantes in 1685. As a consequence of it the Courtauld family of the
day had to flee for their lives from the Ile d'Oléron, near La Rochelle,
with a small baby, Augustine, concealed in a basket of vegetables. That
baby was later to become one of the very early contributors to The
Middlesex Hospital soon after its foundation in 1745. That started a
family connection with The Middlesex which was to result in a direct
descendant, Mr Samuel Augustine Courtauld, serving on the Board
and Council and other important committees and making munificent
benefactions to the School between 1922 and the time of his death in
1953. Mr Courtauld was not only a great figure in the world of finance
and industry, he was also a classics scholar of some distinction and had

25

published a translation of the Odes of Horace which ran to several editions.

Council and Committees

The School Council was so constituted as to have equal representation from the Board of Management and from the teaching staff. In 1935, in addition to the Chairman, Council consisted of eight members nominated by the Board of Management; four members nominated by the Hospital medical and surgical staff; the Chairman and four other members of the School Committee; the Honorary Treasurer of the Medical School; and the Dean. The Secretary-Superintendent of the Hospital acted as Secretary to the Council and the School Secretary also attended meetings.

The School Committee consisted of the honorary medical and surgical staff of the Hospital together with the professors and lecturers of the School. This Committee was the predecessor of the Academic Board formed in 1948. Another committee which existed at that time was a small 'Dean's Committee' consisting of the Dean and five others who were appointed by the School Committee in February each year; at each of its meetings the School Committee 'received and initialled' the minutes of the Dean's Committee.

The Finance Committee of the School was composed then, as now, of an equal number of so-called 'lay' members and 'staff' members of Council. But the terminology in connection with this particular committee is an idiosyncratic anomaly because it has always been recognized that the 'lay' members are the real financial experts and the 'staff' members could more accurately be described as 'lay'. For that reason it became the tendency to refer to the 'non-academic' and 'academic' members of the Committee, although even that might not be completely accurate either.

The great strength of the Finance Committee is evident from the distinction of its membership. The Chairman in 1935 was Mr Richard Davis. His family had been associated with The Middlesex for two generations and his generosity was coupled with a deep personal and abiding interest in its affairs. It is a most appropriate tribute to him that the room in the Hospital provided for the relatives of patients should have been named the 'Richard Davis Room'. In addition to chairing the Finance Committee for several years he played an active role in the

26

students' clubs, especially in the Sailing Club, up to the time of his death in 1950.

Mr S. G. Asher had first joined the Board of the Hospital in 1910 and had been particularly concerned with the promotion of research as one of the Barnato-Joel Trustees. He was Chairman of the Council of the Medical School from 1921 to 1930 and continued to serve on Council until his death in 1938.

Mr Reginald Beddington was a stockbroker who had been a member of the Board of Governors since 1916 and who played a particularly active role on the Nursing Committee.

Mr Edward Meyerstein (Sir Edward Meyerstein, 1938) a London stockbroker and later High Sheriff of Kent, was a great financial figure, a major benefactor of the Hospital and School and served on both the Board of Management and School Council. He brought the Hospital Rebuilding Appeal to an abrupt end at his first meeting of the Board of Management on 17 October 1934. The minutes of that meeting start as follows:

> Prayers were read by the Chaplain.
> The Chairman welcomed Mr E. W. Meyerstein on his taking his seat at the Board for the first time; and expressed to him the deep gratitude of the Hospital for the magnificent gifts he had recently made, the first of £30,000 for a new Department of Radiotherapy, and the second of £70,000 to enable the Board to proceed with the final section of the new Hospital.
> Mr Meyerstein thanked the Board for the honour they had done him in electing him to a seat and said that it came particularly aptly as that day was his birthday. He proposed to give himself a present. He was fond of pictures, and there was a picture outside the Hospital which he desired to possess. That picture showed what was still needed to complete the new Hospital and the price upon it was £85,675. If Prince Arthur and his Board approved, he would give them a cheque for that amount and take the picture down.
> On the motion of Mr Vaughan Morgan, seconded by Sir Edward Penton, it was resolved unanimously that Mr Meyerstein be permitted to purchase the picture, and the Board expressed their heartfelt thanks to him for his wonderful gift.

He subsequently increased the sum required for the Meyerstein Institute when it was found that the actual cost exceeded the original estimate by over 50 per cent. His great generosity to The Middlesex was not to end there, as will be indicated later, but it is worthy of note at this stage that he also made substantial benefactions to other hospitals and medical schools. These included the Westminster for their new medical school; St Mary's for a dental research laboratory; The London for a nurses' swimming pool.

His grand-daughters, Mrs Una Dinnis and Mrs Elizabeth Germaney, recall that when Sir Edward held a garden party as High Sheriff of Kent he had The Middlesex placard on display together with a large model of the main blocks of the new Hospital. The interior had been made to represent the main entrance hall into which people could walk to make donations to the Hospital.

It was a sad irony that one of the first patients to be treated in the new Meyerstein Institute of Radiotherapy was his own daughter Phyllis, who was to die of cancer at the age of forty-two.

In those days there was a post of Honorary Treasurer of the School which had been specially created for Mr A. E. Webb-Johnson (Sir Alfred Webb-Johnson, 1936; Baron Webb-Johnson of Stoke-on-Trent, 1948). During his period as Dean from 1919 to 1925 he had seen the need to establish Chairs in the essential scientific disciplines and had been highly successful in attracting endowments for a number of them. These included the Joel Chair of Physics, the S. A. Courtauld Chair of Anatomy and the John Astor Chair of Physiology. After ceasing to be Dean in 1925 he was appointed to the Hospital Rebuilding Committee and is said to have been responsible for coining the perfectly accurate slogan which was so effective on the placards, 'The Middlesex Hospital is falling down.' His great abilities in attracting financial support led him to be described aptly as a 'most wonderful and successful beggar'. Later he was to use those same attributes to good effect for the benefit of The Royal College of Surgeons of England.

School Buildings

In 1935 the rebuilding of the Hospital had just been completed and discussions had already taken place on the need for expanding the School and on ways in which this might be achieved. In 1933 Council had instructed the Dean

> to proceed with the preparation of a memorandum specifying the ultimate requirements of the School as regards laboratories, lecture theatres, common rooms, administrative and committee rooms, library, accommodation for students, etc., and the approximate cost thereof.

It had been agreed at that stage, however, that no attempt would be made to extend the School until the rebuilding of the Hospital had been completed.

In 1935 the School buildings consisted of the Bland-Sutton Institute of Pathology; the Courtauld Institute of Biochemistry; the Ferens Institute of Otolaryngology, occupying the third floor of the Out-Patient Annexe in Cleveland Street; and old buildings on either side of the Bland-Sutton Institute in Riding House Street (then Union Street). The academic Departments of Chemistry, Physics, Biology (in the Melhado Memorial Biology Laboratories), Anatomy and Physiology were accommodated in a very restricted building to the west of the Bland-Sutton Institute but not extending all the way to Nassau Street, as the corner site at that time was still a baker's shop.

The entrance to the School from Riding House Street led past the Porters' Lodge and the cloakrooms, where overcoats and briefcases were left without any of the lockers which have become obligatory in the modern world. At that time, coats and other articles left hanging in open view did not go missing except very occasionally and inadvertently, when they were returned with apologies. There were no intruders then.

The Porters' Lodge was under the supervision of a formidable character, Charles Hockley, who combined in a curious way all the best qualities of a former regimental sergeant-major with those of an uncle who is only too aware of some of the failings of youth. His large frame and great moustache gave him an appearance which could daunt even the most robust, but which disguised a soft heart for anyone with genuine problems. The way in which he was regarded was well illustrated by a splendid cartoon of him in the *Journal* which was captioned, 'Guide, Philosopher and Friend'.

The offices of the Dean, the Secretary and the secretarial staff occupied three rooms on the ground floor of the Riding House Street frontage, below the museum of the Bland-Sutton Institute. Between them and the Bland-Sutton Lecture Theatre was the Senior Common Room with its elegant leather armchairs. The Junior Common Room for students on the north-east corner was hardly less grand, in the club manner, with its leather armchairs and couches and its splendid panelling, whilst outside were the War Memorial panels recording the names of those Middlesex graduates who had given their lives during the 1914–18 War. Over the fireplace was the fine oil painting of Captain

John Fox-Russell who had been awarded the Military Cross for conspicuous gallantry during the first battle of Gaza in 1917 and was posthumously awarded the Victoria Cross for his valour in action at Tel-el-Khuweilfeh later the same year.

An additional lecture theatre opened off the garden side of the corridor leading from Hockley's Lodge to the Bland-Sutton Lecture Theatre. This was the Round Lecture Theatre and it took the magic of Dr Lakin's weekly lectures, at noon on Wednesdays, to overcome the painful awareness of the hard cramped seating on the tiered wooden benches.

Professorial Staff

At the start of the period covered in this book there were only six professors on the School staff. They were Sidney Russ, Joel Professor of Physics; W. B. Tuck, Professor of Chemistry; Thomas Yeates, S. A. Courtauld Professor of Anatomy; James McIntosh, Professor of Pathology; E. C. Dodds (Sir Charles Dodds, 1954; Baronet, 1964), Courtauld Professor of Biochemistry; and Samson Wright, John Astor Professor of Physiology. Professors Russ, Yeates and McIntosh were appointed in 1920, Professor Tuck in 1921, Professor Dodds in 1925 and Professor Samson Wright in 1930. Except for Chemistry and Pathology, the Chairs were funded from endowments equivalent to approximately £250,000 in 1985 currency but some of them were established before being endowed and when the John Astor Chair of Physiology was endowed in 1920, Major Astor had insisted on anonymity and it was not until 1932 that it was known by the name of the benefactor.

Professor Sidney Russ had been the first of these to be appointed. He had come to The Middlesex on a Beit Fellowship in 1910 and in July 1913 he had been appointed as Physicist to the Hospital. There is every reason to believe that he was the first Physicist to be appointed to the staff of a hospital anywhere in the world and the fact that there are now so many posts in that discipline indicates that his appointment was an important development. His teaching commitment was limited to the 1st MB course and to the Diplomas of Radiology of London and of Cambridge, but he had an active research programme concerned with radiobiological studies of rat tumours. The X-ray equipment in those days was incredibly primitive (and dangerous) but this did not deter the progress of the work. The King Edward Hospital Fund for London kept a stock of radium at The Middlesex in the care of Russ and this was loaned to other hospitals in London as required, together with help and advice on applications and dosimetry. Radon was also supplied to many hospitals.

Professor W. B. Tuck, a tall, large, outspoken man with a big moustache, had come to The Middlesex from University College London where he had been working in Sir William Ramsay's department. In spite of that background he was not research orientated; he taught inorganic chemistry to the 1st MB students and organic chemistry to the 2nd MB course with an anecdotal flair and with frequent references to the rapidity with which chemical reactions occurred as being equivalent to 'the speed of lightning through a gooseberry bush'. He was certainly a dramatic demonstrator of experiments given before lay audiences to illustrate the work of the School.

Professor Thomas Yeates, invariably referred to as 'Tim Yeates', who had come from Queen's College, Belfast, and the University of Edinburgh where he had graduated in medicine in 1893, had contributed much to the Universities of Newcastle and of Birmingham as a senior lecturer before being appointed to The Middlesex as Lecturer in 1915 and then to a Professorial title in 1920. He always put his work first, far ahead of everything else, and his knowledge was ascertained by direct observation and imaginative thought. He was not the ideal teacher of elementary anatomy for students beginning the 2nd MB but contributed greatly to their knowledge towards the end of the course and excelled in enthusing Primary FRCS candidates. Many of these came from Australia and New Zealand and it was commonly said that, in the surgical hierarchy of Australasia, the name of Yeates was better known and more respected than anyone after royalty and Gordon-Taylor.

Professor James McIntosh had had a distinguished record in experimental pathological research at Aberdeen University and then at The London Hospital Medical College before coming to The Middlesex at the age of thirty-seven. He was a microbiologist who had done pioneer work on syphilis and the Wasserman reaction which had been accorded widespread recognition. During the First World War he investigated anaerobic bacteria associated with wound infection, producing a report which was regarded for a long period as the authoritative paper on this important subject. He was an undoubted 'personality' with a stooping powerful figure which appeared even more aggressive because of his boundless enthusiastic energy and his outspoken denunciation of bad work. He did not appear to suffer fools gladly but anyone, fool or not, who turned to him for help always received kindness and sympathy and an apparently unlimited amount of time. He had a penchant for high-powered sports cars and played aggressive golf with great enthusiasm.

Professor Charles Dodds was a Middlesex graduate who had entered the School at the age of sixteen in 1916 along with some thirty-six other students of the same age, including such distinguished figures as Samson Wright and David Patey. He rapidly displayed his talents in such a company by obtaining the class prize in chemistry and a certificate in physics. He was a very rapid reader with a remarkably retentive memory, which included even the facts contained in the footnotes to the text. While still an undergraduate he was appointed as a Student Demonstrator in a department of the Bland-Sutton Institute which had just been established to deal with pathological and physiological chemistry. After qualification with the Conjoint Diplomas in July 1921 he was appointed a Lecturer, before obtaining the MB BS with distinction in May 1922. He was awarded a PhD in January 1925 and in May that year he was appointed to the newly created Chair of Biochemistry, which was later endowed by Mr S. A. Courtauld. That was just seven months after his twenty-fifth birthday and he was to be Professor of Biochemistry for just over forty years. In his early days he used to drive racing cars at Brooklands but abandoned it when most of the drivers became professionals in the sport.

Professor Samson Wright had also entered The Middlesex as a student in 1916 and had qualified with the University Medal (commonly referred to as the Gold Medal) in 1922. He had then become Demonstrator in Physiology and immediately displayed his outstanding abilities as a teacher. There are few who would dispute the assessment of him made later by Professor Cyril Keele that he was undoubtedly the greatest teacher of physiology of his generation. He had an intensely quick mind and a supreme ability to stimulate in the lecture theatre and in conversation – often being provocative in order to obtain an adequate response. His lectures were never dull and were interspersed with searching questions appropriately placed so that everyone remained alert throughout. In the 1935–36 session the sixth edition of his classic textbook *Applied Physiology* was published, the first edition having appeared in 1926 when he was aged twenty-seven. The title of the book summarized his attitude to the subject which he regarded as the essential basis of medicine and not as a remote academic discipline, although it was all firmly based on the scientific method and the elucidation of facts by experimental methods. From the very early stages of the course students were given an insight into the way in which a knowledge of physiology was essential to the understanding of disease processes. Samson Wright was the first to arrange clinical demonstrations on patients during the preclinical years. In 1929 he left The Middlesex to become Lecturer in Physiology at King's College, London, but in the following year he returned to fill the Chair of Physiology, 'for five years in the first instance', as was the practice in those days for professors and readers. He was aged thirty-one at the time of his appointment. His teaching prowess was very widely recognized by students.

The combination of Tim Yeates in Anatomy and Samson Wright in Physiology provided an extraordinarily powerful team which attracted many students taking the Primary FRCS course; there were often about fifty to sixty such 'occasional students', as anyone not following the normal undergraduate course was officially designated. It was widely accepted that nobody would contemplate sitting the examination without having a copy of *Applied Physiology* and studying it intently.

Other School Staff

Although the Bland-Sutton Institute of Pathology and the Courtauld Institute of Biochemistry were better staffed than other departments, because of their clinical service roles and their research programmes, the professors of the School in those days had few assistants. In Chemistry there was one fulltime Demonstrator, Mr W. H. S. Cheavin. In Physics, during the 1935–36 session, the only other academic members of staff were a Research Assistant, Mr F. L. Warburton, and a demonstrator, Mr B. D. Watters. In Biology the only member of the academic staff was the Reader, Dr J. H. Woodger. He had come to The Middlesex in 1922 from University College, London, where he held the Derby Research Fellowship. He had also worked for a year in Vienna at a time when the 'Vienna Circle' of philosophers was at its height; this influenced the direction of his research. He was an experimental embryologist with considerable manipulative skill which he put to good use in the preparation of histological material.

The Anatomy Department had only two Demonstrators at that time, Dr E. A. Rucker, who was to retire from the department in 1936, and Mr P. H. Newman, who had qualified in 1934 and whose appointment in the Anatomy Department was a prelude to a distinguished career in orthopaedics on the staff of The Middlesex and the Royal National Orthopaedic Hospital.

In the Anatomy Department, as in others, there were also one or two student demonstrators who were appointed for a term, or even up to a year in some cases, from students who had recently completed the course with credit and who could help in the dissecting room or in practical classes. They received an honorarium of £10 per term (£200, 1985).

In Physiology there were also two Demonstrators, Dr A. T. Wilson, who was to leave at the end of the 1935–36 session, and Dr C. A. Keele who had qualified in 1928 and who, after holding important clinical posts, including that of House Physician to Dr R. A. Young at the Brompton Hospital, RMO at the Royal Masonic Hospital and Registrar to Dr G. E. S. Ward and Dr Evan Bedford, had been stimulated by Professor Samson Wright to become a Demonstrator in the Department in 1933. In this post he succeeded Dr Michael Kremer who became Medical Registrar. At that time there was no separate Department of Pharmacology and Dr Cyril Keele undertook the teaching of pharmacology as well as of physiology.

In addition to Professor James McIntosh, the Bland-Sutton Institute of Pathology had a Reader in Morbid Anatomy and Histology, Dr Robert Scarff, who was already recognized as an outstanding histopathologist and whose opinions were sought from far and wide on difficult sections. He was to succeed Professor McIntosh as Director of the Institute in 1948.

The other aspects of pathology, bacteriology and haematology, also had an exceptionally able exponent in Dr Lionel Whitby (Sir Lionel Whitby, 1945) who had served with distinction in the First World War where he had been awarded the Military Cross and was seriously wounded, leading to the high amputation of a leg by a Middlesex surgeon then in the Army, Mr Gordon Gordon-Taylor. The first edition of Dr Whitby's well-known textbook, *Medical Bacteriology*, had appeared in 1928 and the first edition of *Disorders of the Blood*, written jointly with Dr C. J. C. Britton, was published in 1935. There were at that time six other medically qualified assistants in the Bland-Sutton

Institute, and working in the Institute was the powerful Medical Research Council Unit of Bacterial Chemistry under the Director Dr Paul Fildes FRS (Sir Paul Fildes, 1946).

In the Courtauld Institute of Biochemistry Professor Charles Dodds was strongly supported in his research laboratories by Mr Wilfred Lawson, who had a very different personality. Whereas Dodds was a man bursting with ideas, enthusiasm and optimism, Lawson was by nature super-cautious and somewhat pessimistic but he was a fine chemist. They complemented each other admirably and in combination they made great advances which neither might have achieved alone. The research on which they were working at the start of this period was about to produce developments of far-reaching consequence, as will be mentioned in the next chapter. Chemical Pathology was under the direct charge of Dr J. Douglas Robertson, a dynamically active worker who was always deeply tanned from ultraviolet light and who was a world-class squash player. The Department at that time had two other assistants on the School staff and there were also two fulltime workers of the Medical Research Council, one fulltime worker of the British Empire Cancer Campaign, a Halley Stewart Fellow, a Leverhulme Scholar and a Mackenzie-Mackinnon Scholar. This gave a powerful research team working under Professor Dodds.

In addition to the School Departments already mentioned, there was one other institute, the Ferens Institute of Otolaryngology, which had been endowed in 1925 with a generous benefaction by Mr T. R. Ferens of Hull. This Institute was concerned with both teaching and research under the direction of the ear, nose and throat surgeons of the Hospital, Mr Somerville Hastings MP (who was later to become Leader of the London County Council, among other things) and Mr F. J. Cleminson. The first Librarian and Curator of the Institute was Dr Albert Gray whose exquisite work on the comparative anatomy of the labyrinth, on theories of hearing and on other complex problems in otology had resulted in his being awarded a number of distinctions including the Guyot Prize of the University of Groningen. He died in 1936. Also in the Institute was Dr C. S. Hallpike, a Foulerton Research Student of the Royal Society who was later to become Director of a Medical Research Council Unit at the National Hospital for Nervous Diseases and be elected a Fellow of the Royal Society in 1956, before returning to the Ferens in 1965 as Director of Research. By 1935 the Institute had already made significant contributions to research over a wide range of projects. The sectioning of temporal bones presented difficult problems because of their dense calcification and the fragility of their soft-tissue contents but a successful technique was developed which attracted visitors from abroad as well as from this country.

The School Secretary in 1935 was Mr R. A. Foley. After serving in the Army during the First World War, and being decorated with the Military Cross, he had worked in the office of the Secretary-Superintendent of the Hospital before being appointed as Secretary of the Medical School. His assistant was Miss Eileen Walton, who had been appointed in 1934 as a secretary/typist. One of her earliest responsibilities was to act as assistant to Dr Campbell Thomson in the preparation of his *The Story of The Middlesex Hospital Medical School, 1835–1935*. In 1949 Miss Walton was to succeed Mr Foley as Secretary of the School and in 1984, in her retirement, she has assisted in the preparation of this book.

Teaching and the Curriculum

Up to 1973 The Middlesex Hospital Medical School provided a course of one year in the 'preliminary sciences' of chemistry, physics and biology leading to the 1st MB BS examination of the University of London. This was the first year of a six-year course. Exemption could be obtained by sitting that examination or its equivalent at school or elsewhere and a number of students did that, although not usually as many as those who took 1st MB at The Middlesex. Students who took the preclinical course at Oxford and Cambridge and then came to The Middlesex entered the clinical course six months later than their London colleagues and it was possible in those days for everyone, after a period of out-patient experience, to begin the clinical clerkships on medical wards and follow this six months later by experience with surgical firms. The arrangements necessary today with a single entry require half the students to begin their clinical course on surgical wards. Few would dispute the advantages of the old system in this particular respect and there was regret that it had to alter with the changes in the curriculum in 1974.

In the years dealt with in the early part of this book it was the usual practice for banks, offices and factories to work on Saturday mornings and that also applied to the Medical School where there were regular routine teaching sessions for that half day. Out-patient clinics on Saturday afternoons had been abandoned only a short time previously.

THE PRECLINICAL COURSE

The 1st MB course started in October each year but some students did not join the School until the following January. The course continued up to the examinations in the following July. Compared with similar courses taken at school it was directed only at medical students and, for that reason, probably had a greater bias towards using illustrative examples which had a medical basis. Also, the main teachers in these subjects were engaged in research having medical aspects.

The 2nd MB course also started in October and continued during five university terms until March or April some eighteen months later. In the first term, anatomy and physiology were the subjects which predominated, with the dissecting room and the practical classes in physiology providing major elements in respect of time. Organic chemistry provided a new dimension in the chemical field and was examined after two terms, in March the following year.

In anatomy the body was divided into five parts – upper limb, lower limb, abdomen, thorax, head and neck with one part being dissected by paired students each term. Lectures obviously played a part in the teaching, but the dissecting room provided the bulk of learning from practical contact with structures and from discussion with, and periodical vivas by, the demonstrators.

In physiology, as has been mentioned already, the regular and stimulating lectures and demonstrations on patients had a very particular role but the practical classes, using apparatus of which much would now be regarded as obsolete, played a large part in stressing the great importance of the scientific method and the need to make deductions based on direct and repeatable observations. Pharmacology was at that time taught as part of physiology and examined with it, and, additionally, the art of practical pharmacy was taught by the Hospital Pharmacist, Mr S. H. White, whose deft fingers could wrap up a bottle or container of any shape or size in a sheet of white paper neatly sealed in place with sealing wax, almost as quickly and certainly more impressively than it can be done today with the aid of instant sticky labels and transparent adhesive tape. He stressed the absolute need for careful precision, tidiness and legibility and particularly for clarity in the instructions in the prescriptions and on the label, points which have become much more important today with the greatly increased range and potency of drugs.

In October 1935 it was decided by the School Committee that, following the successful completion of the 2nd MB examination in March each year, London students would have a short break during April and start the clinical course in May with an attachment as out-patient clerk to one of the assistant general physicians and as dresser to one or more of the assistant general surgeons in Out-Patients. They would attend the Casualty Department, as it was then called, during the same three-month appointment. It had also been decided that the clinical curriculum should include a short course of practical nursing, lectures on general practice and instruction in tropical medicine and helminthology.

The first appointment provided an introduction to clinical work and one of the duties laid on the clerks on Medical Out-Patients was that of testing the urines of all the patients attending the clinic. And this all had to be completed before the 'Chief' arrived. This was in the days when patients were not given appointments and they merely came to the Out-Patient Department on the appropriate day. Almost all the patients arrived before 9a.m. for the morning clinics and before 1p.m. for the afternoon clinics and for a large number this meant a wait of two, three or four hours, or possibly even more. In contrast the appointments system for out-patients, which is now universal for almost all clinics, has replaced the wait *on* the day (not completely, alas!) with a much longer wait *for* a day. Planning has now produced a situation where a patient has cause for complaint if he or she has to wait more than perhaps an hour before being seen but, apparently, does not have any cause for complaint if he or she has to wait several months to obtain an appointment. 'Progress' is not always absolute.

After the three-month period in Out-Patients and Casualty, students were attached as Clerks to a general medical firm on one of the floors of the East Wing of the Hospital for a period of three months, and then to a second medical firm on another floor for a further three months. After that, there were similar arrangements as dressers on two successive general surgical firms on the West Wing. With about thirty-five students entering the clinical course at any one time there were, on average, about nine students on each firm. So, if the out-patient attachment is also included, the first fifteen months of the clinical course were devoted to general medicine and general surgery. It must be remembered, however, that in those days the other specialities were not nearly so highly developed as they are now and the general physicians and surgeons had a much wider remit than they have today. For example, at that time, although there were two outstanding orthopaedic surgeons on the staff, one of the assistant general surgeons held a Fracture Clinic each day in rotation.

MEDICAL FIRMS

Although it has been a long-standing arrangement in the School that Professors continued in post up to 30 September of the academic year in which they reached the age of retirement, that practice was not introduced for the staff of the Hospital until 1966. As a result, at the beginning of the 1936–37 session a major change was brought about by the retirement of the Senior Physician, Dr R. A. Young (Sir Robert Young, 1947). He had joined the honorary staff in 1902 after a distinguished career as a student at The Middlesex which he had entered in 1889. He was also a member of the honorary staff of the Brompton Hospital and had been Censor and then Senior Censor of the Royal College of Physicians.

Dr G. E. Beaumont, until then 'Physician with Charge of Out-Patients', was appointed in 1936 to replace him on the senior staff as Physician, and Dr H. L. Marriott, the Resident Medical Officer, was appointed as Assistant Physician to replace Dr Beaumont.

Following those changes the four general medical firms consisted of Dr C. E. Lakin and Dr T. Izod Bennett; Dr E. A. Cockayne and Dr H. E. A. Boldero (Sir Harold Boldero, 1950); Dr G. E. S. Ward and Dr D. E. Bedford; and Dr G. E. Beaumont and Dr H. L. Marriott.

Dr Charles Lakin's profound knowledge of medicine was based on a keen dedication to the importance of pathology and this featured prominently in his regular weekly open lectures on Wednesdays with a review of the patients he had seen during the previous week. He conducted autopsies himself and any specimens from the post-mortem room were described in detail and then passed round the assembled students. Other happenings might also be referred to at these lectures and a number of philosophical pearls would be delivered while he was rocking forwards and backwards from heels to toes, a movement which was also common at the foot of a patient's bed when he was considering a difficult diagnostic problem or awaiting a student's reply to a question. He was the last member of staff always to come to the Hospital in a morning coat and top hat.

Dr Izod Bennett had been Dean of the Medical School from 1929 to 1934. He had a dramatic style of teaching which was impressive and remembered by students even if only because it stimulated controversy about the accuracy of some apparently extravagant claim. His special interests lay in the alimentary tract and in the field of metabolism and he was also an Honorary on the staff of the Royal National Orthopaedic Hospital.

Dr E. A. Cockayne might reasonably be described as a brilliant clinical geneticist many years ahead of his time. His expertise brought together an extraordinary collection of patients with rare congenital abnormalities, many of them in children, and he had under his care whole families with various disorders. Although he later realised the total absurdity of it, one student who was on his firm really believed at the time that he would never pass the final examinations unless he knew all about gargoylism! He had clerked three patients with the condition and he couldn't understand why there was so little about it in the textbooks. There's not all that much more now. Dr Cockayne was a renowned entomologist with a profound knowledge of butterflies and he was soon to become President of the Royal Entomological Society.

Dr Harold Boldero had been appointed Dean in 1934 in succession to Dr Izod Bennett. He had been an Oxford blue in athletics before coming to The Middlesex as a student where, among other things, he captained the hockey team which brought the Cup to The Middlesex in the 1919–20 season. Before being appointed as Assistant Physician he had held a post which was to remain unique, 'Assistant to the Assistant Physicians'. The creation of such a post for him was a tribute to his abilities, and subsequent events were to illustrate the great wisdom of those who were responsible for that far-sighted innovation.

Dr G. E. S. Ward, a tall, lean figure, impeccably dressed and always with a wing collar, was in charge of the Cardiology Department but he had a wide general interest and students on his firm were not restricted to cardiac problems. They all had impressed upon them how to elicit physical signs and he frequently used anecdotes from the MRCP and other examinations to illustrate his teachings.

Dr Evan Bedford, 'the Old Top' as he came to be known, had been attracted to cardiology while still a schoolboy. He played an important role in developing it into much more of a science than it had ever been before, being at the forefront of the improvements in the electrical recordings and radiological techniques which were being developed. He insisted on undertaking a meticulous post-mortem examination of the heart of any of his patients who died. This is typified by the occasion when he came to the Hospital one morning to be told that one of his patients had died during the night. 'Yes, I know,' he replied in his quiet voice. 'I have his heart in my bag'.

Like Dr Robert Young whom he replaced on the staff, Dr G. E. Beaumont had a special interest in diseases of the lung and was also an Honorary on the staff of the Brompton Hospital. He had a particularly wide knowledge of medicine, however, with an infinite capacity for taking pains. His textbook, *Medicine, Essentials for Practitioners and Students*, was kept up to date by him as sole author through several editions and was rightly regarded as essential reading. In 1950 he was also to produce another great book, *Applied Medicine*. His other major publication, in which he collaborated with Professor Charles Dodds, was *Recent Advances in Medicine* which was produced regularly edition after edition, reaching its eighth edition in 1936. He had an extraordinarily quick mind and a pungent wit which attracted large numbers of postgraduates as well as undergraduates to his open ward rounds at 2p.m. on Tuesdays and he was one of the best after-dinner speakers.

Dr Hugh Marriott had been RMO for nine years when he was appointed to the honorary staff. He had had a very broad experience and in April 1935 had published, together with Dr Alan Kekwick, at that time a House Physician in the Hospital, an article in *The Lancet* describing a method of prolonged continuous transfusions of blood.

In 1985 it may not be easy to realise that, in 1935, large prolonged blood transfusions had not previously been used and they required new special techniques. It must also be remembered that in those days there was nothing like the highly organised blood-transfusion service available today. Although the British Red Cross Society had a blood-transfusion service most of the donors were relatives or friends of the patients. Of the 100 donors to whom Marriott and Kekwick referred in that paper, only seven were Red Cross Society donors. Again, with the multitude of different types of plastic materials available today there is difficulty in appreciating now the mechanical and microbiological problems associated with the use of glass and rubber in drip transfussions.

This development in blood transfusion was rapidly recognised as an enormous advance. It was applicable in a wide range of conditions and in the field of surgery, in particular, it enabled patients to undergo operations which were previously impossible. A few years later it was to save countless lives during the Second World War. Appropriately, on the outbreak of war, Dr Lionel Whitby of the Bland-Sutton Institute of Pathology became the officer commanding the Army Blood Supply Depot at Bristol and he had on his staff a number of personnel from The Middlesex, including for a while Dr Marriott and Dr Kekwick. The depot provided a comprehensive service of quality which received high commendation.

On each firm there was a Registrar (or Junior Registrar) and a House Physician and they were responsible for much of the teaching. Much was also learnt from the Ward Sister who was usually very experienced, having probably looked after the two wards on the floor for several years. In those days the nurses worked more than a fifty-hour week (exclusive of meals and lectures) and it was to be 1948 before the official nursing week was reduced to forty-eight hours. In 1935 virtually all nurses at The Middlesex completed a four-year course leading to the award of a Hospital Certificate in addition to the SRN Diploma obtained after three years.

The hospital rounds by the honoraries were particular occasions. Compared with today's rounds they had a formality which made them special events. Although the details varied a little from floor to floor, everyone concerned was in attendance for the whole of the round – Registrar, House Physician, Sister and students. On some firms the honorary would be met at the front hall of the Hospital by the Registrar and House Physician and accompanied to the wards to be met there by the Sister and the neatly assembled and well-dressed line of students who were all known by name after one or two rounds or, on some firms, after a dinner at the honorary's home. On other floors it was the custom for the students also to assemble in the front hall with the Registrar and House Physician and one student would be deputed to ensure that a lift was waiting for the honorary when he arrived there.

SURGICAL FIRMS

On the West Wing of the Hospital the surgical firms, in 1935–36, were: Mr W. Sampson Handley and Mr W. Turner Warwick; Sir Alfred Webb-Johnson and Mr E. W. Riches (Sir Eric Riches, 1958); Mr

Gordon Gordon-Taylor (Sir Gordon Gordon-Taylor, 1946) and Mr R. Vaughan Hudson; and Mr E. L. Pearce Gould and Mr D. H. Patey.

Mr W. Sampson Handley had been Senior Surgeon to the Hospital since 1928. He had first come to The Middlesex from Guy's as Richard Hollins Cancer Research Scholar to work in the laboratory under the Old Lecture Theatre (Round Theatre) and had been appointed to the honorary staff in 1905. He had a special interest in the field of cancer and, particularly, carcinoma of the breast, and published a large number of important papers in that field. He was a great general surgeon of wide interests, however, had introduced bone plating for fractures to The Middlesex and been the first surgeon in the country to perform arterial embolectomy. He had been elected to the Council of the Royal College of Surgeons in July 1923 and was Vice-President in 1931 and 1932.

Mr William Turner Warwick had been a student at The Middlesex and a Broderip Scholar, after previously obtaining an honours degree in mathematics and an athletic blue at Cambridge. He had been Resident Surgical Officer at Leeds and also at St Mark's Hospital before being appointed to the honorary staff of The Middlesex in 1923. His particular interest was in colo-rectal surgery but he applied his analytical mind and mathematical expertise to a vast range of problems including, for instance, varicose veins.

Mr Gordon Gordon-Taylor had also been a Middlesex student but before that he had been a classical scholar at Aberdeen University where he graduated with honours in 1898. He qualified in medicine in 1903 and immediately became Demonstrator in Anatomy. In the same year the University of London instituted a BSc Honours degree in anatomy and Gordon-Taylor and Victor Bonney were the first candidates. They both attained first-class honours. His surgery was founded on this extensive anatomical knowledge and no operation was too large or too complex for him. He was appointed to the honorary staff in 1907 and rapidly became recognized as an outstanding surgeon with a truly 'general' remit. He was elected to the Council of The Royal College of Surgeons in 1932. He always wore a wing collar and bow tie and had a carnation in his buttonhole, a perpetual daily gift from a grateful patient it was said. His oratory, which so often included pertinent classical quotations, was in great demand on special occasions but his informal comments on events and personalities were even more entertaining.

Mr Rupert Vaughan Hudson had been House Surgeon to Mr Gordon-Taylor in 1924 and Registrar from 1926–28 after qualifying at The Middlesex in 1922, where his father and grandfather had also qualified. As a student he had been a member of the cricket team which won the Cup in 1919 and of the hockey team which won the Cup in 1920, when he scored the winning goal. He was also a superb centre-three-quarter at rugby and Vice-Captain of the United Hospitals Rugby Club. He was appointed as Assistant Surgeon in 1928 and, although his work covered the range of general surgery, his particular interest was in the surgery of the thyroid gland in which he had already established his reputation.

Sir Alfred Webb-Johnson has been mentioned already in respect of his deanship and treasurership. He had come from Manchester and had been appointed Assistant Surgeon in 1911 after being Resident Medical Officer from 1908. In the field of surgery he excelled in the management of difficult problems and his lectures were often illustrated by reference to patients who had been treated under exceptionally difficult circumstances. He was the founder of the Department of Urology which has continued as a strong department since then.

Mr E. W. Riches qualified at The Middlesex in 1925, winning the Broderip Scholarship in the same year, after distinguished war service in which he was awarded the Military Cross. His special expertise lay in the field of urology and he had rapidly established himself in this expanding speciality, even though in the years at the beginning of this book he was very much a general surgeon.

Mr Eric Pearce Gould, son of Sir Alfred Pearce Gould, had a brilliant academic career at Oxford before coming to The Middlesex where he was appointed Assistant Surgeon in 1920. Like his father, who had been Dean from 1886 to 1892, Mr Eric Pearce Gould was also Dean, from 1925 to 1929. Sir Alfred was reputed to be one of the greatest clinical teachers of all time and his son Eric inherited, or developed, the same abilities; those who knew them both said that he had gifts of language which surpassed even those of his father. Certainly, students of the day were keen to put their names down for his firm because of the teaching which they knew they would receive. He took over from his father responsibility for the well-known textbook, *Elements of Surgical Diagnosis*; the eighth edition was published in 1938.

The teaching on the first floor of the West Wing was enhanced by the presence there of Mr David Patey, usually known as Jimmy Patey, who had qualified at The Middlesex with honours and the University Medal, after winning the Broderip Scholarship. He had been an assistant in the Bland-Sutton Institute of Pathology before being appointed as Assistant Surgeon in 1930 and this experience in the pathology laboratories had a profound influence in maintaining his perpetual devotion to the experimental side of surgery. His interest in research was coupled with a similar lifelong interest in medical education and produced most stimulating bedside teaching.

On the surgical wards the rounds by the honoraries perhaps lacked some of the grandeur of those on the medical wards but they were not greatly dissimilar. Assisting the honoraries in the operating theatres was regarded as a privilege by most of the students most of the time, but could be trying for some on a few of the floors. Students then probably had more practical experience than now, both in the theatres and the wards, although the nature of it was obviously different from that of today.

The general anaesthetics available at that time consisted essentially of only nitrous oxide, ether and choloroform and the anaesthetists exhibited great skill in induction which students found difficult to emulate. One of the senior anaesthetists of the day, Dr H. P. Crampton, used to compare the procedure with the starting of a car of those times on a very cold morning – one had to use enough accelerator to get going and increase momentum but not so much that a stall or backfire resulted.

OTHER SPECIALITIES

After completion of the surgical firms students were attached to the Department of Obstetrics and Gynaecology. In 1934 arrangements had been made for midwifery training also at St Mary Abbots Hospital and the normal arrangement was for students to have a fortnight assisting with deliveries at The Middlesex followed by a further two weeks at St Mary Abbots. In those days more women had their babies at home and students used to accompany midwives on such calls, perhaps half a dozen or more during their appointment.

The Senior Obstetric and Gynaecological Surgeon in 1935 was Mr Victor Bonney, a brilliant scholar and expert surgeon who was the first obstetrician and gynaecologist to be elected to the Council of The Royal College of Surgeons. The other two honoraries in the department were Mr Louis Carnac Rivett, and Mr Frederick ('Freddie') Roques. Both were dextrous and quick surgeons and Mr Rivett was a particularly clear and able teacher.

After Obstetrics and Gynaecology, students were attached to the other specialist Departments: Paediatrics (Dr Alan Moncrieff (Sir Alan Moncrieff, 1964)), Neurology (Dr Douglas McAlpine), Dermatology (Dr Henry MacCormac), Psychological Medicine (Dr Noel G. Harris), Ophthalmology (Mr Affleck Greeves and Mr Maurice Whiting), Orthopaedic Surgery (Mr Blundell Bankart and Mr Philip Wiles), Otolaryngology (Mr Somerville Hastings, Mr F. J. Cleminson and Mr C. P. Wilson), Radiotherapy (Dr J. H. Douglas Webster and Mr B. W. Windeyer (Sir Brian Windeyer, 1961)).

The teaching of Pathology took place throughout the clinical course in a series of lectures and practical classes held at noon, when students would be expected to leave the wards while the patients had their lunch. The teaching was augmented by attendances in the post-mortem room. Teaching in Anaesthetics, with practical instruction, was conducted on a rota system during the time when students were surgical dressers. The honorary staff consisted of Dr R. E. Apperly, Dr H. P. Crampton, Dr A. E. W. Idris and Dr B. R. M. Johnson.

QUALIFYING EXAMINATIONS

It was possible to qualify with the diplomas of LRCP MRCS of the Conjoint Board earlier than with a university degree. This time difference induced virtually everyone, even the most brilliant, to take the Conjoint diplomas, en passant if nothing more. Additionally, many of the students had financial difficulties and a considerable number would leave the School at that stage without staying to obtain a degree. A few might take the diplomas of the Worshipful Society of Apothecaries. Of the fifty-two students who qualified in 1936 twenty-one took a university degree and only two of those had not previously qualified with the Conjoint diplomas. Of the sixty-eight students who entered the School in 1936 and completed the course, only twenty-nine took a university degree and twenty-two of them had qualified with the Conjoint diplomas previously.

POSTGRADUATE EDUCATION

Postgraduate education is now so well organised and so closely controlled, by statute in the case of those intending to become principals in general practice, that it may not be easy for a number of recent graduates to realise that, prior to the Medical Act of 1950, it was possible for students to pass one of the qualifying examinations, immediately afterwards become registered by the General Medical Council and without any further training become general practitioners. A considerable number did this although others took house officer and other posts in hospitals before entering general practice and some became Registrars and took the MRCP or FRCS examination even though they had decided not to continue in fulltime hospital practice. As general practitioners with those qualifications they could often combine their practice with hospital appointments if they wished to do so. An appreciable amount of hospital work was undertaken by 'General Practitioner Physicians', 'General Practitioner Surgeons', 'General Practitioner Anaesthetists', etc. There were no such posts, of course, in the teaching hospitals.

At The Middlesex, postgraduate courses were provided for the Primary FRCS examination (at a fee of twenty guineas) and for the Diploma of Radiology and Electrology of the Universities of London and Cambridge (at a fee of eight guineas). In connection with the latter course, it is also worth recording that The Middlesex at that time was one of only eight hospitals in England recognized for the training of radiographers.

THE COURTAULD WARDS

Considerable research work was being undertaken in the institutes and departments of the School and further reference will be made to this in subsequent chapters. There was, however, one feature of the rebuilt Hospital which provided a special facility which was not available previously. Through the generosity of Mr S. A. Courtauld the first-floor crosspiece had been specially designed for teaching and research. A lecture theatre was provided right in the heart of the Hospital, readily accessible to both main wings and suitable for demonstrations on patients. Much of the equipment in the lecture theatre had come from the donations of Middlesex graduates. The remainder of that crosspiece consisted of a number of small wards in which all the patients were under the joint care of an Honorary on the staff of the Hospital and the Professor of Physiology or Pathology or Biochemistry. The policy of the wards was determined by the Cancer and General Research Committee, chaired at that time by Mr Courtauld himself, and patients with particular diseases were admitted for special study in the light of

47

the latest laboratory and clinical knowledge. The London County Council readily cooperated in this work and a number of patients were transferred from its hospitals for their own benefit as well as the advancement of medicine.

At the end of 1934 Council approved the recommendation that, in addition to the Resident Clinical Assistant to the Courtauld Wards, there should be a fulltime Research Assistant appointed to the Department of Physiology to be concerned mainly with research in the Clinical Research Unit. At the beginning of 1935 Dr A. M. Gill was appointed as Resident Clinical Assistant to the Clinical Research Unit (at a salary of £325 p.a.). He was soon to become a Medical Registrar.

Student Arrangements and Activities

An outline has already been given of the teaching arrangements in the School at the beginning of the third fifty years and of some of the staff of the School and the Hospital at that time. One benefit for the students which is now very much taken for granted, but which was then an innovation, was the opportunity of living in the Residency when on duty with the emergency firm and at other times also. This facility had been made possible by the generosity of Mr Edward Meyerstein who, in addition to his other great benefactions, had enabled an additional three floors to be added to the Residency so that thirty-six students could live in the Hospital and have ready opportunity for participating in the care of patients during the night. There were then no telephones in the rooms of either the housemen or the students and a summons to the ward was by means of a book brought by a porter, which would need to be signed on receipt of the message.

The School Refectory at that time occupied the ground floor of the Courtauld Institute with the entrance in Riding House Street and the kitchen at the back. Students could eat a very reasonable lunch and obtain some change from a shilling (5p coin of today). It is of interest to note that, in the 1935–36 session, the Refectory made a profit of £208 3s 9d, of which £200 was handed over to the Students' Amalgamated Clubs (£4000, 1985). In the following year the amount transferred to the clubs was £275 and in 1937 it amounted to £400. A staff table was used regularly for lunch by many members of the academic staff and by the Honoraries. This provided a valuable meeting place for Hospital and School teachers. Lunch there was stimulating and entertaining, frequently being enlivened by vigorous discussions between Sammy Wright and Jimmy Patey on a variety of topics, often political or educational.

AMALGAMATED CLUBS

The various students' sports clubs and the Common Room Society, the Medical Society and the Music Society were grouped together as the Students' Amalgamated Clubs, funded by a proportion of the entrance fee paid by each general student and by 'extraordinary' revenue such as that from the Refectory just mentioned. In 1935–36 the entrance fee for London undergraduates was £25 and, of this, £15 15s represented the subscription to the Amalgamated Clubs. The sports clubs which were active at that time were Cricket, Rugby Football, Association Football, Athletics, Swimming, Golf, Tennis, Hockey, Sailing, Squash, Shooting and Boxing; a Table Tennis Club had just been formed. The sports ground then was a ten-acre (four-hectare) site very close to North Wembley station and was shared with St Mary's.

Hospital and School staff and members of Council played active roles as officers in the Amalgamated Clubs, especially as treasurers, but also in individual clubs, and there is little doubt that this formal association had many advantages for the students and was greatly appreciated by those members of Council and staff who were interested in taking part in the affairs of the School, in addition to their commitments on the Council or in teaching and research.

The rugby coach at that time was a dynamic and talented Australian, Mr B. W. Windeyer, who had been appointed as Radium Officer to the Hospital in 1931. He was a great athlete who had rowed for St Andrew's College of the University of Sydney for four years and had played in the combined Australian and New Zealand Universities Rugby Team. His abundant energy and enthusiasm at evening training sessions will be well remembered by all those who were fortunate enough to participate, however arduous it may have seemed at the time. Four rugby teams had regular fixtures, the First XV, and the A, B and Extra-B XVs, but it must be admitted that the Extra-B fixtures were regarded more as social events rather than serious rugby matches, although the team often included excellent players of previous years who had been unable to retain the fitness required for other teams as Finals approached.

Annual Events

CHRISTMAS CONCERTS

Everyone who has been at The Middlesex will remember the enjoyment of the Christmas concerts produced by students with the help of former students, nurses, physiotherapists, radiographers and others. Those who have known only those mounted with considerable sophistication in the large Edward Lewis Theatre, with its proper stage and theatre lighting, will have difficulty in imagining the concerts produced in the Refectory on the ground floor of the Courtauld Institute, with the front row of the audience sitting almost on the stage and the back row sitting rather precariously on chairs perched on tables in order to be able to see at all.

These productions started in the last century as Ward Concerts and the 'Restaurant Concerts', as they were first referred to in the records, did not appear as extra events until 1930. In 1898 an 'Entertainment' had been organised by students and nurses to amuse the patients in the Children's Ward on New Year's Day. In 1910 two concerts were arranged in the boardroom of the Hospital for patients and nurses and in subsequent years concerts were produced on two of the wards on Christmas Day, with a matinée being given later in the Out-Patients Department. These concerts continued during the Great War of 1914–18 but a few years later they were taken over by the housemen and became known as 'Residents' Concerts'.

By 1926 the cast was beginning to include names which were soon to become household words. In that year Eric Riches was the producer and general manager and he also received great applause for his 'Bassoon Song', while Hugh Marriott was cast as an amorous houseman who insisted on switching off the lights at every opportunity. In the following year students and residents put on a combined concert. The 1928 show included Cyril Keele singing two delightful ditties as well as appearing in a sketch, while in 1929 there was a popular duet by Ralph Winterton and Oswald Lloyd-Davies.

The 1930 concerts (which were the first also to be given in the Refectory) received high praise in the wards, where nearly an hour was spent in each ward; but the Restaurant Concert got off to a very delayed start, while the cast arrived from the Cambridge it was (correctly) alleged, and was criticised in the *Journal*. In that show Richard Handley appeared as a good-looking nurse.

Nowadays, rehearsals for these concerts are spread over a considerable part of the Christmas term and some comments are made on this in various academic discussions. The 1931 and 1932 shows narrowly escaped disaster from a virtual lack of any coordinated rehearsals but, in the following year, the producer, Alan Kekwick, was determined to avoid such a possible catastrophe and started preparing his show the day after Boxing Day, or so he claimed. He also introduced microphones, amplifiers and loudspeakers and changed the name to the 'Annual Christmas Concert'. His thorough preparations were a great success and the show was lauded as 'pithy, witty, libellous and polished'.

SMOKING CONCERTS

There seem to be good reasons for believing that, almost from the time the School was founded, the students used to get together in a local pub or restaurant once a year for a party at which some of them would provide entertainment. These annual gatherings lapsed but, in the latter part of the last century, they were not only revived but changed in character by incorporating professional artistes, by having a member of the staff act as chairman for the evening, by moving to a proper hall (or the Pavilion at Lord's on one occasion), by allowing members of the public to attend and by using the concerts as a means of raising funds for the Cancer Charity, established in 1792 by Mr Samuel Whitbread. In the 1930s the profit from these shows, handed over to the Cancer Charity, amounted to over £400 each year (£8000, 1985). In the light of present knowledge an event known as the 'Smoking Concert' hardly seems the most appropriate for a cancer charity.

Over the years famous names appeared on the programme; these included Seymour Hicks, George Robey, Marie Lloyd, Dan Leno, Albert Chevalier, Eugene Stratton, Edna May (the 'Belle of New York'), Ellaline Ferriss, Phyllis Bedells and a whole host of others. It was a difficult matter to persuade the artistes to appear and to fit them into a programme for an evening, especially as a number had other commitments on the same night, and it is not surprising that the secretaries of 'The Smoker' were made Honorary Life Governors of the Hospital.

By 1935 'The Smoker' had become well established as an annual event in the Queen's Hall in Langham Place but the architectural arrangements there were not ideal for a concert of that type, especially in respect of backstage accommodation, and recent developments in the decorations and scenery added to the disadvantages. As a result the venue was changed in 1936 to the Scala Theatre in Charlotte Street where, among other events, *Peter Pan* was a regular production every year. It was eminently suitable for concerts, was considerably cheaper to hire for one night than the Queen's Hall and the number of seats in the auditorium was only slightly less.

Although these concerts were highly successful and attracted a number of internationally known artistes who had no difficulty in coping with any 'high spirits' that might erupt from the balcony or elsewhere in the auditorium, there were, inevitably, others on the stage who did not always receive a warm welcome and who naturally resented any interruptions when they were appearing by invitation and for charity; this caused some embarrassment to the organisers.

ANNUAL DINNER

The annual dinner is an event which will be familiar to most Middlesex men and women and virtually everyone will associate it with the Savoy Hotel where it has been held since 1927, at the end of September or beginning of October, depending on the start of the academic year.

The first annual dinner was held in St James's Hall in 1867 with about 100 gentlemen present from all parts of England. An account of the event concluded with the statement that 'The meeting passed off with great success, an unanimous feeling prevailing that The Middlesex Hospital College Dinner should become an annual institution'. It certainly has done, apart of course from the war years, and the attendance has been somewhat above, or just below, 300.

There have now been over 100 annual dinners and it is worth considering the significance of their continuing popularity. They indicate a desire for Middlesex men, and now women, to dine together, to recall events of the past, to discuss present trends and to contemplate possible future developments. And that can be no bad thing. It signifies a special affinity for an institution which has played such an important role in so many lives at a crucial stage of their careers and indicates an esprit de corps which can be regarded as desirable and praiseworthy. At the beginning of the period of this book there used to be seven speeches at these dinners but in 1939 the decision was taken to reduce the number to the present figure of four. This came into effect when the dinners were resumed after the war, as the 1939 dinner had to be cancelled.

ANNUAL PRIZEGIVING CEREMONY

By 1935 there was an annual prizegiving ceremony held in the Queen's Hall, Langham Place as a combined event for medical students and nurses and for their parents at which there was an 'Introductory Address' by a member of the staff and a 'Report for the Past Year' by the Dean before the prizes were presented. The event at Queen's Hall was followed by tea in the boardroom of the Hospital and in the School Refectory, and the Hospital and School buildings were open for inspection.

In 1936 the prizes were presented to students and nurses by the Duke of Northumberland, President of the Hospital, and the introductory address was given by Dr G. E. S. Ward. In view of the fact that prizes to students are now presented to them before the Astor Lecture on Founders Day it is noteworthy that Dr Ward began his address by commenting on the change of date of the occasion from October to July and then went on to say that the nursing staff always referred to the day as 'Founders Day'.

OTHER EVENTS

Although they did not happen with the same regularity as other annual events and varied somewhat in respect of timing there were, at the beginning of the period of this book, a number of art exhibitions and Music Society concerts as there are today. In 1936 there were two separate music concerts, in the spring and summer terms, and both seem to have been highly successful. In the art exhibition of 1937 one of the items receiving special mention was a model steam engine which had been machined with superb precision by Richard Handley.

Middlesex Institutions

A number of features of The Middlesex which are very much a part of its life today were already in existence more than fifty years ago and will be mentioned briefly.

THE MIDDLESEX HOSPITAL MEDICAL SOCIETY

The Middlesex Hospital Medical Society was founded in 1774, only one year after the foundation of the Medical Society of London, and is the oldest medical society of its kind in the country, with an unbroken continuity to the present day. It was formed by the students themselves and Dr Campbell Thomson records in his book that they were allowed to use the Physicians' Room on two nights a week on condition that they paid three guineas per quarter to the Charity, and also with the proviso that the society would meet at the expense of its own candles.

During the course of its history the society has been addressed by some of the most distinguished figures in medicine and, in addition, has organised a number of conversaziones on the opening nights of new sessions to which visitors from outside medicine were welcomed to give them an opportunity of learning something about the subject and about hospitals. The vitality of the society can be judged from the fact that well-attended meetings were held at weekly or fortnightly intervals during the Christmas and spring terms. Although it has always been a student society, it has long been customary to elect a member of the staff as President.

THE MIDDLESEX HOSPITAL CLUB

Within twenty years of the foundation of the Medical School there were enough graduates who felt they were losing touch with their alma mater; they therefore formed a club with aims which were set out as follows:

1. To promote and maintain social intercourse amongst past students of The Middlesex Hospital;
2. To promote the welfare of the Hospital and Medical School;
3. To create a reserve fund so as to be able to relieve any deserving case of distress occurring amongst former students and to assist any object immediately connected with the welfare and progress of the School.

The club came into being chiefly at the instigation of Mr Thomas Taylor, Lecturer in Chemistry, and there were fifty founder members. The objects of the club are the same now as they were then but there have naturally been some changes in the practical ways adopted for furthering those aims.

Since its inception, apart from the war years, the club has held a dinner following the annual general meeting, the first being chaired by Dr Francis Hawkins, one of the founders of the Medical School. That and the eleven succeeding ones were held in the Albion Tavern. Since then dinners have been held in Willis's Rooms, Pall Mall Restaurant, Criterion, Café Royal, the Royal Botanical Gardens, the Royal College of Surgeons, the London Zoological Society and in the Medical School itself.

THE MIDDLESEX HOSPITAL JOURNAL

In 1897 a senior student, C. H. Reismann (who changed his name to Rivers by deed poll in 1917), originated the idea that the Hospital should possess its own *Journal* to report the activities of the Hospital and School and particularly the Medical Society. He and Dr Campbell Thomson, who was then a Medical Registrar, became the first joint editors. Five issues per year were produced, consisting mainly of medical contributions. In 1903, however, another Middlesex publication also appeared, the *Archives of The Middlesex Hospital*, which proceeded to publish many of the articles which previously would have appeared in the *Journal*. As a result the *Journal* lost a good deal of support. Shortly before the First World War the Amalgamated Clubs agreed to underwrite any losses incurred in producing the *Journal* but this was obviously not a sound business arrangement and in 1924 the formula was changed so that the Amalgamated Clubs agreed to purchase sufficient copies of every issue to provide one for each student.

In 1936 the *Journal* page size increased to $9\frac{1}{4} \times 7$ inches; even though the number of pages was kept at about 200 per year, the enlargement was achieved without any increase in price, six shillings per year. By then it had become firmly established that it was a student journal with a student editor, assistant editor and business manager but there was also a Business Committee chaired by a member of staff. This was Mr E. W. Riches at that time.

—3—
The Prewar Years

'Normal' activities – Preparations for a possible 'emergency' – Death of Prince Arthur of Connaught – Appointment of Major The Hon. J. J. Astor as Chairman of
the Board – Staff changes – Rebuilding – Stilboestrol –
Sulphapyridine – Sulphathiazole – Academic developments – New sports ground

In retrospect there is no difficulty in describing the period 1935–39 as
'the prewar years'. A number of readers will have their own recollections
of those years and how they regarded them at the time but it is of
interest to note from the minutes of meetings and from other records
the official reactions to events and the steps which were being taken to
prepare for what might happen.

It is recorded in the Council minutes of June 1936 that the Dean
had attended a conference at the Home Office on anti-gas precautions
where it had been suggested that an expert from the Home Office
should visit the medical schools to give lecture demonstrations to
students in their final year, or, alternatively, that the schools should
send members of staff to receive a course of instruction at the Home
Office Anti-Gas School so that they could become 'Gas Instructors'
themselves. Council opted for the lecture demonstrations and regarded
the matter as important enough to recommend the Finance Committee
to make a small contribution to any expenses incurred in the exercise.

In September 1938, along with many others, Middlesex members of
the Royal Naval Volunteer Reserve participated in the mobilisation of
the Fleet. Within a month of the Prime Minister, Mr Neville Chamberlain, landing at Croydon Airport on 30 September 1938 on his return
from Munich with the message 'Peace for our time', the London
teaching hospitals had each appointed one man to act as chief executive
officer of hospital and school in the event of war. Dr Harold Boldero

was The Middlesex officer and he and his eleven colleagues continued to meet on a regular basis thereafter. By March 1939 the general principles for medical education in a national emergency had been agreed and the Finance Committee had been asked to examine the financial implications of the proposals. By June it had been decided that, if an emergency occurred, the preclinical students would continue their studies in Bristol and that a Middlesex Sub-Dean should be appointed there to supervise their activities.

In July 1939 Council noted that the Government had appointed Dr Lionel Whitby as the organiser of a Blood Transfusion Service which would come into operation immediately in the event of war and which would be based at the Southmead Hospital, Bristol. At the same meeting in July Council took note of the advice, issued by the Ministry of Health to all hospitals and medical schools, that it was desirable to discourage people from going so far abroad as Canada or the USA during the holiday period; Council also considered a letter from the University of London enquiring about the funds available to help students who might experience hardship if they were transferred to a 'Reception University'.

The records for the period show that, whatever may have been the personal views of individuals, everyday decisions were taken in almost a normal manner while at the same time arrangements were being made in the School and Hospital to have everything prepared for a possible 'emergency', to use the euphemism current at the time. Such was the background against which other events can be recorded for the years covered in this chapter.

Council and Committees

In 1938 HRH Prince Arthur of Connaught died after serving as Chairman of the Board of Management for fourteen years. To fill that important post the Board elected as its Chairman Major The Hon. J. J. Astor MP (Lord Astor of Hever, 1956) who had been a member of the Board since 1920. His association with The Middlesex first arose through his friendship with Mr Alfred Webb-Johnson whose amputation of his leg had saved his life when he was severely wounded in the First World War. Having become associated with The Middlesex in that way he developed a deep and abiding interest in everything related to the Hospital and School. Anonymously at that stage, he had provided the Hospital in 1929 with an outstanding nurses' home which was the envy of the country, at a cost equivalent to over £6 million at today's prices. The anonymity of his gift was preserved until 1948 but the architect had subtly concealed the Astor monogram in the wrought iron of the staircase balustrade.

On becoming Chairman of the Board in 1938 Major Astor resigned from the School Council and the vacancy was filled by Mr F. H. Doran. He was a prominent member of the Stock Exchange and was to become its Vice-Chairman at a later date. His appointment to Council was a very significant one for the School for he was to play a crucial role in the rebuilding of the School in the 1950s and served as Chairman of the School Finance Committee and on other committees for several years.

The year 1938 also saw the death of Mr S. G. Asher, former Chairman of the School Council and a member of the Board of Governors since 1910. He was replaced on the Council and Finance Committee by Mr Arthur Bull.

In June 1936 a knighthood was conferred on Mr Alfred Webb-Johnson and in January 1938 on Mr Edward Meyerstein.

Staff

In September 1937 Professor Thomas Yeates retired from the S. A. Courtauld Chair of Anatomy and Professor John Kirk was appointed to replace him. For nine years before this John Kirk had been Senior Demonstrator in Anatomy and Sub-Dean of the Faculty of Medical Sciences at University College London. Prior to that he had spent twenty-one years in China.

He had graduated in medicine in Edinburgh where, among other distinctions, he had been awarded a golf blue in 1903. In 1907 he had gone as a ship's surgeon to New Zealand to visit relatives and while there he learned of the New Zealand Presbyterian Mission Society's strong wish to establish a hospital in China. The Canton area being considered had a high incidence of disease and a doctor on a previous mission had died within six months of arrival. The region was also known to be hostile to foreigners but such challenges served only to stimulate the deep Christian spirit of J.K., as he was affectionately known. He completed a year without the death of a single patient on whom he operated, by a combination of wise judgement and meticulous care, and as a result the confidence of the local population was secured and the future of the mission established. He returned to New Zealand for a while to raise funds to build a hospital and, later, a nurses' training school in China where he taught anatomy as well as surgery in Cantonese. This linguistic ability was to prove disconcerting to more than one student from that region sitting examinations in England and pleading difficulty in understanding the questions in the oral section.

In Physiology it was decided at the beginning of the 1936–37 session that the Senior Demonstrator post should be converted to that of a permanent First Assistant with the status of lecturer; not surprisingly, Dr Cyril Keele was appointed, from 1 January 1937. At around the same time Mr W. F. Floyd, with a BSc in physics and with a special knowledge of electronics was appointed a Demonstrator. In addition to his teaching and research in physiology Dr Keele had also been teaching pharmacology. In 1938 the regulations for the London MB BS examination were changed to require a course of elementary pharmacology, to be tested in the physiology section of the 2nd MB examination, and a course of pharmacology and therapeutics during the clinical years, to be examined as a separate subject in the Final MB BS examination. To meet these requirements Dr Keele was appointed to a newly created post of Lecturer in Pharmacology and Therapeutics. As no additional space could be provided in the School at that time, he retained his previous accommodation but the department was officially redesignated the Department of Physiology and Pharmacology. This arrangement was to continue, and with Dr Keele as the only teacher of pharmacology, until the Department of Chemistry was redesigned in 1946 to provide accommodation for pharmacology as well as an electro-physiology laboratory.

In 1936 it was decided that the increased demands for physics services consequent on the work of the Meyerstein Institute of Radiotherapy made it necessary to establish an Assistant Physicist post and this was filled from 1 January 1937 by Dr Eric Roberts. He had been a graduate of the University of Leeds where he had also obtained a PhD and a DSc and in 1932 he had joined the Physics Department of Professor Mayneard at the Royal Cancer Hospital, as it was then named before becoming the Royal Marsden Hospital in 1954. In that Department he had undertaken extensive work on the irradiation of tissues and by the time he came to The Middlesex in 1937 he was already recognized as an important member of a new group of British physicists who had changed the whole concept of dose measurement of radium and X-rays from the previous empiricism to one of practical scientific accuracy.

In the Bland-Sutton Institute of Pathology two notable appointments were made in 1936. In June, Dr F. R. Selbie was appointed as a research worker in Bacteriology. He was a student of the University of Aberdeen where he had graduated with the Gold Medal as the best student of the year; he subsequently received the Thursfield award for the best MD thesis. After that he had worked in the Pasteur Institute in Paris and in the University of Munich.

In 1932 Dr C. J. C. Britton had come to The Middlesex as the New Zealand Scholar and in the following year had been appointed as Assistant Pathologist. He had returned to the Christchurch Hospital in New Zealand in 1934 but in late 1936 he accepted a further appointment to the Bland-Sutton Institute to replace Dr W. H. Mason who had died suddenly while holding the post of Assistant Bacteriologist with special duties in haematology. On his original appointment Dr Britton's association with Dr Lionel Whitby had led them to produce an authoritative and popular textbook, *Disorders of the Blood*, which first appeared in 1935. Their subsequent collaboration was to lead to a further nine editions between then and 1969 in order to meet the widespread demand for the book.

There were also a number of important changes in the honorary staff of the Hospital during this period. In 1937 the Senior Surgeon, Mr William Sampson Handley, retired and Mr William Turner Warwick was appointed to succeed him on the senior staff. Mr P. B. Ascroft was appointed as Assistant Surgeon. He was a brilliant general surgeon with a particular expertise in neurosurgery and with a ready willingness to instruct students in surgical skills and spend time 'assisting' them. With Mr Turner Warwick's interest in colo-rectal surgery it was not long before the two surgical Honoraries on the fourth floor were the subject of a cartoon in the *Journal* laconically entitled 'Tops and Tails'.

Later in 1937 Mr Victor Bonney reached retiring age and joined the consulting staff. The vacancy on the honorary staff was filled in January 1938 by Mr W. Ralph Winterton who had originally come to the School as a Cambridge student and who was on the staff of The Hospital for Women, Soho, and Queen Charlotte's Hospital before being appointed to The Middlesex. He had the reputation of being a forthright debunker of unnecessarily elaborate theories and practices.

Also in 1937 Mr Cleminson retired from the staff of the Ear, Nose and Throat Department on account of ill health and his place was taken by Mr J. P. Monkhouse. He had graduated from St Mary's Hospital Medical School and, in addition to other attributes, he had a fine engineering and watchmaking skill which was to help him make considerable contributions to the design and improvement of surgical instruments. Mr Monkhouse became a pioneer, within a decade, in the microsurgery of the ear.

In 1936 the number of registrars was increased by the appointment of a Fracture and Orthopaedic Registrar and a Dental Registrar. Even with the latter appointment, and with no dental students, the School agreed to follow the normal pattern and meet half the salary cost because of the research which he would undertake. In 1938 two other new posts were created. One was of a Clinical Cancer Research Officer and the other an Anaesthetic Registrar who would have important teaching commitments during the sixth clinical appointment.

Rebuilding

With the completion of the Hospital rebuilding in 1935 the School was able to start giving detailed consideration to its own plans for development which had been envisaged since at least 1922 and, more particularly, since 1933 when the Dean had been asked to prepare a memorandum on requirements. Accordingly, a Medical School Accommodation Sub-Committee was established with a membership of Dr H. E. A. Boldero (Dean), Mr R. C. Davis, Mr E. Pearce Gould, Mr A. E. Webb-Johnson, and with the architect, Mr Alner Hall, in attendance. There was no difficulty in agreeing that the first step towards reconstruction would be the conversion of the baker's shop and the flats above it at the corner of Riding House Street (then Union Street) and Nassau Street. The proposals were readily accepted by the Council and Board of Management and the contract was signed on 6 May 1936. This extension provided an additional lecture theatre for the Anatomy Department and further laboratory space for the Departments of Physiology and Physics. The new accommodation was in use at the beginning of the 1936–37 session.

While this was proceeding the Sub-Committee was considering the main development and no less than forty-one meetings were held between January 1936 and July 1938. The memorandum prepared by the Dean on the School's requirements formed the basis of the discussions and a review was made of virtually all property in the neighbourhood which might be considered of potential value. After thorough investigation it became clear that none of these properties could be considered a practical proposition and the decision was taken to recommend rebuilding on the garden site in line with the West Wing of the Hospital after demolition of the Round Lecture Theatre. This general plan was approved by the School Council and the Board of Management with some overall restrictions but a lot of further discussion was required to determine the facilities which should be included.

It was an essential requirement that the basement should provide accommodation for mortuary chapels of different denominations as well as at least one room for relatives of deceased patients. It was also agreed at an early stage that the third floor should be used as a post-mortem room and preparation room. There were additional requirements for an assembly hall, a new library, a new refectory, a new lecture theatre to replace the Round Lecture Theatre, and laboratory accommodation for biology. After considerable discussion at several meetings it was decided that the second floor should have laboratories and offices for biology, that the library should be on the first floor and that, on the ground floor, there should be two lecture theatres and rooms for the Dean and for the School Secretary together with a records room and secretary/typist's office. It was felt that the other requirements would have to await subsequent developments. The building proceeded but at one stage a short delay occurred as the workmen had to leave the site to undertake some air-raid precaution work elsewhere. In spite of this the work was completed on schedule in July 1939 at a cost, at 1985 price levels, of approximately £1 million. Another plan which was agreed and put out to tender in March 1939 was to build two squash courts in the South House of the Out-Patients Annexe but, unfortunately, when the estimates were received they proved to be much higher than anticipated and it was regretfully decided to proceed no further.

Research

Research is an essential feature of a university's academic activity and The Middlesex has an enviable record in this field. Over many years it has attracted, in relation to its size, a high proportion of the grants awarded in open competition by the research councils and the great charitable trusts and foundations. The research carried out in the School has been widely based and it would be quite impossible to describe the contributions of every department. Instead, a few outstanding achievements have been selected from the 1935–39 period, although even these deserve fuller treatment than can be accorded here.

STILBOESTROL

Diethylstilboestrol (4:4′-dihydroxy-αβ-diethylstilbene) was the first synthetic compound to be used extensively in clinical practice for its hormonal activity. Its synthesis in Oxford and the demonstration of its biological activity in the Courtauld Institute in 1937 gave a great stimulus to endocrinology and, particularly, to the production of a whole range of new compounds with hormonal effects. The research that led up to this achievement was an illustration of deductive innovation combined with methodical perseverance and demonstrated the value of collaboration between various workers in the field.

By the end of the last century a very crude extract of the ovaries had been used in attempts to relieve menopausal symptoms and some success had been claimed. In 1930, Dodds and Robertson in the Courtauld Institute had shown that an ovarian extract then known as oestrin could be used to relieve symptoms in menopausal and ovariectomised women. It was also known that oestrin from different sources contained several active compounds, although their structures had not been determined. Then, using X-ray crystallography in one of its earliest applications to a biological problem, workers deduced the structure of the steroid nucleus. As a result of this Dodds, Cook and Hewett early in 1933 were able to postulate a structure for one of the compounds in ovarian extracts – oestrone.

As soon as this had been achieved attempts to synthesise it began. The Courtauld Institute group, headed by Professor Dodds, took the view that as several active compounds were known to exist it was likely that structures related to oestrone might also be active. Over the course of the next four to five years Dodds and Lawson synthesised a wide range of compounds whose biological activity was then assessed. In this way they hoped to identify that part of the oestrone structure which conferred oestrogenic activity. While this was going on at The Middlesex an investigation was underway in Sir Robert Robinson's department in Oxford to try to synthesise agents which, while non-steroidal, bore a structural resemblance to oestrone. Mr Lawson had previously worked for Sir Robert Robinson when the latter was Director of Research at the British Dyestuffs Corporation. The laboratories in Oxford and the Courtauld Institute decided to join forces to avoid duplication of work. While testing compounds synthesized by Lawson, the Courtauld team discovered an unidentified impurity in one compound which had a very high activity. Robinson postulated a possible structure for the substance and Dr Leon Golberg, who was then working for him, synthesized a pure sample of what is now known as diethystilboestrol. Assessment of its biological activity in the Courtauld Institute showed it to have the highest oestrogenic activity of any substance known.

'Stilboestrol', as the substance soon came to be known, in spite of the recommendation to the contrary of the workers who had produced it, rapidly came into clinical use as an oral oestrogen to relieve menopausal symptoms, suppress lactation and, in early pregnancy, to reduce the risk of certain types of threatened abortion. It also soon found a place in the management of patients with carcinoma of the prostate and some types of carcinoma of the breast.

Natural oestrogens, which had to be extracted from the urine of pregnant mares by an expensive process, were usually administered by injection whereas stilboestrol is almost as active when administered by mouth as by injection. It appeared to reproduce the activities of the naturally occurring hormone in every way and the combination of cheapness with oral administration provided a drug of inestimable value.

There was, of course, no question in the minds of the discoverers of patenting the substance they had produced and all the information about its preparation was published. Years later, however, when it came to be used so extensively in farm animals bred for food production, others were led to calculate the possible financial rewards which would have accrued to the School and Hospital if stilboestrol had been patented. Other British laboratories have probably made similar calculations in respect of penicillin. Mention might also be made here, rather than in the next chapter, of a story relating to the Second World War. It was said that a proposal had been put forward for emasculating the German war effort by doctoring their reservoirs with appropriate amounts of stilboestrol, which could easily be manufactured by the ton. The proposal was supposed to have been rejected on the grounds that it would be 'hitting below the belt'.

SULPHAPYRIDINE AND SULPHATHIAZOLE

In 1935 Prontosil Rubrum was shown to be capable of curing animal and human infections caused by haemolytic streptococci and it was soon determined that sulphanilamide was the active agent. This naturally led to attempts to synthesise derivatives of it which would be more effective against other organisms. Many different sulphonamides were tested in the Bland-Sutton Institute of Pathology by Dr Lionel Whitby and Mr (later Dr) Stanley Bushby. The standard practice of testing at that time was to administer a single dose of the drug to mice on the day of infection but Whitby and Bushby also tested the administration of two doses, in spite of the great inconvenience caused by the lateness of the hour (11p.m.) for the second dose. Using this procedure against pneumococcal infections in mice they demonstrated the curative effect of a sulphonamide then known by its serial number of M&B 693 (sulphapyridine) which had been produced in the May and Baker Laboratories by Dr M. A. Phillips working under the direction of Dr M. A. Ewins. Clinical trials soon followed. One of the first of these, in Birmingham, involved a study of over 100 patients with pneumococcal pneumonia in which there was a mortality of 8 per cent in the patients treated with M&B 693 compared with 27 per cent in the control series. Later, this drug was also shown to be effective against gonococci. Another sulphonamide which was shown by Whitby and Bushby to be highly active against pneumococci and other organisms was M&B 760 (sulphathiazole). This came to replace sulphapyridine as it was better tolerated by patients.

In 1937 and 1938 Whitby's publications in *The Lancet* evoked considerable interest. One newspaper carried an article on the subject under the bold headline, 'Thank you, Dr Whitby'. The story goes that, next day, when he had finished a routine lecture, the whole class rose as one man and said, 'Thank you, Dr Whitby'.

The effectiveness of these sulphonamides was highlighted during the War when Winston Churchill developed pneumonia in the Middle East. He recounted the illness in his own characteristic manner:

This admirable M and B, from which I did not suffer any inconvenience, was used at the earliest moment and after a week's fever the intruders were repulsed . . . The M and B, which I also called Moran and Bedford, did the work most effectively. There is no doubt that pneumonia is a very different illness from what it was before this marvellous drug was

65

discovered. I did not at any time relinquish my part in the direction of affairs, and there was not the slightest delay in giving the decisions required of me.

Lord Moran was, of course, Churchill's physician. The Bedford to whom he referred was Dr Evan Bedford, then Brigadier Bedford, who, as a clinical colleague of Whitby's at The Middlesex, had been keenly interested in the research being undertaken in the Bland-Sutton Institute a few years earlier.

The advent of the sulphonamide group of drugs and their subsequent development was a most important event in the history of medicine but, as Dr Bushby has pointed out, the major scientific value of the work lay in the discovery that chemical agents could be selectively toxic to bacteria *in vivo*. Until then experiences with antibacterial agents had suggested that the biochemistry of bacteria and human cells was so similar that it was not possible to affect invading bacteria with a systemic drug without also affecting the host. The subsequent introduction of pencillin, which had been used for some years as a laboratory tool, was to produce dramatic effects far beyond those of the sulphonamides.

BACTERIAL CHEMISTRY

In April 1934 a Medical Research Council Unit of Bacterial Chemistry had been established in the Bland-Sutton Institute of Pathology to promote a multidisciplinary study of bacteria of medical interest. The Director was Dr Paul Fildes (Sir Paul Fildes, 1946) FRS, and he headed a powerful team of workers, four of them subsequently becoming professors. In 1920 Dr Fildes had founded the *British Journal of Experimental Pathology* which was subsequently edited by Professor R. W. Scarff, later by Dr R. E. M. Thompson, and now by Professor R. Marian Hicks, Professor of Experimental Pathology in the Bland-Sutton Institute of Pathology.

In 1937, Dr B. C. J. G. Knight, Halley Stewart Research Fellow in the unit, was the first person to demonstrate the growth-factor activity of nicotinic acid and nicotinamide in any organism and later showed that Staphylococcus Aureus could be grown in a medium containing only known chemical components. These findings were important not only for promoting further studies on the nutrition of bacteria but also for the treatment of human nutritional diseases.

When Dr Knight left the unit he was replaced as Halley Stewart

Research Fellow by Dr D. D. Woods who worked on the nature of the substances that were able to reverse the bacteriostatic effect of the sulphonamides. He showed that a sulphanilamide antagonist contained an amino derivative of an aromatic carboxylic acid which acted in a competitive manner and he reasoned that the antagonist was closely related to sulphanilamide in chemical structure. After testing a series of compounds he found p-aminobenzoic acid to be active and went on to propose that the sulphonamide resistance of some organisms might be due to their ability to synthesise sufficient p-aminobenzoic acid to antagonise all the sulphanilamide present. This was subsequently shown to be correct and was a discovery of significance in wider fields.

Academic Developments

The most significant changes in the curriculum and in arrangements for teaching in the prewar years were those in pharmacology, described earlier. In view of the associations which have developed in the last few years between The Middlesex and the Institute of Orthopaedics and the Royal National Orthopaedic Hospital it is of interest that, in 1938, the School accepted with pleasure a suggestion made by Mr H. J. Seddon (Sir Herbert Seddon, 1964), Medical Superintendent of the RNOH at Stanmore, that students might be given six lecture-demonstrations four times per year on Saturday mornings. In the same year The Middlesex agreed to the request of the Postgraduate Medical School, Hammersmith, to provide lecture-demonstrations to panel practitioners up to one a month. In that year also, the Dean, Dr Harold Boldero, was appointed Chairman of the Board of Advanced Medical Studies of the University of London. This was just one of many important appointments outside The Middlesex which he was to hold.

At the beginning of these prewar years the generosity of Mr Edward Meyerstein provided two new scholarships for London students to match those already available to Oxford and Cambridge entrants. This was achieved with an endowment of £3000 which he subsequently doubled. The School Committee drew up regulations for the examinations in anatomy and physiology which were approved by Council and the first awards were made in 1936. A Meyerstein Scholar of a subsequent year, after some hesitation and with considerable diffidence, wrote to Sir Edward, as he then was, to express his great appreciation that such a scholarship had been made available. The warm and under-standing response which he received made it clear that his diffidence had not been necessary and that Sir Edward had been deeply touched by this demonstration of what he had been able to achieve.

The necessity to demolish the Round Lecture Theatre at the start of the rebuilding process placed the School in a difficult position and the relationship existing with the Hospital is well demonstrated by the records of the way in which the problem was overcome. The Board of Management offered to lease Sandhurst Ward to the School for a period of eight months for lectures and demonstrations and proposed that the rental should be at the rate of £75 per annum, plus the initial cost of any necessary alterations. The School Council considered this generous offer at its meeting on 2 June 1938 but regarded the rent as inadequate and, on a formal motion proposed by the Honorary Treas-urer, 'it was decided to inform the Board that the School desired to pay £150 per annum, plus the initial cost of the alterations'.

Amalgamated Clubs

It was in the prewar period that the most momentous event in the history of the Amalgamated Clubs occurred. This was the acquisition in 1938 of the School's own sports ground at Chislehurst, made possible by the further great generosity of Sir Edward Meyerstein.

For some time the School had been considering how it could improve its sports facilities and the possibility of obtaining a new ground was being contemplated. Then in 1936 St Mary's purchased a new ground for themselves at Teddington and from 1 August 1937 the School had to assume sole responsibility for the Wembley ground or acquire a new one. A sub-committee was established to examine the possibilities and Mr Edward Meyerstein agreed to serve as Chairman. In October 1937 the Dean reported to Council that Mr Meyerstein had made a generous gift of £14,122 10s to purchase a new athletic ground of 18.83 acres (7.6 hectares) at Chislehurst. This was not all, for, in the following year, Sir Edward (as he had become) not only added a further three acres which had become available but he also agreed to meet the cost of the construction of an access road, as well as the demolition of the riding school which had been stipulated by the vendors.

As a result of this generosity the School received for its sole use a well-drained ground which was double the size of the one on clay soil which it had previously shared. The ground at Wembley was sold and the assets put towards the cost of a two-storey pavilion at Chislehurst. Mr Richard Davis made a gift of chairs; Mr Eric Pearce Gould provided the fine crest for the balcony rail; and the Dean's wife, Margery, presented the special old and large clock face which had been removed from the Ludgrove Preparatory School when it transferred to other premises. That school had been founded by her father. Even with this help there would have been a deficit on the capital account of £1118 10s 10d if that sum had not been contributed most generously by the Dean, Dr Harold Boldero.

The ground and pavilion were formally opened on 21 May 1938. Sir Edward had specifically requested that there should be no ceremony but, not surprisingly, some well-chosen words of thanks were voiced by the Dean during the tea interval of the 'Past *v.* Present' cricket match. On that occasion the 'Present' team won handsomely by seven wickets, avenging their defeat the previous year at Wembley.

The Middlesex Hospital *Journal* of January 1938 published a delightful full-page cartoon of Sir Edward; below it was an appropriate ditty which read:

> To patient first he turned his thoughts,
> His kindness was unbounded,
> But now (great day!) he sees that we
> Are well and truly grounded.

The students' great appreciation of the new athletic ground was further expressed aptly by the captain of the Rugby Club at their annual dinner the following year. He remarked, in the course of his speech:

Chislehurst in its first season has proved more than a joy, in fact a danger; some people being so enamoured of the place as to refuse point blank to play anywhere else, the notable exception being our President (Dr Douglas McAlpine) who has supported us through all the Home Counties, in every sort of weather.

Of the other clubs, the Sailing Club had significant successes in the prewar years. In 1937 it won both the Harvey Gold Challenge Inter-Hospital Cup and the Bourne Trophy and in 1939 retained the Harvey Cup while narrowly losing the Bourne Trophy to Guy's. The Squash Club won both the Senior and Junior Inter-Hospital Cups in 1939.

The Medical Society continued active programmes and the Music Society had some particularly successful concerts in the Refectory while its choral section provided special carol services in the Chapel.

—4—
The Second World War

London and the War – Hospital arrangements for London
– The Middlesex Hospital – Central Middlesex Hospital
– Preclinical education – Clinical education – Academic
developments – Some other events – Awards and distinctions – Deaths – H.M. Forces – Inter-departmental
committee

The plans which had been prepared for the civilian population and for
hospitals and medical education in the event of war had been based on
the assumption that there would be immediate heavy air-raids on major
cities in Britain and, particularly, on London. They were expected on
the first night but they did not come for several months. After the
German onslaught on Poland from 1 September there were six months
of the 'phoney war', as it was called, before the sudden German invasion
of Norway in April 1940 followed by that of Western Europe in May.
This led to the rapid fall of the Netherlands, Belgium, Denmark and
France and the evacuation of the British Forces from the beaches of
Dunkirk at the end of May 1940. Later that month the German air
force attacked Britain in strength and the Battle of Britain began. At
that stage the German bombing attacks were mainly, but by no means
exclusively, on airfields and other military targets and mostly by day.

Then, having lost the Battle of Britain, the Germans began the
intense bombing of London, in September 1940. For a period of two
months London was attacked every night by an average of 200 bombers.
For a further six months, until May 1941, the bombing of London
continued heavily, but not invariably each night and there was considerable variation in the intensity of the attacks on different occasions.

After the bombing raid of 10 May 1941, which was a particularly
heavy one, London experienced another prolonged lull until February
1944 when a 'baby blitz', as it was called, began. Then, later in 1944,

just one week after the D-Day invasion of Normandy by the Allies on 6 June, London and south-east England came under attack from a new weapon. This was a small, fast, pilotless plane carrying a ton of high explosive. After travelling a predetermined distance the power cut off, there was a sudden cessation of the strident obtrusive noise of the ingenious new jet engine and the plane dived to the ground, not always continuing in the original flight path. These 'flying bombs', 'doodle-bugs', or 'buzz bombs' as they were called, might come over at any time of the day or night. From 15 June 1944 they arrived in large numbers – more than 200 within twenty-four hours, over 3000 in five weeks and more than 7500 in all before their launching sites were overrun by the British and Canadian armies early in September 1944.

The Germans referred to these new weapons as the V1 (*Vergeltung*: retribution, retaliation) and the numeration indicated that it was the first of a series of special weapons. No sooner had the V1 been stopped than the V2 was deployed. This was a high-flying rocket travelling at 4000 m.p.h., and so its explosion preceded the sound of its arrival; in this respect it was the exact opposite of the V1. Because of this and because the accuracy of these weapons was no better than about fifteen miles there were good reasons for not broadcasting much information about the damage they produced; for quite a time they were commonly referred to, rather conspiratorially, as 'flying gas mains'. After the first landed at Chiswick on 8 September 1944 about 200 of these rockets were launched against London each month and more than 1000 in all.

All threats of bombing stopped with the end of the war in Europe on 8 May 1945. The war in the Far East against Japan continued until 14 August 1945.

Hospital Arrangements for London

To enable the hospitals in London and the Home Counties to cope with the number of casualties expected, in addition to continuing to provide facilities for ill patients, plans had been drawn up to convert the teaching hospitals in central London into casualty-reception hospi-tals for the immediate treatment of air-raid victims. A number of hospitals in the relatively safer country around London would be expanded to become base hospitals for the subsequent treatment of casualties and for the care of the sick. For these arrangements to run at all smoothly it was clear that hospitals would have to be grouped together and the obvious arrangement was a sector system radiating out from the centre through the suburbs to the country for about forty miles beyond. The ten sectors agreed were very roughly triangular in shape with a teaching hospital, or in some cases two hospitals, at the apex of each. At the outbreak of the War the Emergency Medical Service (EMS) was brought into operation. The honorary staff were employed fulltime in the EMS but a few months later were offered the opportunity of becoming part-time, with the proviso that they would be required to revert to fulltime employment if circumstances required it.

SECTOR V

The Middlesex was the teaching hospital of Sector V which stretched through Willesden, Wembley, Harrow and the south-west corner of Hertfordshire as far as Aylesbury in Buckinghamshire. The head-quarters of this Sector was at Rickmansworth and based there were the Group Officer in charge of the Sector, Dr Harold Boldero, Dean of the Medical School; the Sector Matron, Miss Dorothy Smith who had been Matron of The Middlesex Hospital since 1929; the Sector-Officer, Mr S. R. C. Plimsoll who had been Secretary-Superintendent of The Middlesex Hospital since 1929; together with other officers from the various municipal authorities and voluntary hospitals in the Sector. In the suburbs the other hospitals in Sector V were the Central Middlesex County Hospital (as it was then); Willesden General and Municipal Hospitals; St Andrew's Hospital at Dollis Hill; Wembley Hospital; and the Harrow and Wealdstone Hospital.

The base hospitals were Mount Vernon Hospital at Northwood, and the Royal Bucks Hospital and Tindal House Emergency Hospital at Aylesbury. The last of these was a public-assistance institution which was converted into an emergency hospital. To start with it had only two wards and additional potential bed space was provided in marquees, without any floors, which had been erected in the kitchen garden where the cabbages were still growing. There was no operating theatre and one had to be improvised. Later, huts were built and linked with passages which were covered, but not enclosed, and it was bitterly cold in winter for patients being transferred to and from the theatre or from one hut to another. Staff and students were accommodated in miserably small metal-walled rooms with tiny windows above eye level. Additionally, a large hutted hospital was being created for the Ministry of Pensions at Stoke Mandeville, about two miles from Aylesbury. This was completed during 1940 and, in addition to other facilities, it provided a major plastic surgery and burns unit directed by Professor T. Pomfret Kilner. A few years later it was to become internationally renowned for its pioneering treatment and rehabilitation of patients with spinal injuries. This was accomplished by the imaginative innovation and dedication of Dr Ludwig Guttman (Sir Ludwig Guttman, 1966) who had come to this country from Germany in 1939 to take up a research appointment at the University of Oxford.

The Middlesex Hospital

During August 1939 the increasing tension led to a steady reduction in the number of admissions to The Middlesex Hospital and when the Germans invaded Poland on Friday, 1 September, the emergency plan was brought into immediate operation. All patients who were fit to return home were discharged, many in a fleet of cars organised by the National Emergency Branch of the Ladies Association. Eighty patients who still required hospital treatment, but who were fit to be moved, were transferred in a convoy of Green Line buses which had been converted into multi-stretcher ambulances. These were to become a familiar feature of the arrangements for the evacuation of casualties when the heavy air-raids started in September 1940. As a result of these efficient measures, by the afternoon of 1 September there were only sixty-two patients left in the Hospital and they were concentrated in the wards on the third floor.

The sixth floor, including the theatre block, was closed completely and new theatres and anaesthetic rooms created on the crosspieces of the second and fourth floors. So as to take full advantage of the space and personnel available two operating tables were fitted into each new theatre on the north sides of the crosspieces. The front hall and board-room were cleared and were prepared to receive casualties; the front courtyard was closed off with a formidable hoarding and its gates, which could be opened for the admission of ambulances during raids, were otherwise kept closed in order to divert users to the Casualty Department in Nassau Street, which became the normal entrance to the Hospital. The front doors and other vulnerable areas were heavily protected by sandbags; the official figures gave the number at 20,000 but those involved in filling them considered that that was a considerable underestimate. The Out-Patient Annexe in Cleveland Street was closed, its ground floor converted into a first-aid post and the basement into a gas-cleansing station. An anti-gas unit was also established in the front courtyard of the Hospital and all personnel carried gas masks.

The sub-basement of the Hospital had long been a storage area for equipment which might be required at some time in the future and was regarded as a challenge to intrepid explorers. It clearly provided a well-protected air-raid shelter, however, and so it had been cleared and an emergency operating theatre and telephone exchange installed in a bricked-up area. Nothing could be done about the obstructions from the many pipes nor about the limited height in many places; however, different areas were allocated to various groups of staff who soon learnt the topography of their patches as a result of painful reminders to skulls and legs. When the air-raids started in September 1940, the sub-basement provided well-protected accommodation for the nurses and other members of staff and for patients from the Woolavington Wing, which was much more vulnerable than the rest of the hospital. This was demonstrated in an early raid when a lot of debris fell down the stairway, damaged it and almost completely obstructed it. At the top of the building, at the other extreme of exposure and danger, the Chief Engineer, Mr David Latto, was in charge of a roof patrol to fight fires and give warnings of imminent attack, with Mr Harry Bolton as his deputy. When the first country-wide blackout came on the night of 1 September the Hospital was in a position to receive and treat casualties in the 200 beds which were ready for them.

The broadcast by the Prime Minister at 11.15 on the morning of Sunday, 3 September, declaring that the country was at war with Germany was followed within a few minutes by an air-raid warning. This was a false alarm but it drew attention to a number of deficiencies in the movement of personnel to action stations, so two other practices were held that day. That night there was a further false alarm so that, within twenty-four hours of the declaration of war, the staff had had four practice alerts and were well acquainted with their roles. They were to become even more proficient with further practice and some months later, at an exercise during the blackout on a dark night, forty-eight 'casualties' were unloaded from twenty-four ambulances and admitted in the space of fifty minutes.

In order to run the Hospital effectively during the war new administrative arrangements were introduced. The Board of Management discontinued its monthly meetings and established a small Emergency

War Committee which also took over the duties of the House Committee. A Medical Commandant was appointed and initially this was Dr Hugh Marriott. When he joined the RAMC in November 1939 he was replaced as Commandant by Dr Alan Moncrieff (Sir Alan Moncrieff, 1964) for a period of a year and then by Mr Brian Windeyer for the remainder of the war. Mr Brian Windeyer was also Dr Harold Boldero's Deputy Group Officer for Sector V.

As the Secretary-Superintendent had become Sector Officer at Rickmansworth the administrative responsibilities of the Hospital devolved on his deputy, Mr H. M. Wilkinson, known affectionately and almost universally as 'Wilkie'. He was the epitome of quiet courteous efficiency and with the Chief Engineer and Deputy Chief Engineer, Mr D. Latto and Mr H. Bolton, the Steward, Mr V. Leek, and the Pharmacist, Mr S. H. White, there was a splendid administrative team to cope with the multitudinous and ever-changing problems facing the Hospital. They became resident in the same way as the medical staff. The Courtauld Wards on the first-floor crosspiece were used to provide accommodation for the honoraries.

As the anti-climax of the 'phoney war' dragged on, sick patients naturally wanted to start using the Hospital again and it was obviously not realistic to keep staff standing by merely to deal with casualties at some uncertain time in the future. Accordingly, the Hospital began to undertake some of its usual medical activities. The first floor of the Barnato-Joel Wing was converted for use by out-patients. At the end of the year the First-Aid Post was transferred to Casualty and the Annexe reopened to a limited extent. The hoarding was also removed from the front courtyard and the front entrance re-opened. By August 1940 all the departments of the Hospital were open to some extent, in spite of the Battle of Britain which had been raging since June.

The start of the heavy bombing of London in September 1940 led to the complete closure of the sixth, fifth and fourth floors of the Hospital and all casualties who required admission were accommodated on the second floor. All the windows of this floor were completely bricked in but, even so, some months later, an unexploded anti-aircraft shell penetrated one of the windows on the street side of Northumberland Ward. Fortunately it failed to explode for the ward was full at the time. The wisdom of evacuating the upper three floors was to be demonstrated subsequently and was almost certainly responsible for saving many lives. The glass was removed from the windows on all the floors and replaced with a fabric which often needed renewing but which avoided the risks of flying glass in explosions.

The medical and nursing staff worked in two teams which were on duty on alternate twenty-four hours. The surgeons on one team were Mr Vaughan Hudson and Mr Paul Wilson and, on the other, Mr David Patey and Mr Brian Windeyer. Dr F. W. (Bobby) Roberts was the anaesthetist to both teams. On most nights operating would go on until about 10 o'clock the following morning and in the afternoon all those patients who were fit for evacuation would be loaded into the convoys of Green Line bus ambulances for transfer to Northwood or Aylesbury. The maximum number of casualties treated on any one night was during the heavy raids of 17–18 April 1941 when eighty-four were admitted, in addition to a much larger number who were treated in the boardroom or Casualty Department. It was no easy task to be sure that casualties did not require admission. Virtually all of them were heavily covered in dirt and blood which had to be cleaned off gently and thoroughly to allow adequate inspection. On that occasion in April operations went on all the following day and some of that night as well. The raids on Saturday 10 May were also particularly heavy with many casualties, but nobody at the time was able to envisage that this would be the last for nearly three years until the 'baby blitz' of 1944, followed by the V weapons starting in June 1944.

The V1 flying bombs resulted in many alerts, at any time of the day and night, and some of them landed close to The Middlesex causing a large number of deaths and injuries. One landed at lunch time on a restaurant in Whitfield Street, just a few hundred yards away. The street was crowded at the time and 200 casualties were brought to The Middlesex of whom eighty had to be admitted. Another, also at lunch time, landing a similar distance away, damaged one of the buildings then on the site of the original Middlesex Hospital in Windmill Street.

Some of the V2 rockets also came down close to The Middlesex, but without any warning. One exploded with a very loud bang on a Saturday morning in November 1944 while Professor Samson Wright was chairing a meeting of the Physiological Society in the Bland-Sutton Lecture Theatre. Lord Adrian, Sir Henry Dale, Sir Edward Mellanby and a host of other distinguished physiologists were in the audience. Dr Cyril Keele, who was present, could not help reflecting that a fractional difference of trajectory might well have resulted in the extinction of the cream of British physiologists in a few milliseconds. Other

V2s also brought a number of casualties and one caused damage to the Hospital, as will be mentioned later.

HOSPITAL AND SCHOOL AIR-RAID DAMAGE

The Middlesex certainly did not emerge unscathed from the War but, considering the intensity and duration of the attacks on London and the proximity of many heavy explosions, the casualties and structural damage were mercifully not great. Two factors played a large part in this protection; the enormous strength and sound construction of the steel-framed and concrete building and the courage and dedication of the roof patrol. Without any protection from bombs or flying debris of all types, except for their steel helmets, they stayed at their uncomfortable posts throughout the whole of the prolonged alert periods. They scrambled all over the treacherous roofs in the dark to deal with fire bombs as they fell and it is amazing that there were no fires in the main building. In one episode alone they dealt with a cluster of fifty incendiaries.

The hazards which the roof patrol faced in their exposed positions are well illustrated by the wording of a decision made by the Emergency War Committee at the time of the V1 raids in 1944, when the alerts were so numerous that staff could not stop working every time the air-raid sirens sounded. The minute of the meeting recorded:

> It was decided that a second warning should be given only if Mr Latto or his Deputy on the roof of the Hospital considered that the bomb was likely to fall in the immediate vicinity of the Hospital. It was realised that this would not give adequate time for patients and staff to go to the shelters, but would enable them to take what cover was available from flying glass and blast.

But there was no cover available on the roof!

The only fatal injury to personnel occurred in an early daylight raid in 1940 when a plane suddenly appeared low out of the clouds before any warning could be given and dropped two small bombs on the Hospital. The one which fell on the West Wing did little damage but the other destroyed a sanitary tower of the Radiotherapy Wing. A fragment of this bomb killed instantly a member of the Friends Ambulance Unit who happened to be in the Barnato-Joel Wing at the time. Three others were injured in that explosion, one of whom was a student who was in his room in the Residency. A large splinter of glass slashed his left arm severing the brachial artery and median nerve but the College Sister, Sister Clark, was on the scene very quickly and when she saw the pool of blood outside a door she found the exsanguinated student collapsed on the bed. He was rushed to the operating theatre and his life saved with a massive blood transfusion.

The greatest damage to the buildings occurred in the heavy raids of 17 April 1941. In one attack a 500kg bomb penetrated the roof of the East Wing and the explosion caused severe damage on the sixth, fifth and fourth floors – Strathcona, Maternity and Meyerstein Wards – all of which were empty as there were no patients above the third floor. The solid strength of the building was amply demonstrated that night by the fact that the staff working on the second floor at the time were not aware until later that the hospital itself had been hit, although it was abundantly clear that it was another 'in the immediate vicinity' as the saying went. In a later attack the same night the top floor of the North Wing of the Out-Patient Annexe was destroyed by explosions followed by a fire which could not be extinguished as no water was available in the mains. As a result, the Barnato-Joel Wing had to be used once again for out-patients. During the 1941–44 lull in bombing the Annexe was largely repaired and reglazed but unfortunately it was further damaged by the V2 rocket which destroyed the Whitfield Memorial Chapel in Tottenham Court Road.

Structural damage to the School was not major. Many windows were broken and in the Barnato-Joel Laboratories apparatus and doors were destroyed by the bomb which landed on the sanitary tower of the Radiotherapy Wing. The Ferens Institute lost a large number of irreplaceable records and also apparatus in the raids which seriously damaged the Out-Patient Annexe. There was also some damage to the tennis court, grounds and pavilion at Chislehurst both in the 1940–41 blitz and from the V1 bombs, many of which landed in the south-east of London.

Central Middlesex County Hospital

The hospitals in Aylesbury were not in a vulnerable area and although Mount Vernon Hospital at Northwood was subject to considerable disruption it did not sustain any bomb damage. The location of the Central Middlesex County Hospital, however, meant that it was very exposed to air attack and it suffered severely. In the 1940–41 raids, ward blocks, the ambulance station and part of the nurses' home were put out of action and other residential accommodation was completely wrecked. Fortunately, none of this resulted in any loss of life to patients or staff. The hospital had to be closed for a while because of disruption of the water and gas supply but a few casualty beds were kept open in spite of that. Students were withdrawn temporarily but were able to return on 1 February 1941.

In February 1944, at the beginning of the 'baby blitz', the garage and five ambulances were completely destroyed and F Block with 100 patients, together with two adjacent buildings holding forty patients, were so severely damaged that they had to be evacuated. The V1 weapons led to the decision to close the vulnerable maternity unit and transfer it to Wellingborough in Northamptonshire but it was reopened in November 1944 and some of the chronic patients were also returned. By a fortunate chance a delay in transport arrangements postponed the reopening of the chronic ward in J Block; on 27 January 1945 a V2 rocket caused so much damage to the empty block that it had to be demolished. The maternity unit was also damaged in the explosion and for a period the patients there had to be transferred to other parts of the hospital while new patients were admitted to other hospitals. Once more it was fortunate that there was no loss of life. Throughout the Blitz hundreds of civilian casualties were treated, particularly from the many surrounding factories which continued to work day and night.

Preclinical Education

Short courses are well recognised in universities but few can have been quite so brief as the preclinical vacation course in anatomy and physiology which started on 1 September 1939. By 10.30 that morning news of the invasion of Poland was known in the classrooms and shortly afterwards Professor Kirk summed up the position by saying, 'Gentlemen, I think we may take it that the vacation course is definitely cancelled'.

MOVE TO BRISTOL

In accordance with the plans which had already been made the preclinical students and most of the preclinical staff were evacuated to Bristol and received a warm welcome from the Medical School and University even though it meant more than doubling, and in some cases almost trebling, the numbers in the lecture theatres and the dissecting room. By careful organisation and willing collaboration it proved possible to cope with this influx of nearly 100 extra students for anatomy but there was a need for additional accommodation for practical physiology and biology. Professor John Kirk had been appointed Sub-Dean and after a reconnaissance visit with Dr Cyril Keele the School decided to take a large house at 121 Pembroke Road and adapt it.

Most generously, many of the preclinical staff were accommodated in the homes of the staff of Bristol University or Royal Infirmary or, in some cases, emeritus members of staff. Students had a kind response for billets from the general practitioners in the area as well as from a number of people unconnected with medicine. The strain on homes in Bristol was considerable as other colleges and also a number of government departments had also been evacuated there.

The third-year preclinical students started at Bristol on Monday, 18 September, and the others a fortnight later. Classes were organized and work proceeded well. Clifton College generously provided facilities for chemistry and physics for the 1st MB course. Middlesex students were able to become members of the Galenicals (the medical society) and enjoyed several excellent meetings. They were also able to join the Bristol University Students Union and within a short time of arriving the Rugby Club was in action, first by courtesy of Clifton College and then on the University ground at Coombe Dingle. The Squash and Boxing Clubs were also able to continue their activities in Bristol although there were some problems as the University was in the process of building four new squash courts which would not be opened until the end of the year. The Students Union in the palatial Victoria Rooms provided excellent facilities, with Middlesex students being able to join any of their clubs simply by application to the appropriate secretary. Additionally, dances were held there most Saturday nights.

RETURN TO THE MIDDLESEX

Although the arrangements for preclinical education had gone well in Bristol and those involved had received a most hospitable welcome there were obvious disadvantages in having so many of the staff and students away from the School. As there was still no sign of any concerted air-raids on London, the Council considered the position carefully at its meeting on 7 December 1939 and after a long discussion decided that staff and students should return to London at the end of that term. Most of the other medical schools in London did likewise even though it was recognized that, if subsequent evacuation did become necessary, it might be very difficult to organise.

So the spring and summer terms of 1940 were spent at The Middlesex, with examinations being held in the usual way. A prizegiving ceremony was planned to take place in July, but in the School Library rather than in the Queen's Hall. The development of the Battle of Britain, however, led to the prizegiving being cancelled and doubts arose as to whether it would be possible to continue preclinical studies in London. The start of the London Blitz in September 1940 determined the issue and, at its Special Meeting held on 28 September, the Council decided that the preclinical students should be transferred to Leeds, starting there on 8 October. Professor Kirk was re-appointed as Sub-Dean.

At the same meeting it was decided that the Council would hold future meetings only when the Dean considered that there was sufficient urgent business to discuss but that the Finance Committee should continue to meet monthly. In the event, the Council met on another seventeen occasions between then and the end of the War in August 1945. The School Committee also found it impractical to meet with so many staff away and no meetings were held between September 1940 and November 1943, only two in 1944 and two in 1945 before regular meetings were resumed in September 1945 after the end of the War. In October 1942 it had been decided that, in view of the suspension of the School Committee, all Heads of Departments should be co-opted on to the Council.

MOVE TO LEEDS

The move to Leeds was easier than the one to Bristol the previous year because of the experience that had been gained on that occasion and also because all the facilities could be provided within the University and its Medical School. There was no need to obtain a property outside the campus on this occasion. As an additional help the School Secretary, Mr R. A. Foley, went to Leeds for the first term. Although the University of Leeds was able to provide all the lecture theatres, laboratories and other rooms required for the 90–100 Middlesex students there was still a need for considerable quantities of apparatus to be transferred from The Middlesex and this required two or three journeys.

The staff of the University, from the Vice-Chancellor downwards, extended a warm welcome to Middlesex staff and students and when the time came to leave Leeds two years later there were many regrets at the breaking of so many friendships and professional associations which had been established. One such alliance which was to have particular benefits for The Middlesex subsequently was the collaboration of the physiology staff with Dr Eric Neil who was then working in Professor Albert Hemmingway's department in Leeds.

Examinations were conducted in Leeds for the 1st and 2nd MB and in June 1941, when the Council came to consider the position, it was evident that the move had been a great success and that much more work had been achieved than would have been possible in London. It was also greatly appreciated that with such collaboration The Middlesex contingent had been able to retain a distinct identity. Grateful thanks were also expressed to the University of Leeds for their generosity in making their facilities available on a no-cost basis, apart from out-of-pocket expenses which amounted to only £126 in the first term. Clinical demonstrations in physiology had been a long-standing practice at The Middlesex but in Leeds they were expanded to include anatomy as well. These demonstrations were undertaken at St James's Hospital and proved so successful that they were continued after the return to The Middlesex.

One member of staff had considerable problems as a result of the move. The heavy load placed on Dr Cyril Keele to provide teaching in pharmacology to preclinical students in Leeds as well as to clinical students in the different Sector hospitals meant that he was almost constantly on the move. At any time such extensive travel would be a problem but those who had any experience of trains in wartime Britain, especially at a time of heavy air-raids, will realise only too well what an endurance test it must have been.

By July 1942 London had experienced for some months a relief from the heavy air-raids and at its meeting that month Council decided on a return to London at the beginning of the next term. During the time away there had been no serious raids in Leeds even though there had been heavy bombing in Sheffield and in Manchester only thirty to forty miles away.

Clinical Education

In accordance with the plans which had been drawn up at the outbreak of the War, Middlesex clinical students were distributed widely to all the Sector V hospitals mentioned previously. At that stage the main role of the students seemed to be that of virtually everyone else – helping generally at anything required and filling innumerable sandbags. Teaching was soon established throughout the Sector, however. At the beginning of December 1939 Council considered that clinical students should be concentrated in fewer Sector hospitals. When this was announced those hospitals which would be losing students protested at the decision even though, at the outset, some of them had attempted to resist accepting them. It says much for the exemplary behaviour of the students that they should have produced this reaction during the three months which Dr Harold Boldero later described as being a most trying period, with no war, no patients and nothing specific to do.

At that time there were about 240 students in their clinical years and it was decided that the eighty or so in their first clinical year would spend their time at The Middlesex, those in the second year would be divided between Central Middlesex, Mount Vernon and Tindal House Hospitals and the final year would also be spent at The Middlesex. This plan needed to be modified at intervals during the War as circumstances changed. When the heavy bombing started in September 1940 and there were only about seventy non-casualty patients in The Middlesex Hospital more students were transferred to the Central Middlesex and particularly to the base hospitals. Other hospitals offered help as well and the School gladly welcomed these opportunities. In December 1940 the Royal Hospital, Wolverhampton expressed its willingness to take Middlesex students and this was to provide an important teaching association. Not more than nine students were there at any one time but that enabled them to receive an extensive experience and to benefit from the high-class teaching so willingly and ably given by the honorary staff. Another hospital to offer help was Princess Mary's RAF Hospital at Halton and students based at The Middlesex visited there with advantage.

As a result of these Sector arrangements the students obtained a wide experience in spite of the War and standards were well maintained. It was certainly a more corporate life than had existed before and each of the main hospitals for teaching organised, for instance, their own

84

medical society meetings which tended to be more personal and involve freer discussion than the larger, more formal, meetings held previously at The Middlesex.

At a comparatively early stage of the War it became necessary to appoint student house officers as there were not enough qualified doctors to fill all the posts in the civilian hospitals. The first student house officer to be appointed to The Middlesex Hospital was to the Ear, Nose and Throat Department in February 1941. They were also appointed in other hospitals in a number of different departments. These appointments were limited to three months and the work load was adjusted to be less than that of a qualified doctor.

Student club activities were organised in each hospital and some very entertaining Christmas concerts were arranged throughout the Sector. Sports fixtures were improvised on a local basis and many good matches resulted. In addition a new club, the Archery Club, came into existence within the Amalgamated Clubs as a result of the stimulus acquired by students while at Aylesbury.

The special association between the School and the Central Middlesex Hospital which was found to be so valuable during the War was to develop into a more prolonged arrangement of great benefit. This was fostered particularly by Dr Horace Joules, the Medical Superintendent, and he had the strong support of his colleagues.

They welcomed the links with The Middlesex Hospital Medical School and there was no doubt about the gain for the students.

Although the close wartime associations with Mount Vernon Hospital were to come to an end a few years after the War there are still many links between The Middlesex and Mount Vernon Hospital which are regarded by both as having considerable advantages.

Clinical Staff

A number of the honoraries joined the Forces at various times but others were precluded on medical grounds or because their particular skills were more needed by the civilian population than by the Armed Forces. As the pattern of hospital activity in the Sector changed so members of staff altered their commitments and a number spent part of each week in one hospital and the rest in another. A few members of staff had widely differing roles at different times of day. For example, Dr Cedric Britton spent his days in charge of Emergency Medical

Service (EMS) Laboratories but at night he metamorphosed into an anti-aircraft gunner in the Primrose Hill Battery. Movements of staff were not only outwards to the base hospitals. For example, after the departure of Mr Peter Ascroft into the Army The Middlesex still had need of expert neurosurgical help and the Hospital was fortunate to be able to call on Mr T. G. I. James, Senior Surgeon of the Central Middlesex Hospital.

It is not possible to attempt any comprehensive or detailed account of the roles of the staff during the War and only some brief general indication can be given. Of the general physicians Drs Bedford and Marriott were soon in the Army; Drs Lakin and Ward moved to Mount Vernon Hospital; Dr Beaumont remained at The Middlesex; Dr Cockayne transferred to Tindal House; Dr Bennett joined Stoke Mandeville Hospital when it was opened; and Dr Harold Boldero was Officer-in-Charge of the whole Sector. Of the general surgeons, Mr Gordon-Taylor and Mr Pearce Gould joined the Royal Navy; Sir Alfred Webb-Johnson was based at The Middlesex; Mr Turner Warwick spent most of his time at Mount Vernon but also continued the Rectal Clinic at The Middlesex; Mr Riches had most of his beds at St Andrew's, Dollis Hill; and Mr Vaughan Hudson and Mr Patey became the Surgeons-in-Charge of the surgical teams at The Middlesex.

Of the obstetricians and gynaecologists, Mr Freddie Roques joined the RAF; Mr Carnac Rivett remained at The Middlesex and the Chelsea Hospital for Women; and Mr Winterton had his beds at Tindal House but also continued to work at The Middlesex for part of the week. Of the anaesthetists, Dr Bernard Johnson joined the Army; Dr Roberts remained with the surgical teams at The Middlesex; Dr Crampton and Dr Idris moved to Mount Vernon; Dr Apperly to St Andrew's at Dollis Hill. Dr Graham-Hodgson (Sir Harold Graham-Hodgson KCVO, 1950) continued as Director of the Diagnostic X-Ray Department at The Middlesex.

The Mount Vernon team also comprised, in orthopaedics, Mr Bankart; in neurology, Dr McAlpine; in ophthalmology, Mr Whiting, who also supervised ocular injuries in the casualties at The Middlesex; in otolaryngology, Mr Somerville Hastings; and in general medicine, Dr R. A. Young, who had retired in 1936. At Tindal House there were, in psychiatry, Dr Noel Harris; in otolaryngology, Mr Monkhouse, who also continued to see out-patients at The Middlesex when they restarted; in paediatrics, Dr Moncrieff; in dental surgery, Mr Breese and Mr Packham; in ophthamology, Mr Greeves; in pathology, Professor McIntosh and Dr Scarff, both of whom also retained a very active role in the Bland-Sutton Institute.

Although seven members of the honorary staff of the Hospital reached the age for retirement during the War they continued on the active staff until after the end of hostilities. As a result there were few honorary appointments made during the six years of War. In December 1939 two Assistant Dental Surgeons were appointed. Mr James W. Schofield, after serving as a pilot in the Royal Flying Corps in the First World War, had qualified in medicine and dentistry at The Middlesex, where he had also been Dental House Surgeon, and by 1939 was already on the honorary staff of the National Dental Hospital. Mr Desmond Greer Walker had qualified in medicine and dentistry in Dublin and had subsequently been Dental House Surgeon and Dental Registrar at The Middlesex. During the War he joined Professor Kilner's Plastic Surgery Unit at Stoke Mandeville Hospital.

In January 1940 a speciality new to The Middlesex was introduced with the appointment of Mr Rainsford Mowlem as Honorary Plastic Surgeon to the Hospital. He had qualified in New Zealand in 1924 but had taken the Primary FRCS course at The Middlesex and, after passing the Final FRCS, he had worked for Sir Harold Gillies and had become one of his star pupils. During the War his main unit had to be established outside Sector V, at St Albans, but after the War it was transferred to Mount Vernon Hospital.

In July 1944 two radiologists were appointed to the honorary staff. Dr F. Campbell Golding, 'Cam Golding' as he became rapidly known, had been a contemporary of Mr Brian Windeyer at the University of Sydney where they had both excelled in sport and had been members of the crew of the St Andrew's College boat, with Cam Golding as stroke. He also stroked the University boat. Dr Eric Samuel had been a medical student at Cardiff and then at The Middlesex where he had subsequently been a House Surgeon, Casualty Medical Officer and Assistant in the Department of Radiotherapy. Having qualified with distinction in the London MB BS examination in 1938 he had passed the Final FRCS the following year and obtained the MD the year after that.

An important addition to the School staff in April 1941 was the appointment of Dr A. C. Thackray to the Central Pathology Laboratory at Stoke Mandeville Hospital, transferring to the Bland-Sutton Institute in August the following year. Before coming to The Middlesex as a student he had been at Cambridge where he had obtained 1st-Class honours in the Natural Science Tripos and had been awarded a University Scholarship to The Middlesex. He was later to succeed Dr Scarff.

Another appointment which was to have great significance in the postwar years was that of Mrs Sylvia Simpson as Research Assistant in Biology to the Courtauld Institute of Biochemistry in 1944.

Academic Developments

On 1 October 1942 Mr Brian Windeyer (Sir Brian Windeyer, 1961) was appointed to the Chair of Radiology (Therapeutic). He was the first person at The Middlesex to become a professor with charge of patients and his appointment had a particular significance for that reason. At that time the honorary tradition was strong and it was the view of a number of people that fulltime salaried appointments should not be made. The exemplary manner in which he filled the Chair of Radiology, the recognition which he received nationally and internationally and the credit which this brought to the Meyerstein Institute and to The Middlesex Hospital and School provided a convincing example of the advantages of such appointments.

It was, of course, a most appropriate speciality for the first clinical chair, for The Middlesex had long had a special interest in the field of cancer and was the first hospital in the country to have a cancer charity, founded by Mr Samuel Whitbread in 1792, although the gift remained anonymous until his death in 1796. The Middlesex also had a strong Department of Physics with a particular interest in radiation and there was considerable research on cancer being undertaken in the Bland-Sutton and Courtauld Institutes.

RESEARCH

Not surprisingly, research in physiology and physics had to be severely curtailed during the War and in pharmacology it virtually came to a complete halt. In the Bland-Sutton and Courtauld Institutes, however, it continued actively in a number of areas, some of which were undertaken with clinicians concerning problems encountered in the treatment of casualties. One in particular was the management of crush injuries.

Until the air-raids had made it a common occurrence there had been little experience of this condition and there was much to be learnt in the laboratories as well as at the bedside. With the fall of Malaysia to the Japanese there were fears that opium derivatives might become scarce and Professor Charles Dodds and his team in the Courtauld Institute produced a range of synthetic drugs which were given their clinical tests on radiotherapy patients who had severe pain.

The advent of penicillin as a therapeutic agent constituted a major advance in treatment which well justifies the description of a 'medical breakthrough'. When it first appeared it was in short supply and there was a compelling need to use the limited amounts in the most effective way. Careful documentation was required of all patients treated with this new drug and a Penicillin Registrar was appointed. Valuable research was undertaken in conjunction with the Bland-Sutton Institute which enabled a scientific assessment to be made of the effects of administration and the response of patients with particularly severe infections.

Some Other Events

Staff of the Hospital and students of the School participated in a number of other functions during the War. On an individual basis many took part in a wide range of wartime activities in addition to their official roles. On some occasions groups of people undertook organised duties elsewhere.

On 6 June 1944 two teams were detached from The Middlesex Hospital to help in the care of casualties evacuated by sea from the Normandy landings. Each team consisted of a surgical registrar, one of the resident anaesthetists, a house surgeon, a theatre sister and a physiotherapist with special orthopaedic experience of immobilisation of injured limbs in plaster of Paris. These teams were transferred on the morning of D-Day to the Sutton Emergency Hospital. Later, when that was damaged by a V1 bomb, the teams moved to St Margaret's Hospital, Swindon, which was one of the hospitals in that area about to receive casualties evacuated by air from Normandy when landing strips could be established there. Another team with Middlesex sisters and nurses was formed at Mount Vernon Hospital and went to Shirley Warren Hospital, Southampton, on the day before D-Day, and students helped to staff the trains used for evacuating casualties.

In 1945 eight Middlesex students formed part of a volunteer force from hospitals in London which was flown into Germany on 29 April to help in the Nazi concentration camp at Belsen which had been entered by the British Forces just a fortnight earlier. When the students arrived in the camp, the emaciated, disease-riddled inhabitants were still dying at the rate of over 500 per day. (When the British Forces had entered the camp on 15 April it was estimated that there were about 40,000 people, barely alive, intermingled with a further 10,000 unburied corpses.) The students spent one month under conditions which they subsequently described in a factual manner and which will not be forgotten by those who heard the account or subsequently read it in the Hospital *Journal*.

Awards and Distinctions

During the six years of war a number of Middlesex men achieved high office or received other distinctions, or both. In July 1941 Sir Alfred Webb-Johnson was elected President of The Royal College of Surgeons of England – an office which he was to hold longer than any other President before or since. The Middlesex was well represented on the Council of the College at that time for, in addition to the President, there were Mr William Sampson Handley, Mr Gordon Gordon-Taylor and Mr Victor Bonney.

Further honours were soon to be awarded to Sir Alfred. In December 1941 he was elected a Vice-President of the Hospital, an honour which had never before been bestowed on an active member of the honorary staff. In June 1942 he was created a Knight Commander of the Royal Victorian Order and in January 1945 he was created a Baronet.

Also in January 1945 Dr Lionel Whitby was created a Knight Bachelor. In April 1942 Professor Charles Dodds was elected a Fellow of the Royal Society in recognition of the outstanding research he had undertaken in the Courtauld Institute. In 1942 the Royal College of Physicians elected Dr Harold Boldero as Registrar, Dr Alan Moncrieff as Assistant Registrar and Dr George Ward as Censor.

For many years students of The Middlesex have obtained more Distinctions and more University Medals in the University of London Final MB BS examination than any other school or college of the University, both in absolute terms and expressed as a percentage of the number of students sitting the examination. This will be referred to in more detail in another connection in a later chapter (p. 231). Even in such a setting, however, the achievement of Arnold Burgen (now Sir Arnold Burgen FRS, Master of Downing College) in May 1945 was outstanding. As well as being awarded the University Medal he obtained distinctions in five sections of the examination: pathology, medicine, applied pharmacology and therapeutics, surgery, obstetrics and gynaecology.

In 1944 Mr Somerville Hastings was appointed Leader of the London County Council. It was certainly unusual for a surgeon in active clinical practice to be appointed to such a post.

Deaths

During the War period The Middlesex lost a number of members of staff who had rendered signal service to both School and Hospital. The year 1940 saw the deaths of a distinguished physician and neurologist, Dr Herbert Campbell Thomson, and a distinguished surgeon, Mr Eric Pearce Gould. Dr Campbell Thomson had been an honorary on the staff of the Hospital from 1900 to 1924 and Dean of the School from 1908 throughout the First World War to 1919. His book set out the history of the School's first 100 years. As was indicated in chapter 2, Mr Eric Pearce Gould was a surgeon and teacher on the active honorary staff of the Hospital although, at the time of his death, he was serving as a Rear-Admiral in the Royal Navy.

Another great loss in 1940 was that of Lady Meyerstein, to be followed almost exactly two years later in February 1942 by the death of Sir Edward Meyerstein. His keen personal interest in the affairs of the Hospital and School and his great benefactions had a profound influence on the development of The Middlesex.

In 1943 Lady Bland-Sutton died, six years after the death of her husband whose name is so revered at The Middlesex and at the Royal College of Surgeons. It will never be fully known how much Lady Bland-Sutton herself advanced the cause of the School and Hospital and the Institute which bears the Bland-Sutton name but there is no doubt that she should be regarded as Sir John's close partner who herself had a deep interest in The Middlesex.

That year also saw the death of Frederick Cleminson who had virtually founded the Ferens Institute by persuading his uncle Thomas Ferens of Hull to make his great benefaction, and William Pasteur, at the age of eighty-seven, who had been on the honorary staff as a physician from 1889 to 1919.

HM Forces

Many members of staff, some students and nurses and a large number of graduates of the School served in the Armed Forces during the Second World War. A register prepared several years ago records the names of 536 such people who were known to have been in the Forces in widely scattered parts of the world but it is evident that lack of adequate information prevented a complete file from being prepared. The register identifies twenty-four who were known to have been killed; a few who were known to have been wounded, but obviously there were very many more; twenty-six who were known to have been taken prisoner; and two who were known to have escaped from prisoner-of-war camps and to have reached England. Additionally, the list records sixty-five awards for gallantry.

It would not be possible here to provide even a table of names of people in any of those categories which could be regarded as being reliably comprehensive. It would certainly be out of the question to attempt any account of the exploits and the considerable contributions made in many theatres of war by those who are named. The author greatly regrets this omission as it had been hoped that it would at least be possible to provide some lists of those in special categories.

Inter-Departmental Committee

A time of war might not seem the most opportune period for planning radical changes in the health services and medical education of the country but during the First World War politicians had repeatedly claimed that Britain would be made into 'a land fit for heroes to live in'. But it hadn't happened. There was a view that matters should be planned more effectively on this occasion and so, in spite of the demands of the War and depressing news at times, planning was initiated in a number of different aspects, including medicine and medical education. The exercise reflected a mood of optimism and confidence in ultimate victory. In October 1941 the Minister of Health informed the House of Commons of the Government's postwar hospital policy and in March 1942 he appointed, in conjunction with the Secretary of State for

Scotland, an inter-departmental Committee to enquire into and make recommendations on the organisation of medical schools in Great Britain, particularly in regard to clinical teaching and research. The Chairman of that Committee was Sir William Goodenough and there were nine other members. Along with other medical schools and universities, The Middlesex Hospital gave evidence to the Committee, which reported in 1944. That Report was considered by the School Committee and the Council and will be referred to further in later chapters.

—5—
The Postwar, Pre-NHS Years

Return to peace – Plans for the National Health Service
– Colonel The Hon. J. J. Astor becomes Chairman of the
School – Changes in Council – New departments – Staff
changes – Hospital bicentenary celebrations – Clinical
teaching arrangements – Women students

As was indicated in the last chapter, public debate on future arrangements for health services and for medical education throughout the
country had been proceeding throughout most of the War. Following
the General Election of July 1945 the discussions intensified and
developed a new urgency. They will not be referred to further until the
next chapter but it is important to bear in mind that they formed a
continuing accompaniment to all the other events occurring in the
period covered here.

During the years 1945–48 there was a gradual return to peacetime
conditions. Large numbers of doctors returned from the Forces and a
number of special demobilisation posts were created, usually at registrar
level. The holders qualified for an extra salary, £650 p.a. instead of the
normal £600.

Chairman and Council

From October 1945 Council resumed its practice of monthly meetings,
except in August. At the end of the 1945–46 session Mr S. A. Courtauld
resigned from the chairmanship of the Council of the School after
serving in that office since 1930, also having been a member of the
Board of Management and several important committees of the Hospital
and School for many years. His specific benefactions created the Courtauld Institute of Biochemistry, provided the Courtauld Lecture

94

Theatre and the Special Courtauld Research Wards and endowed the Chairs of Anatomy and of Biochemistry. In addition to all that he had been a constant source of wise advice and encouragement and had contributed in a number of general ways to the School and Hospital.

At the time of Mr Courtauld's resignation, Colonel the Hon J. J. Astor had been Chairman of the Board of Management for eight years and it was a matter of great good fortune for The Middlesex as a whole that he was also willing to become Chairman of the School Council. His acceptance of this dual responsibility would have been most welcome at any time but in December 1946 it had a special significance beyond that of his own great personal qualities for it came in the midst of the political debate on the separation, as legal entities, of the Hospital and School. During those discussions he was able to speak authoritatively for both and after the change had been effected by statute, from 23 June 1948, he fulfilled an important unifying role which gave a continuing meaning to the term 'The Middlesex' in spite of the change in the legal status of the Hospital and School.

Some changes were introduced into the composition of Council in November 1945 to reflect developments in staffing. The balance between the members elected by the School Committee and the Medical Committee was maintained but the number of each group was increased from four to six. Of those elected by the School Committee it was stipulated that no less than four must be professors or heads of departments and, to maintain the balance, the Chairman of the School Committee would no longer be included as an ex-officio member. In view of his many other commitments, notably the presidency of the Royal College of Surgeons, it was agreed to release Sir Alfred Webb-Johnson from the post of Honorary Treasurer, which had been specially created for him in 1925, and to abolish the post. It was additionally decided to appoint the Secretary of the Medical School as the Secretary of the Council but to retain the liberty of the Secretary-Superintendent of the Hospital to attend meetings. The original laws governing the composition of the Council had specified the election of 'six male members of the Board' and, in amending the composition, the opportunity was taken of deleting the word 'male'.

In 1947 Sir Theobald Matthew, Director of Public Prosecutions, resigned from the School Council. In his place the Hon. Thomas B. Money-Coutts (Lord Latymer, 1949) was elected. He was a Director of Coutts and Company and other large companies and had been

95

Treasurer of the Hospital since 1931 and Vice-Chairman of the Board of Management since 1935. Coutts Bank had been the Hospital bankers since 1761. In July 1948 Mr Richard Davis retired from the Council after serving on it and as Chairman of its Finance Committee for many years.

New Academic Departments

The postwar period saw the creation at The Middlesex of two new academic departments – of medicine and of surgery. In March 1945 the Medical Committee had resolved unanimously that it was desirable to establish University Chairs in Medicine, in Surgery, and in Obstetrics and Gynaecology. Draft terms and conditions for the Chair of Medicine were considered at the meeting of the School Council in June 1945 but it was to be July 1946 before the details had been agreed with the University and the post had been advertised. In that period an application was also made in respect of a Chair of Surgery.

In October 1946 the Board of Advisors unanimously recommended that Dr Alan Kekwick be appointed to the Chair of Medicine but there was to be a further delay of six months before the Senate ratified this recommendation while further discussions took place between the School and the University concerning the precise wording of the terms and conditions relating to the coordination of teaching and facilities for research. When the appointment was finally confirmed it was backdated to 1 October 1946. Mr Peter Ascroft was appointed to the Chair of Surgery with effect from 1 July 1947 and, as was still the custom at that time, these appointments were made 'for five years in the first instance'.

Dr Alan Kekwick had come to The Middlesex from Cambridge as a clinical student and after qualification he had held three House Officer posts and been Casualty Medical Officer before becoming Resident Medical Officer for three years. At the outbreak of the War he had joined the Royal Army Medical Corps and spent two years with the Army Blood Supply Depot at Bristol before being posted to East Africa as Officer-in-Charge of the Medical Division of a 1200-bed hospital. As was mentioned previously (p. 41) he had been a pioneer with Dr Hugh Marriott in the introduction of continuous-drip blood transfusion. In East Africa he became specifically interested in the nutrition of the native troops and produced a number of valuable papers on this subject. Nutrition and obesity were to become part of his research interests but he was very much a general physician whose broadly based teaching fitted him admirably for the Chair.

Mr Peter Ascroft had also been a Middlesex student and had been the Broderip Scholar of his year. At the Final MB BS examination he had obtained a Distinction in Surgery and eighteen months later he had been awarded the Gold Medal at the MS examination. As was mentioned previously (p. 60) he had been appointed to the honorary staff of the Hospital in 1937 as a General Surgeon but with a particular expertise in neurosurgery. He had served with the Royal Army Medical Corps throughout the War and had been Commanding Officer of the No. 1 Mobile Neurosurgical Unit which had been heavily involved in the North Africa campaign where he had been closely associated with The Middlesex neurologists, Dr Douglas McAlpine and Dr Michael Kremer.

In addition to the Professor each of these new clinical academic departments had an initial staff allocation of a first assistant, a second assistant, a house officer and a secretary. In accordance with the practice in respect of registrars, the first and second assistants were appointed to the end of a calendar year on an annual basis.

In 1947 Dr J. W. Paulley was appointed as First Assistant and Dr Robert Semple as Second Assistant in the Department of Medicine. Mr R. S. Lawrie was appointed as First Assistant and Mr L. P. Le Quesne as Second Assistant in the Department of Surgery. Dr Robert Semple was a graduate of the University of Aberdeen. The others had qualified at The Middlesex, Leslie Le Quesne having come as a clinical student from the University of Oxford. In 1948 Mr Rex Lawrie resigned his post on being appointed to the honorary staff of Guy's Hospital; Mr R. S. Monro, also a Middlesex graduate, was appointed to replace him.

After the Chairs of Medicine and of Surgery had been filled a joint committee in each of these subjects was established by the School and Medical Committees to review and advise on the teaching of clinical medicine and clinical surgery. At that stage Dr George Ward was elected Chairman of the Clinical Medicine Committee and Mr W. Turner Warwick Chairman of the Clinical Surgery Committee.

Accommodation for the new Departments of Medicine and Surgery was established in the Courtauld Wards on the first-floor crosspiece. The rooms on the south side of the corridor were equipped as research rooms which were under the supervision, at that time, of the Professors of Medicine, Surgery, Pathology, Biochemistry and Physiology while remaining available to the members of the honorary staff. The rooms on the north side of the corridor were allocated to the Departments of Medicine and Surgery for the professors and their staff.

School Staff

In the three years after the War there were a number of staff changes in the School. Some of these were resignations or retirements followed by replacements, whilst others resulted from planned developments.

At the end of the 1945–46 session both Professor W. B. Tuck and Mr W. H. S. Cheavin retired and the opportunity was taken of discontinuing the separate Department of Chemistry and assigning the responsibility for teaching inorganic and organic chemistry to the Courtauld Institute of Biochemistry. Four new members of staff were appointed to the Institute. Dr A. E. Kellie filled the senior post and combined supervision of teaching with that of running the routine Biochemistry Laboratory. The other lecturers appointed in 1946 were Dr J. B. Jepson and Dr D. G. O'Sullivan and in 1947 Dr S. J. Holt.

Professor S. Russ also retired in September 1946 and was accorded the title of Professor Emeritus by the University. Prior to his departure Council had considered the conditions relating to the Joel Professorship and had agreed with the Board of Management and the University that in future the holder of the post would be known as the 'Joel Professor of Physics as Applied to Medicine' and that he would also be Physicist to the Hospital. In practice he had already held that position but it was considered appropriate to stipulate this in the conditions of the appointment. In December 1946, Dr Eric Roberts was appointed to the Chair. Soon afterwards Mr H. F. Cook was appointed as Senior Assistant in the Department and in 1948 Dr J. F. Tait was appointed as Lecturer. He was a graduate of the University of Leeds.

Before and during the War the Department of Physics had been concerned largely with X-rays and radium, in which fields notable advances had been made. In the postwar years the Department's activities were extended, partly with the aid of a large radar transmitter, borrowed from the Royal Navy, which stood on a truck in the yard outside the Barnato-Joel Laboratories. The microwaves from it were piped into the laboratories for investigation of their biological effects, including their heating properties *in vivo*. One of the Department's party demonstrations at that time was to boil an egg in a little water in a cigarette tin – an early, and cheap, prototype of the microwave ovens developed subsequently. Expansion in other fields was soon to lead to dramatic and far-reaching discoveries as will be described later (p. 161).

In the Department of Biology the title of Professor was conferred on the Reader, Dr J. H. Woodger, at the beginning of 1948. In October 1947 Mr R. F. J. Withers was appointed as Demonstrator.

In 1947 readerships were established in anatomy, to which Dr E. W. Walls was appointed, and in physiology, to which the Lecturer, Dr David Slome, was appointed. Dr Eldred Walls, a Glaswegian by birth, was a student at the University of Glasgow where he excelled in both academic and sporting activities, especially rugby football. He qualified with honours at the early age of twenty-one. After some experience of surgery he worked in the Department of Anatomy in Glasgow until his appointment in 1941 as Senior Lecturer in Anatomy at the University of Wales in Cardiff. After being commissioned in the Royal Naval Volunteer Reserve and seeing service with the University Naval Division he returned to Cardiff where his research gained him the MD with honours in 1947.

There were a number of changes in the senior staff of the Bland-Sutton Institute of Pathology following the War. Sir Lionel Whitby resigned on being appointed Regius Professor of Physic at Cambridge in 1945, and later Master of Downing College. In the following year Dr Cedric Britton also resigned. Shortage of space in the Institute and School led to the loss of the Medical Research Council Unit of Bacterial Chemistry directed by Sir Paul Fildes which had been carrying out research in the Institute since 1934 and had earned a high reputation. The Unit was reconstituted at the Lister Institute. Following Sir Lionel's departure, Dr F. R. Selbie took charge of bacteriology in the School and when a readership in that subject was established in 1947 he was appointed to the post. In April 1946 the title of Professor of Morbid Anatomy and Histology was conferred on Dr Robert W. Scarff who was appointed as Director of the Institute and Bland-Sutton Professor of Pathology following the death of Professor McIntosh in April 1948.

A major development in the Courtauld Institute of Biochemistry occurred in 1946 with the establishment and filling of the Philip Hill Chair of Experimental Biochemistry. This was made possible by an endowment from Mrs Philip Hill in memory of her late husband who had been the Chairman of Philip Hill and Partners Ltd and of Beechams Pills Ltd. He was undoubtedly the creator of the Beecham Group. In October 1946 Dr Frank Dickens was appointed as the first Philip Hill Professor. He had graduated in chemistry at Cambridge and his first post-doctoral job (1923) had been as Assistant to Professor Dodds in the Courtauld Institute for research on processes for the purification of insulin for patients. That appointment had been made 'for one year only' but proved so successful that the post was extended into other fields and continued for ten years until 1933 when he was appointed Director of the Cancer Research Laboratories of the North of England Council of the British Empire Cancer Campaign (now the Cancer Research Campaign). In March 1946 Dr Dickens had returned to the Courtauld Institute and in the following month had been elected a Fellow of the Royal Society.

There were other staff changes in the Courtauld Institute. In 1948, Dr Wilfred Lawson had the title of Reader conferred on him. In March 1947 Dr Douglas Robertson resigned after eighteen years on the staff. He was immediately succeeded by Dr Mary Ransome and then by Dr Denis N. Baron (later Professor of Chemical Pathology, Royal Free Hospital School of Medicine).

Hospital Staff

The years following the War saw a large number of changes in the staff of the Hospital. There were, firstly, the retirements of those who had continued beyond the normal retiring age until hostilities had ended. They were Mr A. S. Blundell Bankart, Orthopaedic Surgeon; Dr E. A. Cockayne, General Physician; Dr H. P. Crampton, Anaesthetist; Sir Gordon Gordon-Taylor, General Surgeon; Mr R. Affleck Greeves, Ophthalmic Surgeon; Mr Somerville Hastings, Ear, Nose and Throat Surgeon; Dr C. E. Lakin, General Physician; Dr Harry MacCormac, Dermatologist; Sir Alfred Webb-Johnson, General Surgeon and Urologist. In addition Dr R. E. Apperly had been obliged to resign his anaesthetic appointment because of ill health and, as was mentioned in the last chapter, Mr Eric Pearce-Gould had died.

In 1946 Dr Alan Moncrieff (Sir Alan Moncrieff, 1964) was appointed to the Nuffield Chair of Child Health at the Institute of Child Health.

In July 1946 the general physician, Dr Izod Bennett, died and in July 1947 the obstetrician and gynaecologist, Mr Carnac Rivett, also died.

Mr Somerville Hastings was not replaced in the Ear, Nose and Throat Department until 1950 but the vacancies resulting from the other losses were filled in the period 1946–48 and, in addition, some further appointments were made. In general medicine Dr A. Willcox was appointed to the honorary staff in May 1946 and Dr G. D. Hadley in December that year. Dr Arthur Willcox had been a clinical student at The Middlesex after obtaining a 1st at Cambridge in the natural sciences tripos and after qualification held house-officer posts at The Middlesex and the Brompton Hospital before returning to The Middlesex as Registrar to Dr G. E. S. Ward and Dr D. E. Bedford, a post which was also combined with dermatology with Dr H. MacCormac. Dr Willcox had been a keen member of the University Officers' Training Corps and during the War he served in France and later North Africa and Italy, being mentioned in dispatches. Dr George Hadley was also a Cambridge and Middlesex student who had similarly held house-officer posts at The Middlesex and the Brompton Hospital and those had been followed by an appointment as First Assistant and Registrar at the London Hospital. He had joined the Army at the outbreak of the War, was captured at Dunkirk and spent the remainder of the War as a prisoner-of-war in Germany. He was Resident Medical Officer at The Middlesex when he was appointed to the honorary staff.

In general surgery Mr R. S. Handley was appointed to the honorary staff in March 1946 and Mr C. J. B. Murray in May of that year. Mr Richard (Dick) Handley had been a Cambridge and Middlesex student who had held appointments as House Physician, House Surgeon, and Casualty Surgical Officer at The Middlesex before becoming an Assistant in the Bland-Sutton Institute. He was the son of Mr William Sampson Handley and his career was to follow a very similar pattern. His war service in the Army had led to a mention in dispatches and to the award of the OBE. Mr Cecil Murray had received all his medical education at The Middlesex and obtained his fellowship of the Royal College of Surgeons in the year after qualification and the MS degree of the University of London in the following year. He had held house-officer appointments and been Casualty Surgical Officer before becoming Surgical Registrar, followed by service in the Army throughout the War.

In March 1946, Dr F. R. Bettley was appointed as Dermatologist to replace Dr H. MacCormac, and Mr A. J. B. Goldsmith (Sir Allen Goldsmith, KCVO, 1970) was appointed as Ophthalmic Surgeon to replace Mr R. Affleck Greeves. Dr Ray Bettley had been an undergraduate student at University College, London, and had undertaken postgraduate studies in Vienna and Strasbourg. In 1937 he had been appointed to the honorary staff of the Cardiff Royal Infirmary and had returned there after serving in the Army throughout the War. Mr Allen Goldsmith, almost universally known as 'Twist' until he was knighted, had been a Middlesex student who won most of the available prizes, including the Senior Broderip Scholarship and Lyell Gold Medal in Surgery before qualifying with Distinctions in medicine and in pathology. He was subsequently an Assistant in Morbid Histology in the Bland-Sutton Institute and passed the Final FRCS examination a year before his age would allow him to use the letters after his name.

In May 1946 Mr P. H. Newman was appointed as Orthopaedic Surgeon to replace Mr Blundell Bankart and Dr O. P. Dinnick as Anaesthetist to replace Dr R. E. Apperly. Mr Philip Newman had also been a Middlesex student and Senior Broderip Scholar. After qualification he had worked as a Demonstrator in the Anatomy Department as well as holding house-officer appointments. During the War he remained at Dunkirk to care for the patients who could not be evacuated and after being captured he was one of the very few medical officers to escape successfully from a German prisoner-of-war camp. It was known that he had been awarded the DSO and MC but virtually nothing could be gleaned of the details of his escape until publication of the book, *Safer than a Known Way*, in 1983. Dr Peter Dinnick had also been a Middlesex student who had qualified at the beginning of the War and rapidly became interested in anaesthetics, progressing to become Senior Resident Anaesthetist before serving with the Royal Air Force.

In November 1946 Dr M. Kremer was appointed to the honorary staff in the Department of Diseases of the Nervous System in addition to Dr D. McAlpine, and Dr B. A. Sellick was appointed as Anaesthetist to replace Dr Crampton. Dr Michael Kremer was a Middlesex student who won many prizes including the Broderip Scholarship, the Lyell Gold Medal and Leopold Hudson Prize, in addition to obtaining an Honours BSc degree in physiology and Distinction in medicine at the Final MB BS examination. After qualifying and holding house-officer appointments he was demonstrator in the Department of Physiology and then Medical Registrar to Dr G. E. S. Ward and Dr D. E. Bedford, exchanging jobs with Dr Cyril Keele at that stage. In the Army during the War he served with the No. 1 Mobile Neurosurgical Unit in North Africa and later at the Military Hospital for Head Injuries at Wheatley, near Oxford, in time to deal with casualties flown there from Europe after the Normandy invasion of 1944. Dr Brian Sellick had also been a Middlesex student who had been awarded the Leopold Hudson and other prizes. After qualification in the early part of the War and holding house-officer and Resident Anaesthetist appointments he was a member of one of the teams detached from The Middlesex to help deal with casualties evacuated from the Normandy landings. Subsequently he saw service with the Royal Navy.

Following Dr A. A. Moncrieff's appointment as Nuffield Professor of Child Health, Dr E. W. Hart was appointed in 1947 to replace him as physician in charge of the Children's Department. He had been at Cambridge where he obtained First-class Honours before coming to The Middlesex as a clinical student and Entrance Scholar. After holding house-physician posts to Dr R. A. Young, Dr E. A. Cockayne and the Neurological and Children's Departments he was the last Clinical Assistant to the Courtauld Research Wards before they were closed at the beginning of the War. He joined the Royal Army Medical Corps and after serving with the Army Blood Supply Depot at Bristol became responsible for the transfusion services of the Army in the whole of India.

Before the War, one of the Surgical Registrars, Mr F. J. S. Gowar, had a special interest and experience in thoracic surgery. There was no thoracic surgeon on the honorary staff of the Hospital, however, until April 1947 when the deficiency was remedied in no uncertain fashion by the appointment of Mr Thomas Holmes Sellors (Sir Thomas Holmes Sellors, 1963). He had been a student at Oxford and The Middlesex, and afterwards at Stockholm, and had been awarded by the University of Oxford the degree of MCh in 1931 and DM in 1933. By the time of his appointment to The Middlesex in 1937 he was already recognized as an outstanding pioneer in the developing speciality of thoracic surgery and had been on the honorary staff of the London Chest Hospital since 1934.

The appointment of Professor Peter Ascroft to the Chair of Surgery in July 1947 meant that he had to devote himself to surgery in general and the Hospital saw the need to appoint a surgeon who would be responsible for neurosurgery without having other commitments. This new post having been established, another innovation at that time was the appointment of a woman to the honorary staff of the hospital. Miss Diana J. K. Beck had graduated at the London School of Medicine for Women (now the Royal Free Hospital School of Medicine) and then became a Demonstrator in Anatomy followed by a number of surgical appointments. She then spent some years in general practice in Wales and always regarded this as a valuable part of her training. She started her career in neurosurgery as House Surgeon to Sir Hugh Cairns in Oxford and in 1944 she had been appointed to take charge of an Emergency Medical Service Neurosurgical Unit at Bristol. For some time most people had foreseen the appointment of women to the honorary staff but few, if any, would have picked neurosurgery as the speciality in which this would first occur.

Following the death of Mr Carnac Rivett in July 1947 the vacancy in the Department of Obstetrics and Gynaecology was filled in February 1948 by Mr I. M. Jackson. Mr Ian Jackson had been a student at Cambridge where he had obtained a Double 1st in the natural sciences tripos and also an open scholarship to the London Hospital Medical College. After house-officer appointments he became First Assistant in the Department of Surgery and then in the Department of Obstetrics and Gynaecology at the London Hospital before joining the Royal Army Medical Corps in which he served as a surgical specialist in a surgical parachute team.

In November 1946 the School Committee recommended that a full-time research post in Anaesthesia be created, the holder carrying out his work jointly in the Department of Pharmacology and in the Department of Anaesthetics. This was approved by the Council and in March 1947 Dr A. J. H. Hewer was appointed to this new post. Dr Jan Hewer had been a student anaesthetist. After qualification he had been Junior and then Senior Resident Anaesthetist as well as holding other appointments at The Middlesex and other hospitals. In April 1948, after one year in the research post, Dr Hewer was appointed to the honorary staff of the Hospital.

REGISTRARS

In 1948 the number of Registrars was increased. In April the School Council approved the recommendations of the Medical Committee that a second post should be established in Obstetrics and Gynaecology and that there should be a Registrar in Paediatrics. In May it was agreed that new posts should be created in Dermatology, Ophthalmology and neurosurgery. In July a second registrarship in Otolaryngology was approved.

SECRETARY-SUPERINTENDENT

On the retirement of Mr S. R. C. Plimsoll after the War, Brigadier G. P. Hardy-Roberts (Sir Geoffrey Hardy-Roberts, KCVO, 1972) was appointed as Secretary-Superintendent in 1946. His record was impressive – Eton, Sandhurst, the Ninth Lancers, the reputation of being an outstanding staff officer, the award of the CB and the CBE. But many people were apprehensive of what might be in store until they met him and noted his quiet efficiency, keen interest and quick grasp of essentials. His classic monograph, *Office Manners*, typified his character and his example sustained morale in all grades of staff at a time of uncertainty about the future. His regular rounds with the Matron were no mere formality. They were conducted to enable him to keep in touch with what was happening throughout the Hospital and to make himself available to patients and to staff. Initially, ward sisters and others were surprised to find that when they returned from lunch matters mentioned on the morning round might well have been resolved. It was his expressed view that to a hospital officer letters of complaint were of immense value because, although some were unreasonable, they could give a useful indication of the need for better methods or of an alteration to existing arrangements. This positive approach ensured that all written complaints were handled rapidly and effectively, almost invariably by himself, and there is no doubt that this not only reassured and satisfied those concerned but it prevented a large number of relatively simple matters developing into more serious complaints. It was not long before the title 'The Brigadier' was being used by virtually everyone as a term of affection and respect. He smoked in the privacy of his own office and sometimes at informal meetings but never in public places in the Hospital and he would not allow the staff under his control to do so either. Even some doctors learnt from his example.

His successor as Secretary Superintendent in 1967, Mr Graham Buckley, was to continue the same fine tradition of administration at

The Middlesex and then, from 1974, as Secretary of the Charing Cross Hospital Medical School.

MATRON

Miss Dorothy Smith had been Matron of the Hospital for sixteen years by the end of the War and her contributions to The Middlesex had been recognised by the esteem in which she was held by nursing and medical staff. Her contributions to nursing in general had been acknowledged by the award of the OBE in 1943. She had been trained at Guy's and soon after the end of the War she decided, with mixed feelings, to accept the position of Matron of Guy's.

In the spring of 1946 Miss Marjorie Marriott was appointed as Matron. She inherited the responsibilities of the post at a difficult time because of uncertainty about the future and a change in the opportunities open to girls. There was a need to encourage entrants of quality to nursing and to The Middlesex and Miss Marriott had the attributes necessary to achieve that. With an outgoing personality and a gift for speaking in public to young people she visited schools in widely scattered parts of the country. Applications followed in such numbers that the rejection rate became high but that seemed to increase the demand for places.

Hospital Bicentenary

The Hospital having been founded in 1745, it was not practical to hold the bicentenary celebrations exactly 200 years later but the occasion was marked in 1946. Among other events a series of scientific lectures was arranged and at each the chair was taken by the Duke of Northumberland. It was the Earl, later First Duke, of Northumberland who laid the foundation stone of the Hospital on its present site in 1755 and since that date the head of the House of Percy has been, without a break, President of the Hospital. In an opening address, the Chairman, Colonel Astor, echoed the feelings of many when he said, among other things,

> We who are privileged to be associated in one capacity or another with our Hospital today have good reason to be proud of its history and record of work. It has entered upon its third century at a time when a new era for hospitals and medical schools is foreshadowed by the National Health Service Act. We believe that the experience and traditions that have been

built up by such Institutions as ours in the past will enable us to play not only a valuable but a vital part in the success of the future service.

Lectures were delivered on 'The Middlesex Hospital' by Sir Alfred Webb-Johnson; on 'Chemistry and Medicine' by Sir Robert Robinson, President of the Royal Society; on 'The Middlesex and Medicine' by Sir Lionel Whitby, Regius Professor of Physic in the University of Cambridge; and on 'The Future of Medical Sciences' by Sir Edward Mellanby.

Clinical Teaching outside The Middlesex

Not surprisingly, the Sector arrangements for clinical teaching did not come to an abrupt halt at the end of the War. Because of the distance and other factors the use of the hospitals in Aylesbury was soon stopped but teaching continued at both the Central Middlesex County Hospital and Mount Vernon Hospital during 1946 and 1947. It was then decided that only one of these hospitals was required and clinical teaching outside The Middlesex was concentrated at the Central Middlesex. So the use of the general clinical facilities at Mount Vernon Hospital came to an end but the links with that hospital were not broken. Important associations were maintained and in some areas strengthened, particularly in the fields of radiotherapy and oncology but also in plastic surgery.

Teaching at the Central Middlesex at that stage was mainly in general medicine, surgery and pathology. Senior members of the staff principally involved at that time were Dr Horace Joules, Physician and Medical Superintendent; Mr T. G. Illtyd James, Senior Surgeon and Neurosurgeon; Dr Francis Avery Jones (Sir Francis Avery Jones, 1970), Physician and Deputy Medical Superintendent; Dr Walter T. U. Pagel, Pathologist; and Mr J. D. Fergusson, Surgeon and Urologist. They were enthusiastic in their desire to teach students and to be associated with The Middlesex and the School was delighted to be able to have access to a hospital with such good clinical facilities and with such a strong staff. The foundations laid during the War and in the few years afterwards were strengthened still further in later years and continued as a most valuable association.

Women Medical Students

In 1860 a woman who was determined to become a doctor came to The Middlesex and worked for six months on a surgical ward. Ostensibly she was a nurse, for the Dean and the Treasurer were unwilling to accept her openly as a student. She gradually began to attend lectures and take part in the teaching without objection from the staff or from the male students. And then she took part in the examinations, obtaining a Certificate of Honour in each class examination. In June 1861 the Medical Committee, having received a petition from the students for her dismissal, decided she must leave and she went from place to place, in Scotland and in London, obtaining whatever experience and tuition she could. In 1864, undaunted by her previous experiences, she returned to The Middlesex for a further five months by persuading individual physicians and surgeons to allow her to attend their ward rounds as a visitor. A year later she had completed in stages the curriculum of the Society of Apothecaries but she would not have been allowed to sit the examination if her father had not threatened the Society with legal action. She passed with credit and the name of Elizabeth Garrett was entered into the Medical Register. She was the first woman trained in England to achieve this. (Elizabeth Blackwell had been born in England but trained in the United States. In 1849 she had obtained the right to practise in the United Kingdom and her name appeared in the Register.)

The story reflects credit on only one person, and that in no uncertain measure, but it is impossible now to appreciate the attitudes prevailing at that time. In spite of the expulsion, The Middlesex proved to be much less inhospitable than a large number of other institutions which refused to have anything to do with her under any pretext. Mrs Elizabeth Garrett-Anderson, as she became, would surely have allowed herself a wry smile if she had been able to foresee that, in 1982, The Middlesex Hospital and the Elizabeth Garrett-Anderson Hospital would both become part of the Bloomsbury Health Authority.

It was to be many years before any other women medical students were allowed to set foot inside The Middlesex. In 1874 the London School of Medicine for Women was founded and although this provided at that time an opportunity for women which was not available elsewhere it did establish in London a type of development different from that in other universities with only one medical school. In 1929 the University of London declared its policy of having three types of medical school – some for men only, one for women only and others for both sexes. The last were, in practice, the multi-faculty colleges and their associated medical schools.

In 1937 the School received a request from the University regarding the admission of a limited number of women students to the preclinical courses of the School. After considerable discussion in the School Committee and the Council it was considered best to restrict the entry to students undertaking a complete course of study.

In the 1938–39 session the annual returns submitted by the universities of Great Britain showed that, within the University of London, there were 551 women medical students out of a total of 5064 at all stages of the course. In the rest of England and Wales there were 708 out of a total of 3587 and, in Scotland, 567 out of 2903. The proportion in London (11 per cent) was considerably lower than that in the rest of Great Britain (20 per cent). By the middle of the War, in the 1942–43 session, the figures for London were 604 out of a total of 4418 (14 per cent); for the rest of England and Wales, 1011 out of 3785 (27 per cent); and, for Scotland, 715 out of 2695 (27 per cent).

In 1943 the University of London again considered the question of providing facilities for the medical education of women and, in response to an enquiry, the School informed the University that it wished to remain a School for men only but that, in the event of all the other medical schools in the University deciding to admit women, The Middlesex Hospital Medical School would be prepared to do likewise.

The inter-departmental committee chaired by Sir William Goodenough reported in 1944 and recommended that:

> In the interests of the public and of the medical profession, co-education, which has been the normal and successful practice for many years in all the medical schools in Great Britain outside London, should become the practice in every school.

The committee further recommended that the payment to any school of Exchequer grants in aid of medical education should be conditional upon the school being co-educational and admitting a reasonable proportion of women students.

After the War it was agreed that not less than 15 per cent of new students should be women and the first of these entered the School in

October 1947. Of the twelve entering in that year, six started at the 1st MB stage, three at the 2nd MB, and there were three clinical students, two from Oxford and one from Cambridge. The total of twelve was somewhat less than the 15 per cent specified but was precisely that figure for the preclinical entry. The shortfall in the clinical numbers resulted from the inadequate number of women applicants at that stage of the course.

In subsequent years the proportion of women admitted increased and by 1967 it was 25 per cent. The idea of any quota of women students disappeared and for several years before the sesquicentenary the proportion of offers made to women applicants has been equal to, or slightly above, the proportion for men although the actual numbers admitted have been about 40 per cent of the total because of the difference in the number of applicants.

Other Events

STUDENT HEALTH CENTRE

In November 1944 the School Committee had considered a report on establishing a health centre for students and had agreed with the principle of having a health centre which could provide routine medical examinations on entry and periodical re-examinations, with particular reference to pulmonary tuberculosis. It was also agreed, however, that the introduction of such a centre should be postponed until after the War. The matter was considered again in March 1946 and agreed, a medical registrar acting as the medical officer to the Centre. Thus a start was made on the provision of a new service for students which was to develop later into a more comprehensive scheme.

ANNUAL DINNERS

The annual dinners which had been suspended during the War were resumed in October 1945 with Colonel Astor in the Chair. He was to have been the Chairman at the dinner in 1939 which was cancelled. In 1946 Dr G. E. Beaumont was in the Chair. The 1947 dinner was planned but had to be cancelled because of problems of food rationing and limitation on the numbers allowed at any dinner. Mr Maurice Whiting was to have been in the Chair and he presided at the dinner in 1948.

110

Other Events

The annual variety concerts also resumed after the War at the Scala Theatre. The one held on 1 December 1947 was notable for the calibre of the artistes who were persuaded to appear. The cast included Gracie Fields, Tommy Handley, Billy Tennent, Clarence Wright and Edward Sommerfield, and they certainly had no difficulty in eliciting a warm and enthusiastic response from the audience.

AMALGAMATED CLUBS

In 1943 the Athletics Club came into existence again after a lapse of nine years and immediately notched up notable successes. In 1945 it won the Inter-Hospitals Championship for the third successive year and was narrowly beaten by Imperial College in the Inter-Collegiate Championship, which The Middlesex had won the previous year. The annual sports days were very popular events and, in spite of rain in 1947, over 200 people attended, including many members of staff. In 1948, John Fairgrieve was the star performer on the track. He was selected for the 200-yards event for the XIV Olympic Games held at Wembley that year. Another outstanding athlete at that time was John Havard, now Secretary of the British Medical Association.

In 1945 the Rowing Club won the United Hospitals Challenge Cup for the first time since 1896 and repeated their success the following year. In 1947 the United Hospitals Regatta was held in March in the worst conditions seen on the tideway for several years. Before the start of the heat in which The Middlesex was rowing the umpire warned the crews of the danger of sinking and the St Bartholomew's and Middlesex boats shipped so much water that they could not continue. The St Thomas's crew managed to complete the course.

Although the other clubs may not have had the same success to show in the competitions they all had active programmes in the postwar years.

—6—
The National Health Service

The introduction of the NHS – Legal separation of the
School from the Hospital – Effects on the Hospital –
Board of Governors – District responsibility – Reorganis-
ation, 1974 – Kensington and Chelsea and Westminster
Area Health Authority (Teaching) – Restructuring, 1982
– Bloomsbury Health Authority

Before the War the voluntary hospitals were struggling to find sufficient finance to continue, and the great success of The Middlesex Hospital Rebuilding Fund in raising over £1 million (£20 million, 1985) was in no way typical of the general position at that time. During the War the voluntary hospitals were largely dependent on the funds from the government provided under the Emergency Medical Service arrangements. After the War it was clear that the old system would never be able to find enough money and that public funds would be required in some form. The other parts of the health services also had their problems. There were wide disparities in the municipal hospitals run by different county councils and a large number of municipal as well as voluntary hospitals were old and needed replacing. The General Practitioner Panel Scheme covered only a proportion of the population and there was pressure for it to be broadened to include everybody who wished to use it.

At the 1945 General Election all three political parties included the provision of a National Health Service in their manifestos and by then the debate was not so much about whether such a service should be introduced but about the form which it should take. Following that election, plans advanced rapidly and a Bill was presented to Parliament which became the National Health Service Act of 1946. On the 'Appointed Day', 5 July 1948, the National Health Service came into existence. The general practitioner service was extended to allow everyone to register with a doctor. Some local authorities became local health authorities for the provision of midwifery and dental services and the establishment of health centres. They worked in collaboration with the bodies responsible for the hospital services.

With a few exceptions the voluntary and municipal hospitals of the country became the responsibility of the government. In England, thirteen hospital boards were established on a regional basis to be responsible to the Minister of Health for the hospitals in their areas, with individual hospitals, or groups of hospitals, being managed by local hospital management committees. Each of the thirteen regions had at least one teaching hospital within its boundaries but, because of their special and complex roles, those teaching hospitals were managed by their individual boards of governors which were each responsible to the Minister directly and not through the regional hospital boards.

The division of most of the country into hospital board regions did not produce many difficulties once a decision had been made on their approximate number and size. In the south-east of England, however, holding about a quarter of the country's population, the problem was a complex one because of the size of London and of the presence within it of twelve separate university medical schools and their associated teaching hospitals, together with a large number of postgraduate institutes and their specialist hospitals. The obvious solution of having one hospital board for the whole of London would have created serious problems in establishing satisfactory regions around London, particularly to the south and east of it. Accordingly, in spite of the problems inherent in transecting a large city with regional boundaries, it was decided to divide London and the surrounding counties in south-east England into four 'metropolitan' regions – North-West, North-East, South-East and South-West.

The drawing of the boundary between the North-West and North-East Metropolitan Regional Hospital Boards is of interest in view of the changes which took place subsequently in 1974 and 1982. The proposals put forward in 1946 placed the London Hospital and St Bartholomew's Hospital within the boundaries of the North-East Metropolitan Region whereas Charing Cross, The Middlesex, Royal Free, St Mary's and University College Hospitals were all placed in the North-West, which also included the Hammersmith Hospital with the Royal Postgraduate Medical School and eight postgraduate institutes with their specialist hospitals, all having their own boards of

113

governors. Not surprisingly, the University of London drew attention to this disparity and individual medical schools recommended that the boundary should be moved westwards in order to create more comparable regions. The views of the educational bodies concerned, however, were not heeded at that time and five days after the end of the consultation period the Minister of Health laid a statutory order before Parliament embodying the original proposals.

The Medical School and the NHS

In its Report of 1944 the inter-departmental committee chaired by Sir William Goodenough had recommended that the medical schools of the University of London should be legal entities, separate from their parent teaching hospitals but closely linked to them. It was also implicit in the plans for a National Health Service that the medical schools would not be taken over by the government along with their teaching hospitals and that it would be necessary for those joined to their hospitals to become independent legal bodies. In London this applied to all the University medical schools with the exception of St Bartholomew's Hospital Medical College, which had separated from its hospital in 1921, and the London School of Medicine for Women which had been independent since its inception in 1874.

At The Middlesex, in July 1946, a joint sub-committee of the Council and the Board of Management was established under the chairmanship of Mr F. H. Doran to examine the problems in detail and to prepare recommendations for a 'Charter'. These were considered at meetings of the Council and Board and later at the University and agreement was reached in good time to enable the formalities to be completed before the introduction of the National Health Service.

One of the items requiring resolution was the question of which buildings should become the responsibility of the School and which should be the Hospital's responsibility. In the past there had been a reasonably clear understanding but legal definition had not been required in the unified structure. The National Health Service (Apportionment and Transfer) Regulations stated that:

> Any interests in premises . . . shall be apportioned between the Minister and the other person or persons concerned according to the extent to which such premises are used for each of such purposes.

114

On that basis many of the decisions were obvious and all of them were resolved fairly easily. There was no difficulty in deciding that the whole of the 'First Floor Cross Piece of the main Hospital Building' and 'The Top Three Floors of the Residents' House' were as unmistakably for exclusive use by the School as were the main School buildings themselves. Except for the basement and the equipment installed therein 'the land and buildings known as the Courtauld Institute of Biochemistry' were also a School property. Apportionments were also made in respect of the basement of the School block housing the mortuary and chapels.

The same sub-committee examined and made recommendations concerning the 'contra account' for services provided by the School for the Hospital. That comprehensive review laid down the general principles of the system and these have been adhered to since then. Not surprisingly, there have been some differences of opinion from time to time on the precise figures which were appropriate at any particular period in relation to the level of services being provided and the correct cost in relation to inflation and other factors.

And so, on 23 June 1948, pursuant to Section 15 of the National Health Service Act 1946, the School became a body corporate under the name of 'The Middlesex Hospital Medical School', having a perpetual succession and a common seal. The main objects of the School were set out as:

> To acquire and carry on the Medical School of The Middlesex Hospital for the purpose of the education of students of Medicine and Medical Science. To provide the accommodation and equipment and the academic and other staff necessary for the education and practical training of the said students.
>
> To promote research work and to provide finance and facilities for the advancement of Medical Science.
>
> To conduct organised courses of instruction for the foregoing purposes and to enter into and carry out such arrangements or agreements as the School shall think fit for providing the School with facilities for the promotion of its objects in association with any hospital or institution and in particular with The Middlesex Hospital, subject where applicable to the Statutes and Regulations of the University of London, so long as the School is a School of that University.

The government of the School was vested in the Council which was constituted with two persons nominated by the Senate of the University of London; eight persons nominated by the Academic Board; six persons nominated by the Board of Governors of the Hospital; two other persons, not being members of the teaching staff, to be co-opted by the Council; and the Dean (*ex officio*). The School Secretary continued as Secretary of the Council.

The initial two members on the Council nominated by the University were Professor D. Hughes Parry QC (Sir David Hughes Parry, 1951) who had been Vice-Chancellor since 1945, and Professor R. O. Kapp, Professor of Electrical Engineering at University College. The six members nominated by the Board of Governors were Colonel, The Hon. J. J. Astor, The Hon. T. B. Money-Coutts, Mr F. H. Doran, Colonel Sir Eric Gore-Brown, Mr J. H. Hambro and Mr Walter Morrison. The facility of co-opting members to the Council was not utilised until 1961.

Under the scheme of government it was laid down that

> the Council shall establish an Academic Board consisting of the Dean (*ex officio*); the Professors of the University and Heads of Departments of the School; representatives of the Readers and Recognised Teachers at the School to be elected by and from those Teachers; other Teachers appointed by the Council to the Academic Board on the nomination of the Board.

The Academic Board replaced the previous School Committee and among its functions and responsibilities were those of determining the course of study in the School; considering and reporting to Council upon all academic matters and questions of educational policy; electing annually a Dean, with the concurrence of Council; considering and making recommendations in regard to the appointment and removal of teachers in the School, subject to the University statutes and regulations in the case of appointed teachers.

The Academic Board for the session 1948–49 consisted of the Dean (Dr Harold Boldero); ten professors, of whom nine were heads of departments; two other heads of departments; four readers; and twelve recognized teachers nominated by the Medical Committee. It was decided to defer to a later date any nominations of other members of staff and it was not until 1951–52 that any readers or recognized teachers who were not also members of the Medical Committee were appointed to the Academic Board. At that time recognition as a teacher was a more protracted process than it became later and this caused some problems in election. In 1951 three of the people originally nominated by the Medical Committee were deemed by the Academic Board to be ineligible on that account and apparently it was not considered appropriate to appoint them as 'other Teachers'. Two of the three had been members of staff, and on the Medical Committee, for several years.

In 1950 Mr T. G. Illtyd James, Senior Surgeon at the Central Middlesex Hospital, was appointed to serve on the Academic Board in view of the importance of that hospital in the teaching of Middlesex students. He had played a major role in the development of the association between the School and the Central Middlesex and his nomination by that Hospital to the Academic Board was warmly welcomed.

The Finance Committee of the School was constituted as before with an approximately equal number of (so-called) lay members and staff members. It was unanimously agreed that Mr F. H. Doran should be re-elected as Chairman.

The Middlesex Hospital

THE START OF THE NHS

With the introduction of the National Health Service the existing Board of Management of The Middlesex Hospital was dissolved and its place taken by a Board of Governors appointed by the Minister of Health. The new Board consisted of twenty-nine members, of whom five were appointed by the Minister after receiving nominations from the University; five after nominations by the medical staff; five after nominations by the North-West Metropolitan Regional Hospital Board; and the remainder 'after consultation with local health authorities and other organisations as appear to the Minister to be concerned'. Such organisations included the London County Council and trade unions. In the event, twenty-one of the members of the new Board of Governors had either been members of the retiring Board of Management or were members of the staff. There was further welcome continuity in that Colonel Astor was appointed Chairman of the new Board.

On the afternoon of Wednesday, 30 June 1948, the retiring Chairman and Board of Management held an 'At Home' in the garden of the Hospital to celebrate the complete reopening of the Hospital and to mark the historic change which was about to take place in its affairs. Over a thousand people were present and the costs were borne by a donor who insisted on remaining anonymous. After tea, Colonel Astor addressed the guests and, among other things, said:

This occasion gives me an opportunity of thanking our former subscribers for their wonderful support in the past. This magnificent Hospital was rebuilt by voluntary contribution and is a lasting memorial to the generosity of the British public. It is such support that has made possible the work done here by doctors and nurses for 200 years, and such work makes every one of us feel proud and grateful.

I would like to emphasise that the transfer of the Hospital to the Ministry of Health in the next few days, though it marks the end of a chapter in our history, is in no sense the end of that history. Granted, the buildings and equipment become the property of the Government, but expenditure on maintenance now amounts to over half a million pounds a year. With taxation at its present level that seems beyond the scope of even the most generous public in the world. This burden in future falls on the State, and I see no reason to regret that fact.

But there is a great deal more to a hospital than bricks and mortar; perhaps the most important characteristic is the spirit which animates and inspires all who work here. It is our aim and firm intention that the best in the voluntary-hospital tradition may continue.

To this end we need your help as much as ever. We need voluntary workers in wards, canteens and library. We need money for amenities and comforts for patients and staff. We need money to carry on research, and to ensure that progress in medical knowledge and technique shall not be hampered by the limitations of government support.

It was typical of Colonel Astor that on such an occasion he should have highlighted in a few words so many salient points. He indicated the inevitability of the Hospital becoming the property of the State and did not express regret. He saw clearly, however, that the government would not be able to provide all that was wanted and that there was still a need for voluntary support. How right he has been proved by events. How much has been accomplished since then by voluntary effort and by donations. The endowment funds have had to be used not only to provide amenities and promote research but also to provide basic essentials for the Hospital which would have been regarded by most people in 1948 as being clearly the responsibility of the State.

The fundamental purpose of the Hospital in caring for patients in the best possible way was, of course, unaltered by the introduction of the National Health Service, and might be said to have been encouraged by the potentiality of even greater development. As the Secretary-Superintendent, Brigadier Hardy-Roberts, wrote in 1949:

> It was, and still is, of vital importance that hospitals everywhere should continue to give to the public the same valuable service as before and that confidence in them should not be shaken. One way, perhaps the most effective way, of achieving this was to avoid any drastic change in the policy of management, in spite of the fundamental change involved in the transfer of responsibility to the Government.

The consequences of the fundamental change in the transfer of responsibility were, however, well illustrated by his further observations that:

> The Health Service was launched on a flood of memoranda and instructions from the Ministry of Health. As an initial outburst it was impressive, but it was also a bit bewildering to an administrator who had before been accustomed only to the lucid verbal orders of his Chairman. To the Board of Governors and to the Medical Committee this spate of directives revealed, with unmistakable clarity, that The Middlesex Hospital, after 200 years, was no longer master of its fate. Could it, we wondered, remain captain of its soul?
>
> In various speeches and pronouncements the Minister had said that Boards of Governors were to act as his agents in the management of the hospitals under their control. What, in fact, did this mean and how was it to be reconciled with the tone and substance of the written instructions which were reaching us by every post? Instructions of a very detailed and intimate kind, ranging from the method of appointing medical staff to the scale of charges to be applied in the private wing; requests for information on all sorts of minor domestic matters; guidance about this; restrictions about that. Was everything to be regimented by Whitehall? Were Boards of Governors to be allowed no real authority and no discrimination?

It was well recognized that each Board of Governors and each Regional Hospital Board could not have a free hand and that there needed to be a measure of supervision and control and some standardisation. It is clear from the writings of the period, however, that the degree to which this regimentation was applied came as a surprise to many people. There was also bewilderment at the way in which some directives appeared to have been drafted as if the consequences of applying them had not been fully appreciated and others as if medical education did not require any special facilities or consideration or had been completely overlooked in an overall instruction.

One of the recommendations contained in the 1944 Report of the inter-departmental committee chaired by Sir William Goodenough was that teaching hospitals should become affiliated with other institutions in order to create widely based university-teaching centres. The Middlesex had welcomed this suggestion and had undertaken negotiations which resulted in The Middlesex Hospital Group of Teaching Hospitals being formed and being officially included in the term 'The Middlesex Hospital' in the NHS Regulations. In addition to The Middlesex Hospital and its convalescent home at Clacton-on-Sea, the Group comprised the St Luke's Hospital for Functional Nervous Disorders, Woodside; The Hospital for Women, Soho Square; and the British Red Cross Society's Clinic for Rheumatism, Peto Place. Not only did these affiliations add to the teaching facilities at that time, they were to make it possible subsequently for the School to develop academic Departments of Psychiatry, of Obstetrics and Gynaecology, and of Rheumatology Research.

The inclusion in the Group of the Hospital for Women and the British Red Cross Society's Clinic for Rheumatism was largely due to their proximity to The Middlesex. The Hospital for Women, Soho, had been founded in 1842 as the first special hospital in the world for the treatment of diseases peculiar to women. The British Red Cross Society's Arthur Stanley Institute had been founded in 1930 as a pioneer out-patient centre for research, diagnosis and treatment of rheumatic diseases in adults. In the case of St Luke's Hospital there had been associations previously. The formation of the St Luke's Charity in 1750 had resulted in the founding of a hospital at Windmill Hill and later in Old Street but the latter had closed in 1917. In 1922, while considering the possibilities of starting a new hospital outside central London, a Deed of Agreement was signed with The Middlesex Hospital for the provision of out-patient and ward facilities. In 1930 a new St Luke's-Woodside Hospital was opened in nearly seven acres of grounds at Muswell Hill; the association with The Middlesex did not end then for in 1938 Dr Noel Harris, Physician-in-Charge of St Luke's-Woodside Hospital from 1935, was appointed as Physician to the Department of Psychological Medicine of The Middlesex Hospital.

With the introduction of the National Health Service the former honorary staff became salaried and were known as 'consultants'. The retired members of staff, who had previously been referred to as the 'consulting staff', became known as the 'honorary consultant staff' for several years. Later, a scheme on lines similar to university practice was introduced so that when consultants retired after more than ten years in the post they became eligible for election by the Medical Committee as 'emeritus consultants'. The staff of the School dealing with patients in the wards or in the laboratories needed also to hold an appointment with the Board of Governors and they were given honorary contracts. The term 'honorary staff' then acquired a meaning quite different from that which had applied until then.

In the course of an address to the Medical Society in June 1956, Sir Harold Boldero, who had been Dean from 1934 to 1954, reviewed the events of that period, including the introduction of the National Health Service eight years previously. He drew attention to some of the benefits produced by it, including the better hospital service which had resulted throughout the country and particularly in the small towns and country areas which had seldom seen specialists or consultants in the past. He considered that the Health Service which had been introduced in 1948 had been the best available at that time. Many people clearly shared his view although contemporary records show that a number were also apprehensive of the way in which the service might develop subsequently and some even went so far as to compare the 'opening phase', as they called it, with the 'phoney war' of 1939–40.

DISTRICT RESPONSIBILITY

The Middlesex Hospital was founded in 1745 'for the sick and lame of Soho'. Over the course of two centuries and with the development of other hospitals, The Middlesex, along with the other teaching hospitals, developed specialised skills and facilities which attracted patients from well beyond its immediate environs. The Hospital decided its bed allocations and other clinical activities in accordance with educational requirements laid down by the General Medical Council and on the basis of the quality of the services which it was able to offer in particular fields. At the introduction of the National Health Service in 1948 The Middlesex Hospital, like other teaching hospitals, had insufficient beds to meet the needs of all the patients referred and there was pressure to expand the size of the Hospital to 1000 beds. In that situation it was difficult to undertake any further commitment and the ultimate responsibility for providing a service for local patients, if no other arrangements could be made, rested on the Regional Hospital Board.

That Regional Board, however, was also in difficulties because of the large number of teaching and specialist hospitals in central London. In the early 1960s discussions were started in the North-West Metropolitan Region on the possibility of the teaching hospitals accepting responsibility for providing hospital care for all patients in a defined catchment area if provision could not be made elsewhere. Because of other pressures it was considered that this suggestion could not be brought into operation then, but later it was agreed that, from 1 April 1968, the Board of Governors would accept 'district responsibility' for about 88,500 residents of an area surrounding The Middlesex, extending from St John's Wood to the Thames and from Edgware Road to Tottenham Court Road.

NHS Reorganisation, 1974

From the start of the National Health Service there had been collaboration between the Boards of Governors and the Regional Hospital Boards, particularly in respect of the provision of regional specialities. A good example was provided in the North West Metropolitan Region where, within a few months, it had been agreed that the radiotherapy centres at The Middlesex and Mount Vernon Hospitals should be integrated and that Professors Windeyer, Roberts and Scarff should be given honorary contracts with the North West Metropolitan Board in respect of their responsibilities at Mount Vernon. Collaboration occurred in other fields and, later, joint consultative committees were formed in each of the four metropolitan regions. Later still, a joint working group of these consultative committees was established, under the chairmanship of Dame Albertine Winner, which examined provision for a number of specialities throughout the four metropolitan regions. Collaboration in this way, however, was not considered adequate by everyone.

In 1965, at the instigation of the University Grants Committee, a Royal Commission on Medical Education was established with Lord Todd as Chairman and this reported to Parliament in April 1968. One of its recommendations was that the teaching hospitals in England and Wales should be brought within the framework of administration of the regional hospital service generally and that the constitution of the

regional boards should be modified to provide appropriate representation of those concerned with medical education. It was considered
that normally the university representatives should form one fifth of
the total members of the regional board and that, under the general
responsibility of the board, the main hospitals associated with each
medical school should be grouped under a newly constituted governing
body with about one half of these members being nominated by the
university.

While the Royal Commission had been meeting, the Minister of
Health had been reviewing the structure of the health service and,
particularly, its separate administrative arrangements for general practice, local-authority health services, and hospitals. Coincident with these
discussions the government was also in the process of reorganising the
local-government structure and this became linked with health-service
reorganisation in respect of timing, the date of change for both being
set for 1 April 1974.

In 1968 the Minister of Health issued a Green Paper drawing attention to the divided responsibility for health care and proposing that the
functions of the existing separate authorities should be combined by
establishing about forty 'area boards' throughout the country. It was
recognized that there were particular problems in London which would
need further examination and discussion. In November that year matters
of health in England became the responsibility of a newly created
department of state, the Department of Health and Social Security
(DHSS). The Department was headed by a Secretary of State for
Social Services and there was also a Minister of State for Health. In
1970 the Secretary of State issued a further Green Paper reiterating
the case for unification and the establishment of area health authorities
but also indicating that the areas would be too small for a number of
important functions, such as the overall planning of hospital and
specialist services. To overcome this it was proposed that there should
also be 'regional health councils' covering areas similar to those of the
existing regional hospital boards.

The Middlesex Hospital Board of Governors and the Medical
Committee considered extensively the proposals made by the Royal
Commission on Medical Education and in the Green Papers and there
were also many discussions in the Teaching Hospitals Association. The
Board voiced its strong support for the Association in its view that
Boards of Governors should be retained in some form with a direct

relationship with the DHSS and that they should also retain their endowment funds and responsibility for appointing staff. Underlying this was the essential requirement to maintain the close association between teaching hospitals and their medical schools in the interests of education and research and therefore of the health service of the future. This could be achieved only if the responsibility for the hospitals was retained in organisations, such as a Board of Governors, with considerable common membership with the schools on important committees and with officers of the hospitals and schools having regular contact with one another. There was also the need for the organisation responsible for the teaching hospitals to be directly responsible to the Secretary of State so that he could properly discharge his statutory obligations for medical education and research. As Lord Cobbold wrote in his Chairman's Report for 1968–69:

> There is one point on which the Board of Governors are in no doubt and on which they are whole-heartedly supported by medical and administrative opinion in the Hospital and Medical School – whatever the future pattern of the Hospital Service, very close links must be maintained between the Teaching Hospitals and their Medical Schools in the interest of teaching and research. Anything which could undermine the close association at all levels between The Middlesex Hospital and its Medical School would be only to the detriment of patients, and of students, and thus of medical services and education.

The case for an organisation on these lines was argued forcibly by Lord Cobbold in debates in the House of Lords and on other occasions. Accordingly, there was great disappointment when the National Health Service Reorganisation Act of 1973 abolished the Boards of Governors of teaching hospitals associated with general medical schools. The endowment funds of the teaching hospitals were, however, protected by the creation of 'special trustees' for each hospital. Mr D. B. Money-Coutts was elected Chairman of The Middlesex Hospital Special Trustees.

The same Act abolished regional hospital boards, hospital management committees and executive councils and created fourteen regional health authorities and ninety area health authorities and family-practitioner committees in England. Areas containing a major teaching hospital were specially designated as 'area health authorities (teaching).' They had two of their members, rather than just one, appointed after nomination by the appropriate university and they were responsible for appointing and employing the consultants working in their hospitals whereas, for other areas, the contracts of the consultants were held by the regional health authority. On each of the regional health authorities there was only one, of fifteen to twenty members, appointed after nomination by the university and, as with the area health authorities (teaching), this proportion fell far short of the recommendation of the Royal Commission on Medical Education.

A number of other changes were introduced with the reorganisation of 1974. A significant proportion of the members of health authorities would be nominated by local authorities; there would be a team of officers for each health authority, operating on a basis of 'consensus management'; there would be 'districts' within each area with district management teams, also working by consensus; community health councils would be established for each district, or possibly for more than one district; meetings of authorities would be held in public, although the public might be excluded from discussion of a few items.

There was considerable controversy about the general principle of reorganisation and each individual feature of it. While most people recognised the arguments for some integration, many considered that the administrative arrangements proposed were too cumbersome to achieve any advantage. That point of view was further fostered by the multitudinous diagrams which were produced in an attempt to explain how everybody and every part of the structure related to everybody else, as illustrated by lines of varying breadth or different colours. There was also deep concern that politics might come to dominate discussions; the concept of the Government of 1946 that hospital boards and management committees should be non-political had been strongly approved. There were many doubts as to whether consensus management would do anything to improve efficiency or would merely result in all decisions, however straightforward, being debated needlessly and at great length, with an interminable proliferation of agenda, minutes and memoranda. That would depend to some extent on the individuals concerned, but they had not been appointed at that stage and there were doubts about the qualities of people who might wish to apply for such posts. Looking at Parliament and local government a number of people wondered whether the holding of meetings in public would necessarily bring out the best qualities and wisest judgement of the

125

members. Later they were also to learn that it did not necessarily promote the best qualities of some members of the public.

Overall, at The Middlesex and at many other hospitals throughout the country, there was much more reaction to the prospect of reorganisation than to the introduction of the National Health Service twenty-six years earlier. In 1948, although there had been great debate, many people regarded the introduction of a National Health Service as both necessary and inevitable. Reorganisation was not seen as either.

On the evening of Tuesday, 26 March 1974, many colleagues and friends gathered in the Refectory of the Medical School to mark the occasion of the last meeting of the Board of Governors of the Hospital and to express their appreciation of those who had so willingly given their time to The Middlesex. A presentation was made to Lord Cobbold, the Chairman since 1963, and to Lady Cobbold. In the course of his address Mr R. S. Handley said:

This Hospital has had a Board of Governors since it was founded in 1745. In a few days that Board is to be swept away. Our gathering this evening thus partakes of something of the atmosphere of a memorial service. On such occasions we are told that the service is one of thanksgiving for a useful life and that we have not congregated to mourn a departed friend and benefactor. How difficult, how impossible, it is to obey this admirable injunction. One cannot escape the sense of loss and deprivation.

It is my view that this evening represents the biggest disaster which this Hospital has ever suffered. We have had, in the Board, a boss whose understanding of medical problems, whose intelligence, whose generosity and whose devotion to the highest traditions of the professions of healing have made our work much easier and much more effective than we could have made it ourselves. We have known our bosses as people, and have been able to discuss problems and situations with them face to face. This friendly and fruitful partnership is now to vanish and we are to be more and more at the mercy of the monstrous regiment of politicians. We have been forced by the administration into a hideous and ill-fitting coat of many colours. What now awaits us remains to be seen . . . Nevertheless, whatever befalls us, it is, I know, the resolve of every member of The Middlesex Hospital staff at every level to keep this Hospital a friendly and cooperative place in which we treat our patients as our guests, and not as cases . . .

I come lastly to our reigning Chairman, Lord Cobbold. Words fail me. That a man who was the Lord Chamberlain for eight years, the Governor of the Bank of England for twelve years, and is a Knight of the Garter and a Privy Councillor should find time to lead us, should interest himself in every aspect of our affairs, should often come to sit with us in our informal staff lunches and know most of the consultant (and no doubt other) members of staff by their names marks him out as a very special person . . .

KENSINGTON AND CHELSEA AND WESTMINSTER

The first Green Paper on reorganisation had recognised the particular problems of London and in 1970 the Secretary of State established a London Working Group under the chairmanship of the Minister of State for Health. Although the existence of the Group was dependent on the fact that there were special problems associated with London the Minister ruled, at an early meeting, that there could be no particular solution which did not conform to the general plans applicable to the country as a whole. Various ideas within the framework were considered and the few members of the Group who had experience of medical education strongly supported the views put forward by the Teaching Hospitals Association that the experience of the Emergency Medical Service during the War had demonstrated the advantages of having a sector arrangement. If areas had to be included in the scheme, it was advocated that they should be of adequate size and extend radially in accordance with transport patterns. It was pointed out that this principle had already been accepted on a larger scale by incorporating the Home Counties with London in determining the disposition of regions in south-east England. Details of possible areas based on that approach had been prepared by a team commissioned by the Teaching Hospitals Association and these proposals would have been included in what would have had to be a minority report if the Group had produced any report. It was disbanded, however, without that being done, the Minister having 'taken note' of the views expressed by members.

The decisions made subsequently by the Secretary of State created the Kensington and Chelsea and Westminster Area Health Authority (Teaching) whose boundaries were indicated in its title. It contained three teaching hospital groups – The Middlesex in the North East District (Teaching); St Mary's in the North West District (Teaching); and the Westminster in the South District (Teaching). The Area was, of course, also responsible for those hospitals in the teaching groups which lay outside its geographical boundaries, such as St Luke's-Woodside Hospital. In addition, the Area was given responsibility for two large psychiatric hospitals in Surrey: Banstead Hospital in Sutton, and

Horton Hospital in Epsom. Initially, Banstead Hospital was allocated to the South District and Horton Hospital to the North East District but subsequently, when the possibility of closing one of these hospitals was being examined, Banstead Hospital was also transferred to the North East District.

The first Chairman of the Area Authority was Mrs C. B. Bicknell; the Vice-Chairman was Dr John Dunwoody and among the members at that stage there were Dr L. M. Green, Director of the Occupational Health Centre of The Middlesex Hospital and Chairman of the Family Practitioner Committee; Mr A. J. Macdonald-Buchanan, member of the School Council and a member of the former Board of Governors; Mr D. B. Money-Coutts, Chairman of the School Council and a member of the former Board of Governors; Miss Helen Rowe, Principal Nursing Officer of the Middlesex Hospital; and Professor E. W. Walls, Dean. In October 1974 Professor Walls was replaced by the author of this book when he succeeded him as Dean. In 1978 Dr Dunwoody became Chairman of the Authority and Mr Money-Coutts was elected Vice-Chairman.

The North East District Management Team consisted of four officers of the Authority, an elected consultant and an elected general practitioner. The Dean did not form part of the 'consensus' but he received all agendas and minutes and attended the meetings held fortnightly, or more often if necessary. The officers were the District Administrator, Mr D. J. Knowles; the District Community Physician, Dr P. A. Kitchener; the District Finance Officer, Mr F. S. Jackson; and the District Nursing Officer, Miss K. M. Biggin. Mr W. W. Slack was elected as the first representative of the consultant medical staff and Dr B. C. Lee as the first representative of the general practitioners of the district.

NORTH WEST THAMES REGION

At the reorganisation, the boundary between the North West and North East Metropolitan Regions was moved westwards and the names changed to make them North West and North East Thames Regional Health Authorities. As a result, the Royal Free and University College Hospitals, as well as the Whittington and Royal Northern Hospitals, came within the responsibility of the North East Thames Region. The Middlesex Hospital came just within the responsibility of the North West Thames Regional Health Authority (even though the Out-Patient

Sir Thomas Watson
FRS

Edward W. Tuson
FRS

Sir Charles Bell
KH, FRS

Dr Francis Hawkins

Herbert Mayo
FRS

James Moncrieff Arnott
FRS

THE FOUNDERS, 1835

Reproduced from *The Story of The Middlesex Hospital Medical School 1835 - 1935*
by H. Campbell Thomson, (John Murray, London, 1935)

Right
The Middlesex Hospital in 1835, at the time of the foundation
of the Medical School

Below
The Hospital in 1935, at the time of the centenary of the Medical
School. The rebuilt Hospital was opened by His Royal Highness
the Duke of York on 29 May 1935. On the left of the picture is the
Residency. Another three floors for the use of students of the
Medical School were added through the generosity of Sir Edward
Meyerstein and opened in April 1936. These are shown in the
1985 photograph opposite.

The Hospital in 1985, at the time of the sesquicentenary of the Medical School. The British Telecom Tower in the background is on the north side of Howland Street, opposite the Windeyer Building of the Medical School

Left
The Middlesex Hospital
Medical School in 1835

Right
The old School buildings
and the Bland-Sutton
Institute of Pathology in
Riding House Street in
1978, just before demoli-
tion of the old buildings to
allow construction of the
Wolfson Building

Below left
The Sir Jules Thorn Institute of Clinical Science
as seen from the Courtauld
Institute of Biochemistry.
In the foreground is the
roof of the Bland-Sutton
Institute of Pathology. Between that and the Institute
is the School Building
erected before the Second
World War and contain-
ing administrative offices,
the Boldero Library,
laboratories and the Post-
mortem Room. In the
background, beyond the
garden, is the main
Hospital building.

Right
The Windeyer Building
(Howland Street frontage),
extending from Cleveland
Street to Charlotte Street.
The main entrance to the
building in Cleveland
Street is hidden from view
in this photograph by the
cupola of the Edward
Lewis Theatre. Work on
the building commenced
in 1957 and Phase 1 was
opened by Lord Astor of
Hever on 16 December
1959. The building was
completed in 1962

Mr Samuel Augustine Courtauld
1930-1946

Colonel The Lord Astor of Hever, D Litt
1946-1962

The Lord Cobbold, KG, GCVO, PC, DL
1963-1974

Mr David Money-Coutts
1974-

Sir Harold Boldero
1934-1954

Professor Sir Brian Windeyer
1954-1967

Professor Eldred Walls
1967-1974

Sir Douglas Ranger
1974-1983

Mr William Slack
1983-

Her Majesty Queen Elizabeth on the occasion of her visit to The Middlesex Hospital on 8 September 1939, five days after the outbreak of the Second World War. She is being greeted by Sir Alfred Webb-Johnson and beyond them is Dr Hugh Marriott, Commandant of the Hospital. Behind and to the right of Her Majesty is Miss E. M. Land, Deputy Matron. Everyone is carrying a gas mask. The blackout curtains at the door and a few of the 20,000, or more, sandbags protecting the Hospital can be seen

Sir Edward Meyerstein presenting the Senior Broderip Scholarship to Mr L. L. Whytehead at the prizegiving ceremony in the Queen's Hall in 1938, with Mr R. A. Foley, School Secretary, in attendance. Such ceremonies were held at the Queen's Hall annually before the Second World War

Sir Michael Sobell. His generous benefaction to the School enabled the construction of the Sir Jules Thorn Institute of Clinical Science to proceed and provided the School with the extensive Sobell Laboratories within it

Sir Jules Thorn. His generous benefactions to the School led to the construction of the Sir Jules Thorn Institute of Clinical Science and have supported research by named Fellows in the Institute and in other Departments of the School and Hospital. Reproduced by kind permission of the *Financial Times*

Top: Her Majesty Queen Elizabeth The Queen Mother, Chancellor of the University of London, at the opening of the Sir Jules Thorn Institute of Clinical Science on 30 May 1974. Her Majesty is accompanied by the Dean, Professor Eldred Walls. With them is her lady-in-waiting Lady Elizabeth Basset

Above: The Queen Mother unveils the commemorative wall plaque. To her left are the Dean, Professor Eldred Walls and The Hon. John Astor, Chairman of the Building Committee of the School

Top: Her Royal Highness The Princess Anne, Mrs Mark Phillips, on the occasion of her visit to the School on the day of her inauguration as Chancellor of the University of London, 13 October 1982. On her left is Mr David Money-Coutts, Chairman of the School and on his left is the Dean, Sir Douglas Ranger

Above: Her Royal Highness The Princess Anne, Mrs Mark Phillips, is presented with a bouquet by Miss Melanie Robson. On Her Royal Highness's left are Professor Randolph Quirk (Sir Randolph Quirk, 1985), Vice-Chancellor of the University, Mr David Money-Coutts, Chairman of the School, and her lady-in-waiting, the Countess of Lichfield. Sir Douglas Ranger is on the extreme left of the photograph

Top: Sir Leonard Wolfson unveiling the wall plaque at the opening of the Wolfson Building on 3 July 1979 with Lady Wolfson. Mr David Money-Coutts, Chairman of the Council of the School, is standing in front of the notice board and on his left are Professor Eldred Walls, Dean at the time of the Wolfson benefaction, and Mrs Walls. The Dean in 1979, Sir Douglas Ranger, is behind Sir Leonard's right shoulder

Above: Part of the Boldero Library, opened in 1939, showing the portrait of Sir Harold Boldero on one of the pillars

Right

The Wolfson Building in Riding House Street with the Bland-Sutton Institute of Pathology beyond it. The building provides accommodation for psychiatric out-patients and for the Academic Department of Psychiatry

Below

Part of the Hospital garden looking towards the main Hospital from outside the Bland-Sutton Institute of Pathology with, on the right of the photograph, parts of the School block, the Sir Jules Thorn Institute of Clinical Science and the West Wing of the Hospital. The portion of the garden beyond the steps was excavated and raised in order to allow the construction of the Central Sterile Supply Department. The portion of the garden in the foreground of the garden was a tennis court until 1931.
The Middlesex has won the Best Hospital Garden competition on several occasions

Right
A cartoon of Sir Edward Meyerstein which was published in the *Middlesex Hospital Journal* in January 1938, soon after the announcement of Sir Edward's gift of the new sports ground at Chislehurst – just one of his many munificent benefactions to The Middlesex Hospital and Medical School. The verse under the cartoon read:

To patient first he turned his thoughts,
His kindness was unbounded,
But now (great day!) he sees that we
Are well and truly grounded

Below
The sports ground at Chislehurst, the gift of Sir Edward Meyerstein, opened on 21 May 1938

The upper part of the British Telecom Tower seen through a hole in the roof of the Anatomy Department in the Windeyer Building following the damage caused by the explosion of a bomb in the viewing platform of the tower on the morning of 31 October 1971. The gap in the enclosure of the observation platform is well shown

Annexe on the other side of Cleveland Street was geographically in the North East Thames Region and students living in Astor College who were admitted to the wards were classified, statistically, as 'inter-Regional transfers').

The North West Thames Region contained seven areas (including two teaching areas) and the Central Middlesex Hospital was in the Brent and Harrow Area Health Authority of that region. The Chairman of the Regional Health Authority was Mrs B. F. R. Paterson CBE (Dame Betty Paterson, 1981).

NHS Restructuring, 1982

As was indicated previously (p. 125) the reorganisation of 1974 provoked a considerable amount of antipathy. In 1979 the Department of Health and Social Security and the Welsh Office issued a consultative paper in which it was stated that:

> There has been widespread criticism of the 1974 changes, which the Royal Commission summed up as:
> – too many tiers;
> – too many administrators, in all disciplines;
> – failure to take quick decisions;
> – money wasted.
> The Government is in no doubt that these criticisms are well-founded and that morale in the Service has suffered as a result.

In response to that consultative paper there were over 3500 comments (including one from the School). It is presumed that a large number fully agreed with the government that the criticisms of the reorganisation were well-founded. In 1980 the government published its decisions for a further change in the structure in which the main features would be: the abolition of the area health authorities, to be replaced by district health authorities, each served by one team of officers; retention of the regional health authorities, for strategic planning and to be responsible for implementing the restructuring programme. Their functions, particularly their relationship with the new district authorities, would be reviewed later. It was also proposed to retain the existing arrangements for the administration of family practitioner committees, even if relating to more than one district authority; and to retain community health councils (the necessity of which

129

had been queried in the consultative paper if health authorities at district level were to be introduced).

BLOOMSBURY

The decision having been taken to establish district health authorities, the details became of critical importance. As will be set out in more detail in a later chapter (p. 227), The Middlesex Hospital Medical School and the School of Medicine, University College London, had already agreed in principle to the formation of a Joint School of Medicine but the Hospitals associated with the Schools were, in 1980, in separate districts and in different regions. There was a fear that, with the existing regional boundary running down Cleveland Street, a decision might be taken to move it just a hundred metres or so westwards so that The Middlesex Hospital lay within the North East Thames Region without its associated district. Before reaching any decisions the Secretary of State had one meeting with the Chairman and a few representatives of the existing Kensington and Chelsea and Westminster Area Health Authority and another meeting with the Chairman and a few representatives of The Middlesex Hospital Medical School and Medical Committee. At those meetings, which were candid and constructive, the various possibilities were discussed and evaluated. The Secretary of State decided to amalgamate the district containing The Middlesex Hospital with the district containing University College Hospital to form one new district, named the Bloomsbury Health Authority. This was placed in the North East Thames Region by moving the inter-regional boundary westwards to Edgware Road.

While The Middlesex Hospital was in the North West Thames Region it had, of course, participated in the arrangements made for the location of regional specialities. They were principally in radiotherapy and cardiac surgery. In announcing his decision on district and regional boundaries the Secretary of State made it clear that, as the regional specialities had been determined very largely by the decisions of a working party which had made a comprehensive study of all four Thames regions, he did not anticipate any change in the arrangements which had already been made for those specialities.

One other great change was made in creating the new Bloomsbury Health Authority. For some time there had been discussion in the University about the possibility of associating some of the postgraduate institutes with general medical schools. Three of the institutes which

130

had been considered for an association with The Middlesex Hospital Medical School and the School of Medicine, University College London, in a Joint School of Medicine, were the Institutes of Laryngology and Otology, of Orthopaedics and of Urology. In view of this the Secretary of State also decided to transfer the management of the Hospitals associated with those Institutes into the Bloomsbury Health Authority. They are the Royal National Throat, Nose and Ear Hospital, the Royal National Orthopaedic Hospital and the St Peter's Hospitals.

Thus the Bloomsbury Health Authority has a unique concentration of facilities for medical education and research, and within the boundaries of the District there is also a unique concentration of other educational resources.

Dr John Dunwoody was appointed Chairman of the Bloomsbury Health Authority and Mr D. B. Money-Coutts was elected Vice-Chairman.

—7—
Hospital Developments

Building development plans, 1948 – Marlborough Court
– Institute of Clinical Research – Athlone House –
Macdonald-Buchanan School of Nursing – James Pringle
House – St Luke's-Woodside – Arthur Stanley House –
Schools of Radiography – General Hospital developments
– Medical developments – Regional specialties – New
departments

There have been considerable changes over the years in the medical practice of The Middlesex Hospital Teaching Group and in its buildings. Developments up to 1948 have already been considered to some extent in previous chapters. Since 1982 there have been some rearrangements brought about as a result of the restructuring of the National Health Service and the Faculty of Medicine of the University and these will be mentioned in the final chapter rather than here.

Buildings

Following the successful rebuilding of the Hospital in the 1930s the Board of Management was concerned to provide better accommodation for the Out-Patient and Casualty Departments; to provide new facilities for the ancillary Schools of Physiotherapy, Radiography and Radiotherapy; to extend the nurses' home; and to provide new School buildings. After the War these ideas were set down formally as the plans for future development and they were endorsed by the new Board of Governors in December 1948. It was realised, of course, that the School had then become the responsibility of the Council but the Hospital and the School still had to plan in unison and there was every wish to do so. There was strong cross-representation between the Board of Governors and the School Council and also between the Plans Committee of the Hospital and the Building Committee of the School.

This is well illustrated by the fact that Sir Harold Boldero, the Dean, was Chairman of the Hospital Plans Committee from 1943 to 1952. He was succeeded in that office, until 1959, by Mr C. P. Wilson who was also a member of the School Building Committee and played a very active role in the extensive planning of the new School buildings described in the next chapter.

For the Out-Patient and Casualty Departments it was planned to provide a new building on the east side of Cleveland Street opposite the main Hospital; this was regarded as the major priority. The area was already zoned for hospital development by the London County Council and the plan was later extended to include a suite of operating theatres, as the pressure on the existing theatres became too great for their capacity. The new building would be linked with the main Hospital by a bridge across Cleveland Street at the second-floor level as there did not seem to be any prospect of closing the street. Eventually the proposals were included in the Ministry of Health's Hospital Plan of 1961 and in 1963 the Board was informed that 1971 had been set as the starting date. Detailed plans were drawn up in many meetings but it was not to happen. By 1971 the radical reorganisation of the Health Service was underway. The original plan had to be abandoned but the necessity for redevelopment was still very evident from the fact that the Out-Patient Department had been built in 1788 as St Paul's Workhouse. After some further years a scheme for the complete rebuilding of the Out-Patient Department on its existing site was agreed by the North West Thames Regional Health Authority. Work was scheduled to start in 1981–82 on a £3.2 million redevelopment but that was also prevented – this time by the restructuring of the NHS of 1982. The transfer of the Hospital and its District into the North East Thames Region has meant that the Health Authorities who are now responsible for the Hospital have to examine the details afresh and slot it into a separate capital-development programme. No starting date has yet been set for the rebuilding and a few pessimists are wondering whether it will ever happen. The optimists are pointing out, however, that equally no date has yet been announced for any further reorganisation or restructuring of the Health Service.

Although that major plan has not been accomplished much else has been achieved. As will be seen in the next chapter, the School buildings have been increased enormously. Additionally, the Schools of Physiotherapy, Radiography and Radiotherapy have been rehoused; the nurses' home has been extended and provided with a new School of Nursing by a generous benefaction; new operating theatres have been developed in the main Hospital building; additional accommodation has been developed to provide new facilities; and the existing structures have been well maintained and upgraded.

All this was achieved in times of great financial difficulty. The Annual Reports contain repeated statements referring to 'a greatly restricted allocation for capital work'; 'a steady reduction in the size of the grant for capital work'; and explanations for lack of expansion in terms such as 'the money available was sufficient for only a few relatively trivial modifications to the Hospital's buildings'. However, although money was in short supply there was no shortage of wisdom and skill in using available resources to the greatest advantage. It is clear that, with Mr Jack Hambro as Treasurer, the Finance Committee made the most of all the opportunities available and the Plans Committee, Architect and Chief Engineer showed considerable ingenuity in devising schemes for improving facilities at minimum cost and with the least possible disturbance to other services. In particular, with so much to be done and with plans of variable extent well prepared in advance, they became adept at coping with the 'Stop–Go' system of capital allocation adopted by the NHS. That system provided limited annual capital grants which might or might not be supplemented towards the end of the financial year. When a windfall was offered later it usually came with the proviso that the work must be completed and the account settled within a specified period of a few weeks or months and with restrictions on the type of project which could be undertaken. Such a system had one merit – it certainly stimulated ingenuity and rapid reflexes. On occasions the Ministry of Health, to the surprise of its officers at first, received detailed proposals almost by return of post followed by a telephone call twenty-four hours later asking for permission to proceed.

MARLBOROUGH COURT

As Colonel Astor had predicted at the start of the National Health Service, it was still necessary for the Hospital to rely on non-Exchequer resources. In 1949 the Board used its endowment funds to purchase Marlborough Court at Lancaster Gate, overlooking Hyde Park, to enable a number of staff and students to live at reasonable cost within easy reach of The Middlesex. This property was sold in 1980 when circumstances changed.

Buildings

In 1951 the Board took a major innovative step of great importance not only to The Middlesex but also to medicine in a much wider context by the research it made possible and by the example it set to other hospitals and medical schools. Using its endowment funds it purchased a property close to the Hospital, Latimer House in Hanson Street, to provide an Institute of Clinical Research and Experimental Medicine for the consultants of the Hospital and their junior staff. The purchase was in doubt for a while because the British Broadcasting Corporation, with much greater resources at its disposal, was also interested in the property but it withdrew when it learned of the far-sighted project proposed by the Board of The Middlesex. Although the facilities were to be provided for the benefit of the Hospital staff it was considered that the Institute could be managed best as a School department. Accordingly an agreement was made to lease the building to the School and to covenant to the School an annual amount from the endowment funds for the costs of general maintenance. Research projects would need to find individual funding. The first Director of the Institute when it opened in November 1953 was Professor Alan Kekwick and its subsequent development is described in a later chapter (p. 202).

ATHLONE HOUSE

The pressure on beds and the increasing cost of hospital stay led the Board in the early 1950s to search for a building which would serve as a recovery unit. In 1953 the Ministry of Health was asked to purchase a property which had been found and was well suited for the purpose. Instead the Ministry offered The Middlesex Caenwood Towers in Highgate which it had acquired some time previously and which the Treasury was pressing them to put to proper use. It seemed clear that the Ministry would not purchase any other property and the building had a superb location overlooking Hampstead Heath and standing in twelve acres (nearly five hectares) of what had once been lovely gardens and were to become so again. The rooms were large and capable of conversion to wards but when this work got underway extensive dry rot and other problems became evident. The Treasury refused to sanction any adequate grant for restoration and the Board was faced with either abandoning the project or meeting the costs from endowment funds. The expenditure was felt to be justified and on 1 January 1958 the first patients were admitted to the new recovery unit which was renamed

Athlone House after the first Earl of Athlone, brother of Prince Francis of Teck, whom he had succeeded as Chairman of the Hospital in 1910. He had remained a very popular Chairman until 1924 when he was appointed Governor-General of South Africa. He was subsequently the first Chairman of the British Empire Cancer Campaign and was Chancellor of the University of London from 1932 to 1955.

The acquisition of Caenwood Towers with its spacious grounds enabled the Hospital subsequently to develop a much-needed unit for elderly patients. In 1969 a sixty-bed unit was opened at Athlone House with forty-five geriatric and fifteen orthopaedic recovery beds, together with a building for resident staff. This unit was also financed in part from the endowment funds and was opened on 11 May 1970 by Baroness Serota, Minister of State for Health.

MACDONALD-BUCHANAN SCHOOL OF NURSING

In 1955 a site in Ogle Street adjacent to John Astor House became available and, in view of its plans to extend the nurses' home, the Board purchased the site even though at that stage it was unable to proceed further. Four years later an outstanding event of the year was a magnificent gift of £140,000 (£1 million, 1985) by Major R. N. and the Hon. Mrs Macdonald-Buchanan (Sir Reginald and Lady Macdonald-Buchanan, 1964) for the purpose of building a new training school for student nurses, as the existing accommodation was no longer adequate. The site was already available from the prudent purchase made four years previously and the Macdonald-Buchanan School of Nursing was constructed. It was Lady Macdonald-Buchanan's father, Lord Woolavington, who made a large benefaction to the Hospital in 1928 to provide the private-patients' wing which bears his name.

JAMES PRINGLE HOUSE

In 1963 the Ministry of Health requested The Middlesex to take over responsibility for the treatment of venereal diseases which was currently being provided by St Peter's and St Paul's Hospitals at the Endell Street Clinic. The Middlesex agreed and obtained a lease on a building which was being built on the corner of Charlotte Street and Tottenham Street. In 1965 the necessary conversions were completed and the building was opened on 1 May that year by Lord Cobbold. It was named James Pringle House after Dr James Pringle who had been physician to the Skin Department from 1888 to 1920 and had founded during the First World War a department specifically for the treatment of syphilis. He was a great linguist and was regarded internationally as an authority on diseases of the skin and on syphilis. He was a regular attender at the Covent Garden Opera and conducted the Hospital orchestra for many years. He had also developed a pink pick-me-up concoction for the alleviation of hangovers which was still listed in the Hospital Pharmacopoeia of the 1930s and 1940s as the 'Pringle Mixture'.

ST LUKE'S-WOODSIDE HOSPITAL

Some important developments were accomplished at St Luke's Hospital to meet the changing needs in psychiatry. In 1963 an acute unit was established from endowment funds and named the Noel Harris Ward in recognition of the great services rendered by Dr Noel Harris both to St Luke's, where he had been on the staff from 1935, and to The Middlesex where he had joined the staff in 1938. He had retired from both hospitals and died in 1963, the year in which the ward named after him was opened. In 1968 a ten-bed unit for adolescent drug addicts was opened in response to the demand created by a growing national problem.

ARTHUR STANLEY HOUSE

When the Arthur Stanley Institute became part of The Middlesex Hospital Group it was in Peto Place, close to Great Portland Street Station. In 1961, when the termination of the lease was approaching, the decision was made to amalgamate it with the Hospital's Department of Physical Medicine. A site was found in Tottenham Street, between Cleveland Street and Charlotte Street, and it was planned to provide accommodation for the Department of Rheumatology and Physical Medicine, for the School of Physiotherapy and the Department of Occupational Therapy. A hydrotherapy pool was also provided in the basement.

The close collaboration existing between the Hospital and School proved of great advantage in connection with this development. The School obtained substantial grants from the Arthritis and Rheumatism Council and the Nuffield Foundation which enabled a further three floors to be added to what was already a substantial building. As a result Arthur Stanley House was built very close to the Hospital and School and combined on one site facilities for patients, for the School of Physiotherapy, for the Department of Occupational Therapy and for research into rheumatic and other diseases. The building was opened on 22 June 1965 by the Chairman, Lord Cobbold, and a few months later, on 10 November, was visited by Her Majesty The Queen during her much appreciated tour of the Hospital complex.

SCHOOLS OF RADIOGRAPHY

Even in the 1930s the Board of Management had recognised the need to provide adequate accommodation for the School of Radiography which was one of only eight schools in England at that time training radiographers. In 1948 the development was listed by the new Board of Governors as a priority but it was to be a long time before a way could be seen to accomplish it. In 1950 the School was housed in the basement under the Hospital forecourt and practical training had been separated into that for radiography and that for radiotherapy instead of the combined training which had been practised previously. In 1967 new accommodation was found for the Schools in a building in Foley Street opposite John Astor House, the nurses' home. The building was opened by Lord Cobbold in November that year and for the first time provided accommodation which could be regarded as anything like appropriate. It is self-contained and extends over four floors providing libraries, classrooms, and administrative, domestic and social facilities.

OTHER DEVELOPMENTS

In spite of the greatly restricted annual allocations for capital expenditure the Plans Committee of the Board brought about many improvements to The Middlesex and other hospitals in the Group over the course of several years. Wards were upgraded and often divided into more suitable units; new operating theatres were created on the sixth floor by the ingenious device of constructing changing rooms on what had been the roof but became a new seventh floor; an extra operating theatre was established on the fifth floor by closing the small Bischoffsheim (gynaecological) Ward; the open balconies were enclosed in stages; the children's ward was extended; an Intensive Therapy Unit was created on the fourth-floor crosspiece; the Diagnostic X-Ray Department was extended; the garden was excavated to provide a Central Sterile Supply Department and the terrace outside the Board-room reconstituted so that the Hospital could still continue to win the Best Hospital Garden Competition; the Radiotherapy Department was

138

extended and new, more powerful equipment installed; a new telephone exchange was installed in 1959; a special-diet kitchen was built and equipped; the building on the corner of Mortimer Street and Nassau Street which was owned by the Hospital (but leased to a fireplace company) was taken over (by negotiating to purchase the unexpired portion of the lease), the ground floor being incorporated into the Casualty Department and the upper floors being converted into offices for the Finance Department; a Department of Clinical Measurement was established; a Hearing Aid Distribution Centre was developed; the Pharmacy was extended to provide a manufacturing unit and a sterilizing unit; an extension to the Out-Patient building provided facilities for pathology; piped gases and piped suction to theatres and wards were installed; a building in Riding House Street, opposite to the School entrance, was obtained to provide facilities for the engineering services and was named Doran House in recognition of all that Mr Frank Doran had done for The Middlesex; additional residential accommodation for staff was provided in York House in Berners Street in 1946, and, in 1970, the Emerson-Bainbridge Building in Cleveland Street, where the ground floor was used for offices for social workers; and many other modifications and innovations were made in addition to maintaining the existing fabric and equipment.

Medical Developments

Since the introduction of the National Health Service and the formation of The Middlesex Hospital Teaching Group an integration of the services and staffing of all the units in the group has been achieved even though St Luke's-Woodside Hospital and the Hospital for Women Soho remain physically separate. As was mentioned previously, the Arthur Stanley Institute was incorporated into The Middlesex Hospital and fused with the existing Department of Physical Medicine in the new Arthur Stanley House in Charlotte Street in 1965.

Over the years there have been changes in the titles of departments in the Hospital and of the staff working in them. In a number of cases this has been simply a matter of terminology, such as the change from 'Diseases of the Skin' to 'Dermatology' and 'Physician to the Department for Nervous Diseases' to '(Consultant) Neurologist'. In other cases the alterations to the titles of departments have reflected changes in medical practice. The 'Department of Physical Medicine' became the 'Department of Rheumatology and Physical Medicine' on fusion with the Arthur Stanley Institute to indicate the change in its scope and its current title of 'Rheumatology' most accurately reflects its present role. Similarly, the title of 'Oral Surgery and Dentistry' indicates the present activities of that Department better than the former title of the 'Department of Dental Surgery'. For convenience, throughout this section, the titles in use in 1984 will generally be used even though they may not be correct for the period to which they refer. To use an historically accurate nomenclature would result in a cumbersome and confusing text in what is already a highly compressed account of a large number of developments.

As would be expected from the changes in medicine which have occurred generally there has been increasing specialisation of medical practice within the Hospital not only by the establishment of new departments but also among the general physicians and general surgeons. As was made evident in chapter 2 of this book there was already a considerable degree of specialisation in 1935 but over the course of fifty years that has become greater as scientific knowledge has increased and as many new diagnostic and therapeutic measures have become available. In these changes the Hospital and School have worked in close cooperation, the School developing new departments providing direct patient care or extending its existing laboratory facilities.

There has been a considerable increase in the number and seniority of School staff directly involved in the work of the Hospital. In 1935 there were no members of School staff who had clinical responsibility for the care of patients and there were only two Professors in those laboratories which provided laboratory services for the Hospital. In 1982 there were seven Professors, five Readers and several Senior Lecturers and Lecturers treating patients in the wards and seven Professors and six Readers responsible for laboratory-based clinical services, with a commensurate increase of other School staff. (The figures for 1982 are quoted, rather than later figures, because in that year certain changes occurred in connection with restructuring within the University of London which prevent a direct comparison being made with 1935. Those changes are mentioned in the final chapter of the book.)

REGIONAL SPECIALITIES

The appointment in 1947 of Mr Thomas Holmes Sellors (Sir Thomas Holmes Sellors, 1963) led to striking developments in cardiothoracic surgery and particularly open heart surgery. This was very much a team effort involving cardiologists and anaesthetists as well as surgeons. In 1954 Dr Walter Somerville was the first person to be appointed to the Hospital designated as a Cardiologist and he joined Dr Evan Bedford who was an outstanding cardiologist but was classified as a General Physician. Mr J. R. (Jack) Belcher was appointed as Cardiothoracic Surgeon in 1955. The anaesthetist in the team was Dr B. A. (Brian) Sellick who had a particular interest and expertise in respiratory and cardiac problems as a result of research undertaken in conjunction with the Department of Physiology. In 1958, following operations using hypothermia, a Mayo-Gibbon Pump Oxygenator (heart-lung machine) was brought into use following extensive research and a visit to the USA by Mr Holmes Sellors and Dr Sellick. This development led to major advances in the field.

In 1967 Sir Thomas Holmes Sellors retired from the staff and in the following year he was elected a Vice-President of The Royal College of Surgeons. In 1969 he was elected President and served in that office until 1972. He was replaced at The Middlesex by Mr M. F. (Marvin) Sturridge. In 1977, as a result of a generous benefaction, the School was able to appoint Mr D. N. (Donald) Ross as the Charles Wolfson Cardiac Surgeon within the Department of Surgical Studies. On his retirement in 1982 Mr Belcher was replaced by Mr Tom Treasure, who was also appointed to the staff of University College Hospital.

On Dr Evan Bedford's retirement in 1963, after thirty-six years on the staff and having been with the Department of Cardiology since its inception, Dr R. W. (Richard) Emanuel was appointed as Cardiologist.

The other field in which The Middlesex has a recognised regional specialty is in radiotherapy and some reference to the role played in this by Professor Sir Brian Windeyer and his successors in the academic department of the School is made in chapter 9 (p. 197). In the Meyerstein Institute of Radiotherapy Miss M. D. (Margaret) Snelling was appointed to the staff in 1949 as Deputy Director of the Institute. In 1956, Dr A. M. (Tony) Jelliffe was also appointed to the staff and on Sir Brian Windeyer's retirement in 1969 Miss Snelling became Director of the Institute and Dr Jelliffe Deputy Director. In 1971,

Dr M. F. (Margaret) Spittle was appointed to the staff. In 1980 the Area Health Authority decided to phase out radiotherapy at St Mary's and arrangements were made for their patients to be treated in the Meyerstein Institute. Dr H. C. Hodges and Dr N. A. Sharples, who were already on the staff of St Mary's, were accorded honorary contracts at The Middlesex and Dr Carmel Coulter was appointed jointly between The Middlesex and St Mary's.

Over the years the equipment available in the Institute has increased greatly in its power and capacity with great benefits to the patients. In 1971 a remote loading cathetron unit was installed with the great advantage of eliminating all irradiation of staff.

New departments

In addition to the great developments made in existing departments, some new departments have been created in the Hospital since 1935. Some of these have been mentioned in previous chapters, such as the appointment of Mr Rainsford Mowlem as Plastic Surgeon in 1940 and Miss Diana Beck as Neurosurgeon in 1947.

The Department of Urology was founded by Lord Webb-Johnson (then Mr A. E. Webb-Johnson) who had been appointed as a General Surgeon. He was followed by Sir Eric Riches who was also a General Surgeon but came to spend virtually all his time in the practice of urology. In 1960, Mr Richard Turner-Warwick (son of William Turner-Warwick) was also appointed as a General Surgeon and Head of the Department of Urology, becoming in 1975 responsible for urology without commitments to general surgery. In 1963, Mr I. H. (Iorwerth) Griffiths was appointed as Surgeon to the Department of Urology and in 1974 Mr E. J. G. (Euan) Milroy was appointed Consultant Urologist to this Department. Although not exactly new, it acquired a status independent of general surgery and its scope has extended considerably.

Until 1964 patients with venereal diseases were treated in the Skin Department but in that year a Department of Venereology was established with Dr R. D. (Duncan) Catterall as the Consultant. In 1966 Dr J. R. (John) Seale was also appointed to the staff and on his resignation in 1976 he was replaced by Dr J. S. (James) Bingham. In addition, as is mentioned in chapter 9 (p. 199) Professor Adler was appointed to the Duncan Guthrie Chair of Genito-Urinary Medicine in 1978; the Department by that time having become known by that name.

In 1969 a new Department of Geriatrics was created with the appointment of Dr John Wedgwood and the opening of the sixty-bed unit in Athlone House. In 1980, Dr Wedgwood resigned his appointment on becoming Director of Medical and Research Services of the Royal Home and Hospital for Incurables and Dr G. P. J. (Gareth) Beynon was appointed to replace him at The Middlesex. In 1981 Dr J. R. (John) Croker was appointed an additional Consultant in the Department.

In 1965 a new Department of Clinical Measurement came into being under the Director, Dr A. J. H. (Jan) Hewer who had been appointed Anaesthetist to the Hospital in 1948. While working in the Institute of Clinical Research in 1953 and after much thought he put forward proposals for the establishment of a department to tackle a multitude of problems of measurement affecting many specialities. The idea found favour in the Hospital and School and Dr Hewer was obviously well equipped to direct such an enterprise. Space was found initially in the Ferens Institute and a grant for capital equipment was provided by the Board of Governors. The concept also appealed to the Ministry of Health as a prototype unit and revenue resources were made available to extend the work. The expansion of the Department was accomplished in accommodation made available in the basement of the Residency. The value of the Department rapidly became apparent; it became a ready reference point for clinicians in all disciplines who wished to consult experts and provided a source of expertise on a wide range of problems. It was not long before the Department became responsible for most of the scientific equipment used in the Hospital and Dr Hewer became a whole-time Director until his retirement in 1982.

For a number of years the need for an intensive therapy unit was apparent in the Hospital but the difficulty was to find space in a central location. In 1973 it was decided that accommodation should be provided on the fourth floor crosspiece so that access would be readily available from all parts of the Hospital. As cardiological in-patients were already located on that floor on the east wing, where there was a coronary care unit, there would be a concentration of facilities. As it was anticipated that the Cardiothoracic Surgical Department would be a major user of the unit it was also decided to locate those patients on the fourth floor west wing so as to be in immediate proximity to the unit. One of the wards was converted to make it suitable for patients of both sexes and was renamed the Holmes Sellors Ward in recognition of his great services to the advancement of cardiac surgery and to the Hospital. In 1974 Dr Jack Tinker was appointed as whole-time Director of the unit and in April 1975 the new unit was formally opened by Dr John Dunwoody, Vice-Chairman of the Kensington and Chelsea and Westminster Area Health Authority (Teaching).

—8—
School Building Redevelopment

The Windeyer Building – Astor College – Arthur Stanley
House – School of Pathology – Institute of Nuclear Medi-
cine – Sir Jules Thorn Institute of Clinical Science –
Wolfson Building – Bland-Sutton Institute of Pathology –
Horace Joules Hall – General developments

By 1935 it was well recognised that the buildings in which the School
was housed were inadequate and outdated. Most of the accommodation
had been constructed in the previous century and could no longer meet
existing requirements. An overall scheme was therefore formulated in
1936 and a start was made by erecting the main School building
containing the Dean's office, School administration and lecture theatres
on the ground floor and the Boldero Library, scientific laboratories and
post-mortem room on the floors above. Further progress was halted
abruptly by the Second World War and the financial position of the
country after the War precluded any progress for some years. By the
early 1950s, however, the problems of accommodation were serious and
prevented full advantage being taken of the opportunities for sponsored
research for which members of staff were able to attract grants from
research councils and the great charitable trusts and foundations. It
became clear that a bold and imaginative major development
programme was required if the School was to maintain and develop its
high status in teaching and research.

To meet this challenge, in December 1954, six months after his
appointment as Dean, Professor B. W. Windeyer submitted to Council
a memorandum on the possibility of rebuilding the School. This was
based very largely on the overall scheme which had been formulated in
1936 but took account of the information which was then available that
planning permission was unlikely to be obtained for a building of

145

the requisite size on the area of the existing School buildings. The memorandum raised the possibility of development on a site between the Out-Patient Department and Howland Street, called the Cartwright Estate, which had been purchased by the Board of Management of the Hospital and School during the War, with a view to future development. The Ministry of Health had indicated that it would be most unlikely to allow a major development of the Hospital there within the next twenty-five years, whereas it had intimated that more limited schemes, particularly those involving existing buildings, might be contemplated. Accordingly it was considered that the School should develop on the Cartwright Estate and that, when building had been completed, the School would relinquish some accommodation, for use by the Hospital, on the 'Island Site', i.e., on the area containing the main Hospital and bounded by Mortimer, Cleveland, Riding House, and Nassau Streets.

The principles of such an arrangement were approved by the Council and by the Board of Governors and a small Building Committee was established consisting of Colonel Astor, Sir Harold Boldero, Mr F. H. Doran, Professor E. W. Walls, Mr C. P. Wilson and Professor B. W. Windeyer. At the second meeting of the Committee, in May, the Dean reported that Colonel Astor had made a munificent gift to the School of £400,000 (over £3 million, 1985) so that building could start as soon as possible. At that stage he had asked for his donation to remain confidential as he thought it would be more appropriate to make an announcement later. It was not his only contribution to this project. In 1960 he made a further benefaction of £200,000 in order to prevent any delay in proceeding from one phase of construction to the next.

Thus began a development scheme which was to continue and which would mean that in 1984 no less than 80 per cent of the teaching and laboratory areas of the School had been built within the previous twenty-five years. Each project presented its own particular problems and for most of them there were the difficulties of trying to ensure minimum inconvenience while building on a very congested site where clinical work and teaching had to continue. And, of course, every project was dependent on the support of generous benefactors and charitable trusts and foundations, the National Health Service and, in particular, the University Grants Committee. A measure of that support is provided by the fact that, in the twenty-five years between 1959 and 1984, the School brought into use some 14,000 square metres of new accommodation for teaching, research and clinical services and was enabled to

146

provide new residential accommodation for 266 students together with considerable recreational facilities.

WINDEYER BUILDING

Following Colonel Astor's initial generous gift, realistic planning could proceed. Mr S. E. T. Cusdin, of Messrs Easton and Robertson, was appointed as architect; extensive and detailed discussions with staff took place regarding the accommodation to be provided; an application for support from the University Grants Committee was submitted to the University; and an appeal was planned, to be launched at the most appropriate time. The whole project was divided into smaller integrated projects, or phases, as it would not be possible to sign a contract or commence any building work until the necessary capital had been ensured for each particular phase.

In respect of the detailed planning of the building the proposals of the architect were approved that all fixtures and fittings should be coordinated throughout the laboratory areas to save costs and to allow easy modifications in the future if necessary. It was also agreed that all laboratory services should be provided on ring mains or networks so that maintenance could be readily undertaken with minimal disruption of the laboratory work. This was a new development at the time but was to become common practice.

From the outset the building was planned to comprise the Preclinical Departments. The Clinical Departments of Medicine and Surgery were considered for inclusion but, after discussion with the Heads of those Departments, the Academic Board and Building Committee decided that the distance of the new building from the wards was too great. The provision of residential accommodation for students was an essential part of the development and given a very high priority by Colonel Astor and others but in the event it had to become the final phase of the development. There was a need for new lecture theatres, including one theatre capable of accommodating a large audience in comfort and having facilities for more than just lectures.

The provision of such a theatre became possible through the generosity of Mr E. R. Lewis (Sir Edward Lewis, 1961), Chairman of Decca Ltd, who was at that time supporting research in the Ferens Institute. When it was built the Edward Lewis Theatre provided a facility not enjoyed by many colleges, having commodious and comfortable seating for 390 people and a stage which could be raised or

147

lowered. Initially this had to be done manually which was a tedious and very time-consuming exercise, taking two people two days to accomplish. After a few years it was decided that an electric motor should be installed to reduce the time to a minute. The cost of £4000 was met from the Dean's Discretionary Fund, the prime source being the Whitbread family – friends and benefactors of The Middlesex for more than two centuries. The theatre was equipped with a formidable array of stage lighting and had backstage changing rooms which the architect had enclosed in a special cupola designed to overcome some planning constraints. This theatre was eminently suitable for formal addresses and routine lectures to large classes; it also enabled fairly lavish stage productions to be mounted by the Dramatic Society, the Musical Society and the producers of the Christmas concerts.

Other parts of the building also received specific funding. In response to an application by Professor C. A. Keele the Wellcome Trust made a generous grant to provide research accommodation and facilities for the Department of Pharmacology and Therapeutics. This grant reflected the reputation of Professor Keele and the Senior Lecturer in the Department at that time, Dr F. Hobbiger, who was later to have the title of Professor of Experimental Pharmacology conferred on him by the University; he subsequently succeeded Professor Keele as Head of the Department and Professor of Pharmacology.

The site presented a number of problems, one of which was overcome by extensive excavation. This brought the base level down to the good London blue-clay stratum and enabled a quadrangle and garden to be constructed immediately outside many of the public rooms. Construction started at the end of December 1957 and the first phase of the building, at the Cleveland Street end of the site, was opened by Lord Astor of Hever on 16 December 1959. That phase contained the teaching laboratories and lecture theatres and also the Edward Lewis Theatre in which the opening ceremony took place. In his address Lord Astor stressed the privilege he felt in being associated with such a worthwhile venture which was so full of promise. It was with a spirit of thankfulness and hope that he was carrying out the unveiling ceremony and he hoped that the new School would be a place where it would be learned how best to benefit mankind. He was delighted that the building was being put to use, good use, within an hour or two and he said that the opening had become almost a matter of urgency, for the producers of the Christmas concert were holding the dress rehearsal that evening on the new stage.

The second phase of the building had to be divided into two stages, the first being completed in April 1961 and the whole phase in September 1962. So by 1963 the School had in use a fine new building, the Windeyer Building, of eight storeys extending along Howland Street from Cleveland Street to Charlotte Street. In providing over 7000 square metres of usable area its construction had doubled, in the space of five years, the total accommodation of the School and had provided substantial teaching and research facilities for the Departments of Biology as applied to Medicine, Physics as applied to Medicine, Biochemistry, Anatomy, Physiology, Pharmacology and Therapeutics. In addition there was a large refectory and a staff dining room as well as lecture theatres and various other rooms for study and reading. The separate common rooms for the staff, their assistants and the students were transferred there as well as the Finance Department of the School. Provision was also made for the Medical Officer of the Students' Health Service and his secretary. One third of the cost of the building had been met by the University Grants Committee and the remaining two thirds by the substantial specific benefactions and grants referred to previously, augmented by further benefactions and donations from a large number of people in response to the appeal.

ASTOR COLLEGE

In 1965 Mr J. R. Burden became a partner of Mr Cusdin and he was the architect responsible for the design and planning of Astor College, with Mr Cusdin remaining as consultant architect. Phase III of the Cartwright Estate development was the construction of the residential college in Charlotte Street adjoining the Windeyer Building at its eastern end. The delay in proceeding with this phase was due to the fact that that site was not available any earlier and it was not possible to start building until 1965. The first students moved into the college on 24 April 1967 and on 31 May Her Majesty Queen Elizabeth the Queen Mother, Chancellor of the University, formally opened the building and unveiled the delightful portrait of Lord Astor by Mr Edward Halliday which hangs in the Lodge at the front entrance. The College provided 170 study-bedrooms along with common rooms, recreation, music and billiard rooms, two squash courts and flats for the Warden and Bursar. Dr P. A. J. Ball was appointed as the first

Warden and Miss R. Boucher as Bursar responsible for the day-to-day administration.

Although Astor College provided 170 study-bedrooms which had not been available in any form previously the demand for such accommodation still exceeded the availability. In 1977 it was decided to build an extension to the College and this became available for use in 1978. As a result there are a total of 236 study-bedrooms and the College can guarantee accommodation to all students in their first and final years in the School. A considerable and most welcome grant for this extension was obtained from the University Grants Committee but over 60 per cent of the cost was met from other sources, including the Astor Foundation, the Wolfson Foundation and individuals.

GYMNASIUM AND EXAMINATION HALL

In 1973, as a further consequence of Lord Astor's generosity, aided by a grant from the University Grants Committee, it proved possible to construct in the space alongside Astor College a building which fulfils a dual role. For most of the year it is a gymnasium and games hall but as and when required it converts to an examination room large enough to accommodate all the students of any year. When not in use for examinations it is a centre for recreation – basketball, badminton, indoor football, weight lifting etc. It has proved to be a most valuable asset.

ARTHUR STANLEY HOUSE

The development of Arthur Stanley House in Tottenham Street has been mentioned in the previous chapter (p. 137). The School involvement in this project consisted of the addition of the top three floors which was made possible by a substantial grant from the Arthritis and Rheumatism Council and another from the Nuffield Foundation. Strong support was also obtained from the University Grants Committee and, as a result, the School was able to open two new Departments, those of Rheumatology Research and of Immunology. The facilities on the three School floors consist mainly of laboratories specially designed and equipped for research, supplemented by rooms for small-group teaching.

SCHOOL OF PATHOLOGY

The Bland-Sutton Institute of Pathology was built in 1913 at the suggestion of Sir John Bland-Sutton and as a result of his generosity, to provide accommodation for the Departments of Morbid Anatomy and Histology (Histopathology today), Haematology and Medical Microbiology. After the First World War an extra floor was added but over the years it became clear that the advances taking place in laboratory diagnosis were creating demands for space and for specialised facilities which could not be met within the buildings comprising the Bland-Sutton Institute. After the Second World War these pressures became much greater and in 1968 a warehouse in Riding House Street almost opposite the entrance to the School and extending through to Foley Street, became available and was purchased to provide further space for the rapidly growing Institute. Two thirds of the cost of purchase was met by a grant from the University Grants Committee and the other third from the National Health Service, in recognition of the work undertaken in the Institute for NHS patients. Extensive reconstruction was required to convert the warehouse for laboratory use and the School was able to accomplish this as a result of receiving a large grant of £250,000 from the National Fund for Research into Crippling Diseases.

The façade of the building was not changed and is unimpressive but the interior was adapted to provide the maximum usable accommodation on its five floors. Haematology and Medical Microbiology were accommodated in the building, which was named the School of Pathology. In addition, space was provided there for the Cell Pathology Research Group of the Department of Histopathology. The basement, which was linked to the 'Island Site' by a new tunnel under Riding House Street, contained two communicating teaching laboratories which were together able to accommodate all the students in any one year's class. The benefit obtained by this development can be judged by the fact that the capacity of the School of Pathology is one-and-a-half times as great as was the capacity of the Bland-Sutton Institute at that time.

The conversion of the building was completed in the summer of 1971 and the School of Pathology was opened on 17 December that year by HRH Prince Philip, Duke of Edinburgh, Patron of the National Fund for Research into Crippling Diseases.

INSTITUTE OF NUCLEAR MEDICINE

In 1968, most people looking at the Hospital and School on the 'Island Site' would have felt convinced that there was no space left in which any substantial building could be erected. Fortunately, someone could see a gap running east and west between the West Wing of the Hospital and the School building erected before the War. In 1967 with the Preclinical Departments well established in good accommodation in the Windeyer Building the School turned its attention to providing new purpose-built accommodation for the Clinical Departments. A comprehensive start could not be made immediately but a generous grant from the Nuffield Foundation enabled part of the site to be used to construct a building to accommodate the Institute of Nuclear Medicine. With a grant from the University Grants Committee to cover the cost of furnishings and new equipment the building was completed and occupied in 1968. This was planned as the first phase of a considerable development, but it was not clear then how or when the next stage could be undertaken.

THE SIR JULES THORN INSTITUTE OF CLINICAL SCIENCE

Whilst outline schemes had been prepared for the second phase of the development following the completion of the Institute of Nuclear Medicine, the lack of resources prevented any further progress. Then in 1970, as a result of highly persuasive approaches made by Dr Michael Kremer, Sir Michael Sobell and Sir Jules Thorn converted a long-term hope into a reality by munificent donations. A substantial grant was also obtained from the University Grants Committee which covered nearly a quarter of the total cost. With the building being sandwiched into the space between the Hospital and the School there were obvious reasons for increasing the Hospital facilities as well as those of the School if it proved possible to do so. It did, and the sixth floor was built as a Hospital ward to provide particular facilities for patients with problems of metabolism. It was named the Hardy-Roberts Ward in tribute to Brigadier Geoffrey Hardy-Roberts who had been Secretary-Superintendent of the Hospital for twenty-one years until 1967.

The construction of this building presented a number of seemingly insuperable problems. The site was a network of underground steam mains, cables and service corridors, all of which had to be kept intact during construction. The old Chemistry Block had to be demolished without interfering with the telephone exchange frame room in the basement. The new building joined on to three existing buildings, all of which had been built using 'Imperial measures', whereas regulations required that the new building was 'metric'. The shape of the building meant that laboratories on either side of the central corridor on each floor could not be both large and square. Once this had been accepted, however, the various users on the different floors found that there was sufficient flexibility in design to meet their diverse needs.

When the building was completed in 1974, in addition to the Institute of Nuclear Medicine and the Hardy-Roberts Ward mentioned already, it provided specially designed accommodation for the School Departments of Medicine, Surgical Studies, Obstetrics and Gynaecology, Neurological Studies, Oncology, Medical Physics, and the Institute of Clinical Research. The last moved from Latimer House in Hanson Street into the seventh floor of the new building which was named the Cobbold Laboratories in recognition of the enormous services rendered to the School and Hospital by Lord Cobbold who was Chairman of the Board of Governors and School Council from 1963 to 1974.

On 30 May 1974 the Sir Jules Thorn Institute of Clinical Science was opened by Her Majesty Queen Elizabeth the Queen Mother, Chancellor of the University.

THE WOLFSON BUILDING

When the academic Department of Psychiatry was established in 1961 it was accommodated in the old block of School buildings in Riding House Street which had been vacated by the Preclinical Departments on their move to the Windeyer Building. The facilities were substandard and inadequate then and they became increasingly difficult to maintain over the years as the fabric deteriorated. In 1972 the Dean, Professor E. W. Walls, approached Sir Isaac Wolfson who expressed an immediate interest in establishing a building which could provide adequate facilities for the work of the Department. As a result the Wolfson Foundation offered a large benefaction of £300,000 for that purpose. Following this offer in respect of psychiatry the School wondered whether it would be possible to raise other funds to enable the Bland-Sutton Institute, and thus the whole of the School buildings in Riding House Street, to be redeveloped at the same time. A working party was established to explore this possibility, with the approval of the Wolfson Foundation, but in 1975 it was decided that such an extensive scheme would not be feasible at that stage and that redevelopment would have to be

153

confined to the buildings to the west of the Bland-Sutton Institute. Accordingly, plans were drawn up on that basis.

The rebuilding also offered the opportunity of arranging a collaboration between the Hospital and School in respect of psychiatric out-patients which had not been achieved previously. Until then the patients of the Academic Department had been seen in the Department while the Hospital consultants saw their patients in the Hospital annexe in Cleveland Street. In the new building the first floor was designed for out-patients of all the psychiatrists while the second and third floors provided the facilities for the Academic Department – offices, interview rooms, seminar rooms, laboratory areas and common room. Work began in January 1977 and the Wolfson Building was opened on 3 July 1979 by Sir Leonard Wolfson.

In addition to the great benefits to the School and Hospital in the important field of psychiatry the generous gift of the Wolfson Foundation helped The Middlesex in a problem which was facing all similar institutions in London. As was indicated in a previous chapter (p. 123), 1972 was a year of great uncertainty for all hospitals in the country and particularly for teaching hospitals. Accordingly it was considered prudent to seek formal reassurances about the future before the Wolfson benefaction was utilized. A letter was written by the Dean, Professor E. W. Walls, to the University which was forwarded to the University Grants Committee. That body sought an authoritative statement from the Department of Health and Social Security in respect of The Middlesex Hospital. Having received it, the University Grants Committee was able to write to the University of London setting out the assurance from the DHSS about the Hospital and stressing the 'very heavy investment in buildings for teaching and research on and around The Middlesex Hospital site'. The letter ended with the clear statement that '. . . the UGC feel that the University of London can safely assure The Middlesex Hospital School that it has a long-term future in its present location'.

Such an assurance should not have been necessary for the facts set out in the UGC letter were well known and obvious. The need to ask for such a statement reflects the great state of uncertainty occasioned by the projected NHS reorganisation. Within a few years the assurance was to have even greater significance when subsequent NHS actions led to further rumours of widespread closures of teaching hospitals in London. Virtually every one of them was mentioned by at least one national newspaper as being under threat. The assurance was also relevant in relation to later discussions on restructuring in the University of London. There were strong academic and other arguments for expanding The Middlesex Hospital Medical School rather than reducing it, but it was also clear that if the DHSS and UGC were to break faith so rapidly with a foundation which had contributed so enormously to universities and hospitals throughout the country they would risk jeopardising future benefactions, not only from that foundation but from all others. Such a thought must have been present in the minds of the Vice-Chancellor and Principal of the University at the opening of the Wolfson Building for, in his address, Sir Leonard Wolfson reminded them of the exchange of letters even though he did not elaborate on the significance he attached to them.

BLAND-SUTTON INSTITUTE OF PATHOLOGY: DEPARTMENT OF HISTOPATHOLOGY

In spite of the commissioning of the School of Pathology building in 1971 the Bland-Sutton Institute still had difficulty in meeting its commitments in respect of service and research. Three new research laboratories were created on the first floor by a rearrangement of existing space and in 1981 derelict space in the basement was redeveloped to provide an electron microscope suite equipped with scanning and transmission electron microscopes and backed up by preparation and cutting rooms and three darkrooms. And then in 1983–84 it proved possible to proceed with a conversion which had been under consideration for a long time but for which it had not been possible to find the large capital sum which was necessary. This was the scheme to build a new floor across the Museum at gallery level and equip it as a histopathology laboratory to replace the existing main service laboratory which was grossly overcrowded and lacked many of the facilities essential to modern practice. This was completed in 1984 as a consequence of generous grants from the North East Thames Regional Health Authority and the University Grants Committee.

HORACE JOULES HALL (CENTRAL MIDDLESEX HOSPITAL)

Middlesex students had been receiving a substantial proportion of their clinical teaching at The Central Middlesex Hospital since the beginning of the Second World War and in 1968 the Vice-Chancellor of the University, Sir Owen Saunders, opened a new building there named after Dr Horace Joules who had been Medical Superintendent when the association with the School started and who had done so much to promote the teaching of Middlesex students and the close collaboration between the two institutions. The building provided considerable teaching facilities as well as residential accommodation for students. In 1972 the Hall was extended to provide facilities for the School's newly formed Department of Community Medicine and later the residential accommodation was further increased so that there were thirty study-bedrooms.

General Developments

The major projects already described created new buildings and greatly increased the accommodation of the School. But whilst these large constructions were going ahead there was also a continuing programme of reconstruction and upgrading of the existing facilities to meet the needs of advancing scientific developments and methods of teaching. The last few years have seen the construction of a specially designed laboratory for the safe handling of carcinogenic materials, which was then recommended by a Medical Research Council committee as a model for others to follow; the development of a new studio and recording centre for audio-visual aids in what was formerly the Junior Common Room; the upgrading of lecture theatres to meet modern teaching requirements; a complete refurbishment of the fume cupboards in all laboratories to satisfy the increased safety standards required under recent legislation; the construction of a new Computer Services Unit and also an enlarged Electron Microscopy Unit; and the modernization of many laboratories and patient services with special facilities and equipment.

One hazard has been discovered which caused alarm some years ago but which, fortunately, did not produce any injury or permanent damage to the building. Opposite the Windeyer Building, on the north side of Howland Street, the General Post Office had erected a communications tower 190 metres high having an observation floor and a revolving restaurant at the top. This dominates the landscape and provides an excellent view of London and the surrounding countryside and, almost immediately beneath it, the Windeyer Building and other parts of the School and Hospital. At approximately 4a.m. on 31 October 1971 the peace of that sleeping Sunday morning was shattered by the explosion of a bomb, or a 'device' as it was described officially, which had been planted on the observation platform and which blew out a large segment of the enclosure to the platform. Much of the debris fell on the Windeyer Building and Astor College. There were nearly 200 holes in the roof, varying in size from small slits up to one over the dissecting room which was 80 centimetres in diameter. Fortunately there was no damage to structural roof members and each case of penetration occurred in a panel, without permanently deforming the steelwork, although it was necessary to cut away some plaster encasements to verify this. There was also damage to a number of windows and some interior structures. Fortunately the four days after the explosion remained fine and repairs were undertaken rapidly following an immediate inspection by the architect, and by the insurance assessors the following day.

It was a fortunate chance which prevented a fatality or serious injury resulting from the effects on Astor College. The room most damaged, with the bed being covered by debris and sheets of glass, would have been occupied if the student there had not been admitted to the Hospital two days previously. At the time, the enforced admission to hospital had seemed an unfortunate interruption of the studies of an academically distinguished student who was subsequently to become a Broderip Scholar.

—9—
Academic Departments

Physics – Nuclear Medicine – Molecular Endocrinology
– Biology – Anatomy – Physiology – Pharmacology and
Therapeutics – Bland-Sutton Institute – Courtauld Insti-
tute – Ferens Institute – Rheumatology Research – Immu-
nology – Medicine – Surgical Studies – Obstetrics and
Gynaecology – Psychiatry – Neurological Studies –
Oncology – Genito-Urinary Medicine – Community
Medicine – Institute of Clinical Research and Exper-
imental Medicine

As was indicated in the second chapter, in 1935 there were only six professors on the staff of the School, in the Departments of Chemistry, Physics, Anatomy, Physiology, the Bland-Sutton Institute of Pathology and the Courtauld Institute of Biochemistry. There were two other Departments, Biology (with a Reader as Head) and the Ferens Institute of Otolaryngology. By 1948 Chemistry had been incorporated into the Courtauld Institute, there was a Department of Pharmacology and Therapeutics and there were three professorial clinical Departments – Medicine, Surgery and what was then called 'Radiology (Therapeutic)'. Some account has already been given about the Departments up to 1948 in previous chapters and here, although some short references will be made to a few events prior to that date, it is the developments between 1948 and 1982 which form the main part of this chapter. As will be seen in the final chapter, since 1982 there have been a few further changes associated with the restructuring of the Faculty of Medicine in the University and those developments will be discussed there. In 1982 there were twenty-one Academic Departments in the School and twenty-three professors on the staff.

Over the years the structure of some Departments has changed. In some cases parts of them have become administratively separate while others have been merged under a single Head of Department. No significance should be attached to the order in which the Departments are mentioned; the scheme adopted has been based partly on history, partly on convenience and partly on a desire to achieve some continuity in moving from one department to another. The space devoted to different departments does not reflect any opinion on their relative importance to the School, to the Hospital or to medicine in general. It would be most unfortunate if any such comparisons were made for it is obvious that all the accounts are incomplete and merely indicate some of the changes which have taken place over the years. Some of the research which Departments have been pursuing is mentioned but the accounts are inevitably superficial and do not do justice to the quality and quantity of the research.

Although the Departments are treated individually there has been continuing close collaboration between them and also with the Hospital. Over the years many visitors and newcomers to the staff have commented favourably on the spirit of friendship and happy working relationships pervading The Middlesex. For easy reference a list of Departments and their Heads since 1935 is included as Appendix 12.

Physics as Applied to Medicine

The Barnato-Joel Laboratories were opened in 1912 by Her Majesty Queen Mary and the Joel Chair of Physics was endowed in 1920 in the first academic department of medical physics in the United Kingdom. In 1946 the title of the Department and the Chair was changed to that of Physics as Applied to Medicine and Professor Eric Roberts became Head of the Department until 1969. On his retirement the School persuaded a former distinguished member of the Department to return from the USA where he was then working. He was Dr J. F. Tait who was at that time, as well as his wife Sylvia, a Senior Scientist at the Worcester Foundation of Experimental Biology, Massachusetts. He was Joel Professor until 1982.

Up to 1974 undergraduate teaching was mainly concentrated as one of the subjects in the Premedical (1st MB) year, with a short course in applied physics for the 2nd MB class. In 1974 the Premedical entry was discontinued and the 2nd MB was replaced by a two-year course in Basic Medical Sciences and Pharmacology. With this change the teaching of Physics as Applied to Medicine became more widespread and a lot was undertaken in combination with other disciplines. Biometry and Biophysics formed significant parts of the course. Post-graduate education has been provided for many years in the form of courses for the Diploma of Medical Radiology. Following the Windscale nuclear reactor accident there was considerable pressure to provide graduate training in the uses and hazards of ionising radiations and the Physics Departments of The Middlesex and St Bartholomew's quickly got together to provide an MSc course in radiation physics.

The Physics services provided for the Hospital have been mainly in the field of radiation. In addition to the involvement of staff in the planning of patients receiving treatment the Department has always provided the statutory Radiation Protection Adviser to the Hospital and School as well as providing the film badge service for over 300 people. The Department has been responsible for computer services in the School and the expertise available in this field has also been made available to Hospital Departments.

The Physics Department has always been active in research and this has become more diversified with each new Head of the Department. In many cases this research has been undertaken in collaboration with other Departments and a striking example of the benefits of this was provided in the field of radioactive isotopes which formed an important part of the Department's research activities from the late 1940s onwards. That particular example will form the next section of this chapter. In addition to studies of radioactivity in its many forms much work has also been done on microwaves, ultrasound and lasers, with particular reference to their applications to medicine.

Since 1970 the field of cytophysics has become of increasing importance and the Department has developed methods of cell separation; Coulter counting; flow cytometry with light-scattering measurements; and general fluorescent investigations in both dynamic and static systems. A new method for the physical separation of cells (column filtration) has been devised and an original method (involving gating) has allowed measurements of the properties of mixed cells without their physical separation. Zona glomerulosa, fasciculata and reticularis adrenal cells have been purified and characterised and preparations of dispersed cardiac cells have been obtained which have led to important studies of their contractility and electrical activity.

Some of this work has been funded by large support grants from the Medical Research Council, leading to the formation within the Department of a Biophysical Endocrinology Unit under the Co-Directors Dr Sylvia Tait and Professor J. F. Tait.

ALDOSTERONE

One of the most dramatic stories of the early radioisotope period is that of Aldosterone. This started in the early 1950s when radioactive sodium and potassium became readily available and it was possible to make precise studies of electrolyte metabolism in animals. Working in the Department of Physics as Applied to Medicine at that time was Dr James Tait and in the Courtauld Institute of Biochemistry, engaged on biological research, was Mrs Sylvia Simpson; they collaborated in their research on microbioassays for steroids with mineralocorticoid activity.

They developed jointly a microbioassay measuring the effects of steroids on the $^{24}Na/^{42}K$ urinary ratio of adrenalectomised rats after injection of the isotopes. Bovine adrenal extract had a high activity in this assay and 95 per cent was chromatographically identified with cortisone. However as they were sure that cortisone was only weakly active and that steroids in mixtures acted unidirectionally in the assay they reasoned that there was an unknown, previously unidentified compound present. A chromatographic system had recently been devised by Dr I. E. Bush at the National Institute for Medical Research at Mill Hill which readily separated the cortisone from the active compound. The chromatographic properties of the acetyl derivative, inactive until after mild hydrolysis, also demonstrated the presence of a new unique compound but it was still not clear whether it was secreted and therefore a true hormone. By then Dr Ian Bush had devised *in vivo* perfusion methods for the adrenal cortex and in a collaborative study it was shown in 1952 that the active steroid, which was then termed 'electrocortin' was secreted by dog and monkey adrenals, and it was later shown to be secreted by several species and was therefore of great interest in human physiology and pathology as a major factor in the control of salt excretion.

The basic structure of the newly discovered salt-retaining hormone was worked out at The Middlesex but the precise and unique structure was subsequently determined in Basle, Switzerland by Reichstein and his colleagues. Soon afterwards, with the identification of an aldehyde group at position 18 in the molecule, the name was changed to aldosterone and the substance was synthesized in the Ciba Laboratories in Basle. It was not long before it was shown that aldosterone could maintain patients with Addison's Disease and that an adenoma of the adrenal gland could preferentially secrete aldosterone and cause hypokalaemia and hypertension. The precise site of the secretion within the adrenal was determined in collaboration with other members of staff of the School including Mr P. J. Ayres of the Physics Department, and subsequently the Courtauld Institute, and Mr R. P. Gould of the Anatomy Department. These studies showed that aldosterone was produced by the zona glomerulosa and cortisol by the zona fasciculata, thus confirming the theory of functional zonation.

James Tait and Sylvia Simpson married in 1956 and received innumerable awards and distinctions in recognition of their joint work. They are the only husband and wife who have been elected to the Fellowship of the Royal Society in respect of work undertaken jointly, and few husbands and wives have been elected for any reason.

Nuclear Medicine

In addition to the work which led to the discovery of aldosterone, much other research on radioisotopes was undertaken in the Department of Physics as Applied to Medicine. In 1954 Dr Roger Ekins evolved a concept of radioisotopic microanalytical techniques which was to lead to a dramatic publication in 1960 and which will be mentioned further in the next section of this chapter. Research was expanding in other radioisotopic fields also and this led Professor Roberts to put forward the idea that a new Department should be created to combine a number of people from different disciplines to carry forward the work which had already led to such important developments. This concept was strongly supported by the Dean, Sir Brian Windeyer, and the idea found favour within the School. This led to the establishment of the Institute of Nuclear Medicine in June 1961. The Nuffield Foundation showed particular interest in this new project and provided a substantial grant for a new building.

Professor Roberts initially acted as Director of the new Institute as well as continuing as Head of Physics. The Deputy Director was Dr Edward Williams, who had originally graduated in physics at King's College London and had then graduated in medicine at The Middlesex. He worked in the Department of Physics as Applied to Medicine, having also been a Registrar in the Meyerstein Institute of Radiotherapy, and his research was concerned with isotopes. The Institute started with a considerable staff, of whom some were seconded from the Physics Department and some from Radiotherapy. In addition there were scientists from the Medical Research Council and British Empire Cancer Campaign as well as visiting workers from abroad. In 1964 Dr Williams became Director of the Institute and in recognition of his researches the University conferred the title of Reader on him in 1966 and of Professor of Nuclear Medicine in 1971.

In addition to the work of Dr Ekins to be described shortly, the Institute has been at the forefront of many advances in nuclear medicine. It developed probe renography to become firmly established as a bedside method of studying renal disease and developed deconvolution analysis to the point when it was routinely applied in renal physiology and pathology, with two members of staff producing the standard reference book on these aspects. Digital computer analysis was applied to radioisotopic image data and digitization of analogue displays was also pioneered. Much work has been done in evaluating and developing computerised axial emission tomography and comparing the value of such examinations with the better-known computerised axial transmission tomography. Digital techniques have also been applied to medical image analysis with particular emphasis on the evaluation of cardiac function, renal function, gastric emptying, liver function and brain function.

MOLECULAR BIOPHYSICS

Following his 1954 concept, in 1957 Dr Roger Ekins began applying radioisotopic microanalytical techniques to thyroid hormones. His concept of 'saturation analysis' was ideally suited for these measurements where there was, and still is, a great need for such estimations which cannot be made by any other means. When Dr Ekins published his first paper in January 1960 it was followed within a few months by another from two workers in New York who had been applying similar methodology to insulin, with curious simultaneity and totally independently. There was a difference in that Ekins had concentrated upon naturally occurring binding agents while Berson and Yalow worked on antibodies. For this reason they called their method an 'immunoassay' and this was the term which became rapidly associated with the procedure, whereas it would seem to be more accurate to reserve that nomenclature for one particular variant of the overall principle of the method to which Ekins gave the very descriptive title of 'saturation analysis'. Ekins then extended his method to other hormones, Vitamin B_{12} and a host of other substances of biological importance. The extent to which the concept of saturation analysis could be applied led to the creation within the Institute of Nuclear Medicine of a Sub-Department headed by Dr Ekins which was entitled the Sub-Department of Molecular Biophysics. In 1968 the University conferred on Dr Ekins the title of Reader in Medical Nucleonics and in 1972 the title of Professor of Biophysics. In 1968 the School appointed him as Deputy Director of the Institute of Nuclear Medicine.

Medical Physics and Institute of Nuclear Medicine Molecular Endocrinology

In 1978 the School Council established a Planning and Resources Committee 'To review the objectives and long-term aims of the School and to recommend any necessary changes'. Although it was not included in the terms of reference it was implicit that the main work of the committee would be to prepare plans to adapt to reduced staffing levels consequent upon the sudden and severe reduction in the School's recurrent grant. Every Department of the School came under review. While the committee was considering the Department of Physics as applied to Medicine and the Institute of Nuclear Medicine, Professor Tait indicated his desire to retire from the Joel Chair of Physics in order to concentrate on research. In view of this and other considerations the Planning and Resources Committee recommended, and the Academic Board supported the recommendation, that from the date of Professor Tait's retirement much of the Institute of Nuclear Medicine should be merged with the Department of Physics as applied to Medicine and that, after some modifications, the Sub-Department of Molecular Biophysics should become a full Department. Some changes of title were also proposed.

The School Council adopted these recommendations and in 1982 the new departmental structure came into being with Professor Williams as Head of the Department of Medical Physics and Institute of Nuclear Medicine and with Professor Ekins as Head of the Department of Molecular Endocrinology. It was recognised that the title of the former of these two Departments was somewhat cumbersome but it was clearly important to retain the word "Physics" and there were sound reasons for continuing to include "Institute of Nuclear Medicine" as it is still uniquely the only University Department of Nuclear Medicine in the kingdom and Edward Williams is the only Professor of the subject.

Other hospitals have NHS Departments but it has always been the policy of The Middlesex that the School should provide scientific services for the Hospital in order to promote an amalgam of patient services, teaching and research within a single department.

Biology as Applied to Medicine

In 1922, Dr J. H. Woodger was appointed as a Reader to the staff of the School and in 1948 the title of Professor of Biology was conferred on him. He retired in 1959 and at that time it was decided to change the title of the Department to 'Biology as Applied to Medicine' and the University agreed to establish a Chair, to which Professor D. R. Newth was appointed in 1960. In 1965 he resigned the post to become Regius Professor in the University of Glasgow and he was replaced at The Middlesex on 1 January 1966 by Professor Lewis Wolpert. In 1982, in response to recommendations made initially by the Planning and Resources Committee, the Department merged with the Department of Anatomy to become the Department of Anatomy and Biology as Applied to Medicine, with Professor Wolpert as Head of the new Department.

Professor Lewis Wolpert had graduated with a BSc Degree in Engineering at the University of Witwatersrand in South Africa but a few years later took part of a special Honours course in Zoology and then a PhD at King's College London. From 1958 he was a Lecturer and then Reader in Zoology at King's College before being appointed to the Chair of Biology as Applied to Medicine at The Middlesex.

TEACHING

Initially the Department was responsible for the teaching of biology in the premedical year and histology in the second year and, before the War and shortly after it, Dr Woodger used to teach histology in the popular Primary FRCS course. Later, histology teaching was taken over by the Department of Anatomy and certainly from the time when the title of the Department was changed, and possibly earlier, teaching for the First MB Examination itself was regarded as filling a rather minor role, the real purpose of the Premedical Course being to give medical students an insight into the biology which would have relevance for them for at least another ten years and hopefully more. And whatever the timetable may have indicated there is no doubt that successive

165

Heads of the Department with their broadly based concepts exerted an influence on thinking and attitudes within the School which extended well beyond the confines of the curriculum.

For that reason the Department was retained when the First MB course in Biology came to an end in 1974 and because of its developing research programmes it has actually expanded since then. With the introduction of the basic medical sciences course in 1974 the Department had responsibility for Cell Biology and Genetics and, like other Departments, became involved in a considerable amount of interdepartmental teaching. In addition, progressively over the years an increasing number of courses have been made available for the Intercalated BSc Honours degree. Throughout its existence the Department has played a major role in teaching postgraduate science students.

RESEARCH

Research has always been a prominent feature of the work of the Department but its pattern has changed considerably over the years. In his very small Department Professor Woodger developed the tools of symbolic logic which he used to good effect to advance biological concepts and it was this, coupled with his creation of the influential 'Theoretical Biology Club' (or 'Woodgerie' as it was often called) which led to him being frequently referred to as 'Socrates' by his friends. The appointment of Professor Newth occurred shortly before the move of the Department into new accommodation in the Windeyer Building and he succeeded in having some modifications made to the plans so that there would be greater laboratory facilities than had been intended originally. This was to play a decisive part in the subsequent development of the Department.

Considerable diversification of the research programme followed the appointment of Professor Wolpert to the Chair in 1966 and increasing support was obtained from the research councils and charitable trusts and foundations. The invasiveness by cell movement was investigated using an assay based on the chick limb bud and cells from carcinomas were found to behave quite differently from other invasive cells. Genetic damage caused by chemical and environmental mutagens/carcinogens was detected using different systems and a rapid cytogenetic screening method was evolved which proved capable of detecting carcinogenicity within twenty-four hours of exposure rather than the many months required for the induction of tumours. From work with bacteria some

166

understanding was achieved of the importance of protein synthesis and growth in relation to the damage caused by ionizing radiations and ultraviolet light. Experiments were directed to test the hypothesis which suggested the presence of oxygen-sensitive radiation targets in cell membranes. A comparison was made of the damage caused by bleomycin which showed distinct differences in the biochemical effects from those produced by irradiation. Theoretical physical analyses of intercellular forces in cell adhesion led to several fruitful experimental approaches using a new quantitative interference microscope technique.

One major research project has been concerned with the cellular basis of pattern formation in development. Following extensive work on hydra, the chick limb bud has been studied intensively to discover the basis of the positional value specified by a signal from a particular region, with the ultimate aim of identifying the biochemical nature of the signal. Such research is highly relevant in relation to the deleterious effects of drugs such as thalidomide, and others which may be developed in the future.

In 1980 Professor Lewis Wolpert was elected a Fellow of the Royal Society in recognition of the research he had carried out in the Department of Biology as applied to Medicine.

Anatomy

The famous Great Windmill Street School of Anatomy founded by William Hunter was taken over by Sir Charles Bell in 1812 and became virtually a school of The Middlesex Hospital, even before the Medical School had been established. So the history of anatomy at The Middlesex goes back a long way. In 1924 a University Chair of Anatomy was established in the School and this had been endowed by Mr S. A. Courtauld. There have been five S. A. Courtauld Professors of Anatomy: T. Yeates, 1920–37; J. Kirk 1937–49; E. W. Walls, 1949–74; P. H. S. Silver, 1974–82; B. A. Wood from 1982. As was mentioned in the previous section, in 1982 the Department merged with Biology as Applied to Medicine, Professor Wolpert being Head of the combined Department.

Professor Yeates and Professor Walls have been mentioned in previous chapters (pp. 31, 99). Before becoming S. A. Courtauld Professor and Head of the Department, Professor Silver had been Reader in the Department since 1957 and in 1964 had the title of

Professor of Embryology conferred on him in recognition of his research in that particular field. Professor Wood had been Reader in Anatomy since 1979 before being appointed to the Chair in 1982.

In addition to running the Department three of the Heads also held other important appointments in the School. Professor Kirk was Sub-Dean during the War, first at Bristol and then for two years in Leeds. In 1946–47 he also became Acting-Dean for a few months during the absence of Dr Boldero on account of illness. Professor Walls was elected Sub-Dean of the School in 1965 and this was followed by his election as Dean in 1967 and annually thereafter until 1974. His period in that office was one of intense activity in the School, and with extensive building developments culminating in the opening of the Sir Jules Thorn Institute of Clinical Science in the year of his retirement. Professor Silver was Sub-Dean of the School from 1976 to 1981 and Mr R. P. Gould, Reader in Histology in the Department was Warden of Astor College from 1974 to 1978 and Sub-Dean of the Medical School from 1981 to 1984.

Professor Walls also had commitments outside the School as President of the Anatomical Society of Great Britain and Ireland, 1963–65, and as President of the Society of Blind Chartered Physiotherapists from 1967 onwards. He was elected a Fellow of the Royal Society of Edinburgh in 1957.

TEACHING

The Department has always had considerable teaching commitments but their nature has changed considerably over the years. With the introduction of the Basic Medical Sciences Course in 1974 the hours of anatomical teaching were greatly reduced from those available previously. The dissecting room is still the most important source of anatomical knowledge but the new course places considerable emphasis on living anatomy and the students are taught how to use their anatomical knowledge when examining patients and reaching a diagnosis. The great clinical advances in imaging have led to an increased emphasis on this aspect which forms an integral part of the clinical anatomy course in the second year, in which Hospital consultants participate. As was mentioned in an early chapter, Professor Samson Wright started clinical demonstrations on patients during the preclinical years as part of the teaching in physiology. During the Second World War this was extended to Anatomy by Professor Kirk at St James's Hospital in

Leeds, and the practice has been continued since. In recent years the combination on the lecture theatre platform of the Professors of Anatomy and Physiology and consultants of the Hospital has provided a stimulating experience of great learning value. A number of aspects of anatomy now form part of integrated courses such as those in neurology and endocrinology.

A major development in the Department was the establishment and subsequent expansion of the electron microscope unit which also provides extensive services for other departments such as physiology and physics. Between the two world wars the Primary FRCS course in anatomy and physiology was renowned and when it resumed in 1946 the demand was greater than ever. In 1950, however, such teaching was considered to be more appropriate to a postgraduate institution and the course at The Middlesex ceased when the Institute of Basic Medical Sciences was developed at the Royal College of Surgeons.

RESEARCH

Not surprisingly, much of the research by members of staff of the Department has been undertaken in collaboration with workers in other disciplines and mention has already been made of the contribution made to the identification of the zone of production of aldosterone in the adrenal. There has been considerable work done in association with the Department of Neurological Studies on the biology and pathology of myelinated nerve fibres, and particularly in relation to demyelinating diseases, and also in studies on peripheral nerves. The autonomic nerves in the pelvis have also been closely studied in relation to surgical strategy in that region. There has been an extensive study of male reproductive biology, including the developmental cytochemistry and fine structure of the testis and epididymis. Substantial contributions have also been made in the field of electromyography and in experimental embryology.

For over twenty years the Department has been involved in the study of human evolution. Professor Bernard Wood has undertaken field research in East Africa and he heads a research group which is evaluating the fossil remains from the Pleistocene hominid site in Kobi Fora, Kenya. He is currently completing a monograph which is part of a multi-volume publication about the major East Africa fossil remains. Professor Wood's enthusiasm for palæoanthropology had been kindled by Dr M. H. Day (whose BSc student he was) prior to Dr Day's appointment at St Thomas's Hospital Medical School as professor.

Physiology

Between 1930 and 1984 there were only two occupants of the John Astor Chair of Physiology, Professor Samson Wright until 1956 and Professor Eric Neil after that. Some mention of Professor Samson Wright has been made already in Chapter 2. Professor Neil graduated at the University of Leeds in 1942 and two years later obtained an MD with distinction. He was a lecturer in the Department of Physiology in Leeds for part of the time when Middlesex students were there during the Second World War and made a deep impression on both staff and students. In 1950 he was appointed a Senior Lecturer in the Department of Physiology at The Middlesex and in the following year was appointed to the Readership in the Department.

In addition to his responsibilities at The Middlesex Professor Neil was elected to a number of important positions on national and international bodies. He was a member of the Committee of the Physiological Society from 1956 to 1961 and its Honorary Treasurer from 1961–67. He was Honorary Treasurer of the International Union of Physiological Sciences from 1968 to 1974 and the President of that prestigious body from 1974 to 1980, the only President in this century to be re-elected for a second three-year term of office.

In 1968 the title of Professor was conferred on Dr J. H. Green who had been a Reader since 1960. He had been a Cambridge and Middlesex student whose studies had been interrupted by the Second World War and who, soon after qualification, joined the staff of the Department of Physiology.

TEACHING

The study of normal function has naturally required an extensive part of the curriculum and from the early days of Professor Samson Wright the distortion of function seen in disease has formed a significant part of the teaching to illustrate the general principles involved. Throughout the years there have been lectures, demonstrations, practical classes and clinical demonstrations but the subject matter has advanced rapidly as scientific knowledge has increased. With the introduction of the basic medical sciences course integrated teaching was introduced on a large scale and while the word 'Physiology' might have appeared less frequently on the timetable the staff have been heavily engaged in combined courses such as neurology, endocrinology, environmental and nutritional studies, and in embryology and developmental biology.

Although mention has been made in an earlier chapter of the BSc Honours degree in Anatomy taken by Mr Gordon Gordon-Taylor and Mr Victor Bonney in 1903, they were exceptional. On the other hand, an outstanding student might well take such a degree in Physiology and the reputation of The Middlesex in this field was considerable. In the present arrangements for the Intercalated BSc courses the Department of Physiology figures prominently in the list of those available to students.

RESEARCH

The heart and circulation have figured in the extensive research of the Department for many years, and particularly in respect of the regulation of the cardiovascular and respiratory systems, cardiovascular and respiratory afferent and efferent fibre activity, and blood gas carriage and physicochemical equilibria of biological fluids at different temperatures. Many studies have also been made of renal function and sodium excretion and also of neurohypophysial hormones. In conjunction with the Department of Surgical Studies detailed investigations have been made of factors influencing water metabolism after anaesthesia and surgery.

Pharmacology and Therapeutics

Dr C. A. Keele was appointed to the Department of Pharmacology and Therapeutics when it was established in 1938 and he remained its Head until 1968, becoming Reader in 1949 and Professor of Pharmacology and Therapeutics in 1952. He remained the only academic member of staff of the Department until 1946 when Dr A. S. V. Burgen (now Sir Arnold Burgen, FRS) was appointed as Demonstrator, and then in 1948 as Assistant Lecturer. He resigned in 1949 on appointment as Professor of Physiology at McGill University, Canada. In 1948 Dr Franz Hobbiger from Vienna joined the Department on a World Health Organisation Fellowship; he was appointed to the staff in 1949, became a Reader in 1959, and Professor of Experimental Pharmacology in 1964.

In 1968 he succeeded Professor Keele as Head of the Department and Professor of Pharmacology.

TEACHING

A medical student has to acquire a sound understanding of the scientific basis of drug action which is relevant to man and which enables him to use drugs in the most efficacious way for the treatment of disease. To accomplish this a course is needed which lays a foundation during the preclinical period and which builds upon it during the clinical period of the undergraduate medical course. This was accomplished by introducing during the clinical period a course which had a defined syllabus and which was vertically fully integrated with the preclinical course. Since the allocation of staff to the Department was small, recruitment of medically qualified staff became more and more difficult with time, and clinical students became more and more dispersed between hospitals, the provision of a vertically integrated pharmacology course meant that individual members of the department had to take on a heavy teaching load, particularly as far as senior members of staff were concerned. That the courses provided were effective is shown by the number of distinctions awarded in the final MB, BS examinations, where Middlesex students have done exceptionally well on many occasions in the clinical pharmacology and therapeutics component of the examinations.

Since its inception the Department has consistently contributed to intercalated BSc teaching, with students usually opting for a combination of neuropharmacology with either an area of physiology or neuroanatomy. Many of the students who have taken this course are now in senior positions within the University or the NHS.

RESEARCH

In spite of the limitation in the number of staff members and their considerable teaching commitments, the Department has made significant contributions to research, as judged by the frequency of citation in scientific journals and text books.

Studies of the actions of botulinum toxin threw new light on its site and mechanism of action. New methods for testing algogenic substances in man were developed and were then used in studies of potential endogenous algogens. Kinetic and pharmacological studies of the interaction between acetylcholinesterase and carbamates and organophosphates led to a better understanding of the mechanism by which these anticholinesterases act as enzyme inhibitors, the synthesis and assessment of novel anticholinesterases, some of which are amongst the most potent known enzyme inhibitors, and the synthesis and assessment of therapeutically effective antidotes (such as TMB–4; trimedoxime) of organophosphates, particularly those which nowadays are used extensively as insecticides. Electrophysiological studies on isolated myocardial cells and the effect of drugs upon them opened up a new field of investigation. Studies of mechanisms controlling the response of smooth muscle to post-ganglionic adrenergic stimulation also provided new information.

Amongst various studies involving patients and control subjects were investigations which delineated the role of atypical cholinesterase in suxamethonium-induced apnoea in patients and gave information on its genetic inheritance. Factors determining blood levels of digoxin and its methyl derivative were studied in control subjects and patients, with particular relevance to optimal prescribing practice. Methods were also developed for studying effects of centrally acting drugs on human performance and then used for assessment of established and new drugs.

Bland-Sutton Institute of Pathology
School of Pathology
(HISTOPATHOLOGY – MEDICAL MICROBIOLOGY – HAEMATOLOGY)

Sir John Bland-Sutton's zeal and generosity, anonymous initially, created the Institute named after him and based on his stated belief that 'Fifty years ago the pathway to surgery lay through the dissecting room. Today it lies through the Pathological Institute'. From its opening in 1914 until 1975 the different disciplines within Pathology (Morbid Anatomy and Histology, Microbiology and Haematology) were grouped together under the overall responsibility of one Director, initially within the Institute itself and, from 1971, also within the School of Pathology. In 1975 the post of Director was abolished, the three disciplines becoming separate School Departments, each with its own Head. A chairman of those Heads was elected to represent them on various committees where necessary.

A Chair of Pathology was established in 1919; its title being changed in 1945 to the Bland-Sutton Chair of Pathology. The first Professor was James McIntosh who was appointed in 1920. On his death in 1948 he was succeeded by Professor R. W. Scarff. Reference has been made to both of them in previous chapters (p. 31 and p. 99). On Professor Scarff's retirement in 1965 Professor G. W. A. Dick was appointed as Bland-Sutton Professor of Pathology and Director of the Institute. He had graduated from the University of Edinburgh where he subsequently obtained a gold medal in the MD. After service with the Royal Army Medical Corps almost throughout the War he spent three years as a Rockefeller Foundation Fellow at the Rockefeller Institute, New York, and at the Johns Hopkins Hospital and was Professor of Microbiology at Queen's University Belfast for ten years before being appointed to the Bland-Sutton Institute. When Professor Dick retired in March 1973, Professor A. C. Thackray acted as Director until his retirement in December 1974.

Within the Institute, and under the overall direction of the Bland-Sutton Professor, senior members of staff were responsible for particular aspects of its varied activities. In 1935, Dr R. W. Scarff was in charge of morbid anatomy and histology and when he became Director in 1948 this aspect of the work became the everyday responsibility of Dr A. C. Thackray, who had joined the staff in 1941. He was appointed Professor of Morbid Histology in 1966. In 1935 Dr L. E. H. Whitby (Sir Lionel Whitby, 1945) was in charge of Bacteriology and Disorders of the Blood. On Sir Lionel's resignation in 1945 to become Regius Professor of Physic at Cambridge (and in 1949 Master of Downing College, and in 1951 Vice-Chancellor of the University of Cambridge) he was succeeded by Dr F. R. Selbie, who was appointed to a newly established Readership in Bacteriology in 1947 and became Professor of Bacteriology in 1949. He died suddenly in 1954, at the age of 49, and on his death Dr R. E. M. Thompson became responsible to the Director for bacteriology (including virology), being appointed to the vacant Readership in 1959. Dr J. W. Stewart became responsible for haematology, becoming a Reader in 1959 and Professor of Haematology in 1969.

When the post of Director of the Institute was abolished in 1975 Dr R. E. M. Thompson was appointed as Head of the Department of Microbiology and Professor J. W. Stewart as Head of the Department of Haematology. As Sir John Bland-Sutton's major interest in pathology had been in morbid anatomy and histology it was decided that the

Bland-Sutton Chair should be allocated to that discipline and renamed the Bland-Sutton Chair of Histopathology. That post was filled by Professor Neville Woolf who had graduated at the University of Cape-Town where he was later awarded an M.Med. degree in pathology. As a William Shepherd Research Fellow at St George's Hospital Medical School, London, his work led to the award of a PhD degree by the University of London and he was subsequently Lecturer, Senior Lecturer and Reader at St George's before being appointed to the Bland-Sutton Chair.

In 1979 the title of Professor of Experimental Pathology was conferred on Dr R. M. Hicks. She had graduated in physiology at University College, subsequently being awarded a PhD in biochemistry and later a DSc, and joined the staff of the Bland-Sutton Institute in 1959 where her research led to her being elected a Fellow of University College.

CLINICAL SERVICES

From the outset it has been the policy of the Hospital that laboratory services should be provided in School Departments so that the essential correlation of patient services, teaching and research could be achieved most readily and most effectively. These services were naturally extended to The Middlesex Hospital Teaching Group when that was established and the specialised facilities available in the laboratories have been utilised by other hospitals also. Not surprisingly, there has been a progressive increase in the demands made on the service in respect of the numbers and complexity of the tests; the most dramatic increase occurred in the postwar years when, between 1945 and 1948, the number of specimens sent to the Institute rose from under 20,000 per annum to over 50,000. By 1972 the figure had risen to over 200,000.

In histopathology, to use the present designation, a major development occurred at the beginning of the 1960s when a cytology service was introduced. This rapidly expanded so that in the ten-year period from 1962 to 1972 the number of specimens examined increased from 2,000 per annum to 20,000. In the 1960s also a specialised neuropathology service was developed and extended. In bacteriology the introduction of an ever-increasing number of antibiotics has led to a much greater demand for a wider variety of tests on each specimen. The development of virology, and the particular expertise available in the

175

School laboratories, has resulted in the service being extended well beyond the Middlesex Hospital Group.

In haematology, in addition to the work undertaken for the Hospital and for general practitioners, the designation of the Department as a haemophilia centre has greatly increased the number and complexity of the investigations undertaken in the haemorrhagic disorders. The management of patients with leukaemia and the increasing requirements for blood transfusion have resulted in increasing service responsibilities. As in other laboratories serving different functions, every effort has been made to reduce the demands on the personnel and Professor Stewart, in conjunction with the Department of Physics as applied to Medicine, was at the forefront of the developments in electronic blood cell counters.

TEACHING

The teaching of pathology has always presented problems in respect of the timetable because of the difficulties of fitting it in with students' responsibilities for patients on the wards and the system of 'firm' teaching. From the 1930s to the 1960s, lectures were given at noon, when students are normally expected to leave the wards during the patients' lunch, but it did not enable all students on surgical wards to attend the classes on operating days, and it meant that as students could not return from the Central Middlesex Hospital for the lectures it was necessary to duplicate them there, making heavy demands on the staff. When the new curriculum was introduced in 1974 much of the lecture course was incorporated into 'Topic Teaching' sessions undertaken with clinicians. In addition, a course in general pathology of sixty hours was incorporated into the three terms of the second year of the preclinical course to provide a bridge between the basic medical sciences and clinical medicine. Cell pathology provides a one-year course for the Intercalated BSc degree.

RESEARCH

As the foundation of the Institute was based on the desire to advance knowledge of disease and improve the outlook for patients, research has always been a major feature of the activities of the Institute and School of Pathology. One illustration of this commitment is the part played by members of the staff in the editorship of the *British Journal of Experimental Pathology*. Sir Paul Fildes, who was Head of the MRC

Unit of Bacterial Chemistry in the Institute from 1934 to 1946, was directly responsible for founding the journal in 1919 and edited it himself from the first issue in 1920 until 1940 when Professor Scarff became editor, until 1950. From 1958 to 1979 Dr R. E. M. Thompson was editor and in 1983 Professor R. M. Hicks was appointed.

Professor Scarff also founded the *British Journal of Cancer*, in 1961, as the official journal of the British Empire Cancer Campaign, of which he became Secretary of the Scientific Advisory Committee in 1935, becoming Honorary Secretary of the Campaign in 1954. Professor A. C. Thackray edited the journal from 1963 to 1971.

In 1792 The Middlesex was the first hospital to open a ward for cancer patients and in 1925 it participated in the formation of the British Empire Cancer Campaign (now the Cancer Research Campaign). It is not surprising therefore that cancer research has featured so largely in the activities of the Institute and School of Pathology. The approaches to this have been histopathological and experimental. An example of the former of these systems lies in the classification of tumours, based on an understanding of their nature as a result of painstaking and dedicated research. In 1958, the World Health Organisation decided to establish twenty-two reference centres in various countries for the nomenclature and classification of tumours of different parts of the body and these centres have now published their reports. Two emanated from the WHO Reference Centres in the Bland-Sutton Institute; 'Histological typing of breast tumours' by Professor R. W. Scarff, 1968, and 'Histological Typing of salivary gland tumours', by Professor A. C. Thackray, 1972.

An illustration of the experimental approach is provided by the establishment of the Cancer Research Group in the late forties which included Dr M. A. Epstein (now Professor M. A. Epstein FRS, Professor of Pathology, University of Bristol). In addition to his particular research on anaerobes and other bacteria, Professor McIntosh had a great interest in viruses and in the Rous sarcoma and the development of the electron microscope led Dr Epstein to continue this work. Later he was struck by the epidemiology of the lymphoma described by Dr D. P. Burkitt in Uganda and obtained material from a patient there which he studied with Miss Yvonne M. Barr. This research resulted in the discovery in 1964 of a new herpes virus now known as the Epstein–Barr virus and subsequent work has also shown its connection with infectious mononucleosis and its implication in some way with nasopharyngeal carcinoma.

Experimental pathology has continued actively and the first morphological identification of lysosomes was provided by Professor Marian Hicks working in collaboration with Professor Stanley Holt of the Courtauld Institute. The research of Professor Hicks on the structure of the bladder and on changes in the luminal plasma membrane led to a recognition of diagnostic markers of neoplastic transformation in these cells. More recent work has been on the potential value of retinoids as chemotherapeutic agents in bladder cancer. Much of this work has been undertaken as part of contracts awarded in open competition by the National Cancer Institute of the USA.

While much of the research effort of the Department of Histopathology continues to be devoted to various aspects of cancer, the last ten years have seen the introduction of a new range of interests. A multidisciplinary group is applying the techniques of cell culture, untrastructural histology and biochemistry to the study of a number of problems related to disorders of arterial endothelium and heart muscle. Immunohistology is also now firmly established.

Courtauld Institute of Biochemistry

In 1919 a special department of Pathological Chemistry was established in the Bland-Sutton Institute of Pathology under Dr E. L. Kennaway (later Professor Sir Ernest Kennaway, FRS) and in the following year the department was also given responsibility for physiological chemistry. In 1921 Dr Kennaway was appointed to the Cancer Hospital and Dr Charles Dodds, who had just qualified but had previously been a Student Demonstrator in the department, was appointed as a Lecturer to succeed him. In May 1925 he was appointed as the first Professor of Biochemistry, at the age of twenty-five. The foundation stone of the Courtauld Institute of Biochemistry was laid in July 1927 and the building was opened on 14 June 1928. In that year also Mr Courtauld endowed the Chair.

In 1965, after forty years as Professor of Biochemistry, Sir Charles Dodds retired from the directorship of the Institute and Professor R. H. S. Thompson was appointed. At Oxford he had been awarded both DM and DSc Degrees and, among other things, he had been a Fellow of University College and Dean of the Medical School. He subsequently became Professor of Chemical Pathology at Guy's Hospital Medical School. He was elected a Fellow of the Royal Society in 1974.

When Professor Thompson retired in December 1975, he was replaced by Professor P. N. Campbell, who had taken an Honours BSc degree at University College London and had subsequently been awarded a PhD and later a DSc degree in Biochemistry. After appointments at University College and at the National Institute for Medical Research he moved to the Courtauld Institute in 1954, becoming a Senior Lecturer in 1957 and Reader in 1964. In 1967 he became Professor and Head of the Department of Biochemistry at the University of Leeds.

The directors of the Institute have all played active roles in international bodies. Sir Charles Dodds played a large part in the organisation of the first Congress of Biochemistry in Cambridge in 1949 and soon afterwards was appointed Chairman of the Biological Chemistry section of the International Union of Pure and Applied Chemistry. Robert Thompson was the first Secretary of the International Union of Biochemistry and Peter Campbell has been closely involved in its educational activities in widely scattered parts of the world.

In addition to the Courtauld Chair of Biochemistry there is also in the Institute the Philip Hill Chair of Experimental Biochemistry to which Professor Frank Dickens, FRS was appointed on its foundation in 1946 (p. 99). On his retirement from the Chair in 1967 to become Director of the Harrogate Laboratories of the Tobacco Research Council he was replaced by Professor P. N. Magee who had graduated in medicine from Cambridge and University College Hospital Medical School, London. In 1976 he moved to Philadelphia as Director of the Fels Research Institute, Temple University. In 1977 Professor S. J. Holt was appointed to the Philip Hill Chair. He had come to the Courtauld Institute in 1947 and received wide recognition for his work in the field of cytochemistry, being appointed a Reader in that subject in 1963 and a Professor in 1970.

In addition to the established chairs in the Institute, other members of staff have had the title of Professor conferred upon them. In 1968, Dr A. E. Kellie became Professor of Steroid Biochemistry in recognition of his extensive research in that field. In 1969 the title of Professor of Biochemistry was conferred on Dr J. B. Jepson, a science graduate of the University of Oxford who joined the staff of the Institute in 1946 and who, in addition to his personal research, designed and developed a new continuous course of teaching from inorganic chemistry, through organic chemistry to biochemistry merging into chemical pathology. He was appointed Sub-Dean of the School in 1975 but died in May the following year at the age of fifty-three. In 1978, Dr Patricia McLean was accorded the title of Professor of Biochemistry in recognition of her research on carbohydrates and in 1981 the title of Professor of Biochemistry was conferred on Dr Brian Ketterer, Ralph Bateman Life Fellow of the Cancer Research Campaign. In 1984 the title of Professor of Biochemistry was accorded to Dr R. K. Craig in recognition of his research in molecular biology and genetic engineering.

SUB-DEPARTMENT OF CHEMICAL PATHOLOGY

In most medical schools chemical pathology has developed in departments separate from biochemistry but at The Middlesex it remained a Sub-Department within the Courtauld Institute of Biochemistry until 1984. This difference would seem to be explained by the fact that the large Courtauld Institute was founded in the early stages of the development of biochemistry and the expertise of the Directors has embraced all facets of the subject. Sir Charles Dodds, the first Courtauld Professor, was not only elected a Fellow of the Royal Society in 1942 but, among a whole host of honours, was elected President of the Royal College of Physicians from 1962 to 1966, a unique distinction for a laboratory-based physician. His successor in the Courtauld, Robert Thompson, was elected a Fellow of the Royal Society in 1974 and had been Professor of Chemical Pathology at Guy's Hospital Medical School for eighteen years before moving to the Courtauld Institute. The present Director, Peter Campbell, has been particularly interested in the biosynthesis of proteins.

Within the Courtauld Institute the work in chemical pathology of Dr Douglas Robertson and others has been referred to in previous chapters (p. 35). Since 1957 Dr A. L. Miller has been head of that section of the Institute responsible for chemical pathology. He was a Middlesex graduate who, after holding House Officer and Registrar appointments in the Hospital and elsewhere and serving in the Royal Air Force, was appointed to the Bland-Sutton Institute and then the Courtauld Institute, becoming a Senior Lecturer in 1964 and a Reader in Chemical Pathology in 1974.

HOSPITAL SERVICES

Since its inception the Courtauld Institute had been responsible for providing the chemical pathology service to The Middlesex Hospital and later The Middlesex Hospital Teaching Group. From the beginning the number of investigations carried out has increased every year, sometimes by over 20 per cent in a single year, resulting in an enormous increase over the course of fifty years. As elsewhere, the introduction of automatic analysers has made it possible to absorb the increase in demand. Due largely to the vision of Sir Charles Dodds, who had seen the machine in use in the USA, the Courtauld Institute acquired one of the first Technicon auto-analysers to be introduced into this country. This machine revolutionised the practice of hospital biochemistry. In 1972 one of the first five Vickers M300 analysers capable of measuring up to twenty parameters on each of 300 samples per hour was installed. This British-built machine probably represented the zenith in design of fast analysers even though it has now been superseded by more compact machines with fewer moving parts.

The Sub-Department of Chemical Pathology has also been much involved with the design and programming of a laboratory data-processing system for use throughout the North West Thames Regional Health Authority.

TEACHING

In 1946 the Institute took over responsibility for the teaching of chemistry in addition to biochemistry and a progressive co-ordinated programme of teaching was evolved, including BSc course units and leading on to chemical pathology which is included in both the preclinical and clinical courses. In the latter there are a number of contributions to the Topic Teaching sessions. The Institute attracts a large number of postgraduate students.

RESEARCH

The publications emanating from the staff of the Institute testify to the extent and diversity of the research undertaken during the fifty-seven years since its foundation. Reference has been made already to some of these, such as stilboestrol and aldosterone, but others include the elucidation of the pentose phosphate pathway and the changes in metabolism occurring in tissues in diabetes and carcinoma by Professor Dickens; the co-discovery of the carcinogenic activity of nitrosamines and their mode of action and interaction with DNA by Professor Magee; the discovery of Hartnup disease during research on the inborn errors of metabolism by Professor Jepson; the discovery of autoimmune thyroid disease by Professors Roitt, Doniach and Campbell, which will be referred to further in relation to the Department of Immunology. In collaboration with the World Health Organisation considerable work has been done on the control of fertility.

One of the important features of the Institute has been the close relationship between individual units and research groups which has stimulated collaborative research, contributed to success in postgraduate education, led to integrated teaching throughout the undergraduate medical course and has provided a continuing stimulus to all members of the staff.

Ferens Institute of Otolaryngology

The Ferens Institute was opened, on the third floor of the Out-Patient Annexe in Cleveland Street, on 8 February 1927 following a generous benefaction in 1925 by Mr T. R. Ferens of Hull. At the opening ceremony it was also announced that Mr Bernard Baron had endowed a postgraduate research scholarship in the Institute and that an anonymous donor had ensured that in the rebuilt Hospital there would be a separate ear nose and throat ward and operating theatre.

The Directors of the new Institute were the Senior ENT surgeons of the Hospital, Mr Somerville Hastings MP and Mr F. J. Cleminson. In 1937 Mr Cleminson had to retire on account of ill health but was appointed Director of Research. During the Second World War, because of its location, the Institute had to be closed. It reopened in 1945 with Mr C. P. Wilson and Mr. J. P. Monkhouse as Directors until 1962 when Mr Wilson retired. Since then the Senior ENT surgeon of the Hospital has been the Director: Mr J. P. Monkhouse 1962–64; Mr D. Ranger (Sir Douglas Ranger, 1978) 1965–83; and Mr R. A. Williams since 1983. It became the practice to invite ENT Surgeons from other hospitals to become honorary librarians and curators of the museum and in addition to those duties some of them also undertook research projects. There was also one general surgeon appointed to that post, Mr S. S. Beare, a Middlesex graduate. Since 1982 Mr D. F. Bishop has been Honorary Curator of the Museum, having just retired as

Senior Chief Medical Laboratory Scientific Officer precisely fifty years to the day since he had joined the Institute as a young assistant.

The research work of Dr Albert Gray and Dr Charles Hallpike in the early days of the Institute has been mentioned in a previous chapter (p. 35). In 1949 the Institute received a generous benefaction from the John Edward Lewis Memorial Trust which led to the appointment of Dr J. C. Seymour to carry out research on sensorineural deafness. This was producing results of significance when he was killed in a road accident in 1960. In 1965, Dr C. S. Hallpike, FRS returned to the Institute as Director of Research and Dr S. K. Bosher was appointed as Research Assistant. A generous grant from the Wellcome Trust enabled the Institute to be almost entirely rebuilt and to be equipped with an electron microscope and with an anechoic chamber which, when it was built, was reputed to be the second quietest room in London. A Readership in Otology was established and Dr Bosher was appointed to that post in October 1970. His research has been concerned mainly with the control of the chemical composition of the endolymph, a fluid which appears to be unique amongst the extra-cellular fluids.

In the Institute's research there has been close collaboration with workers in other Departments, particularly Dr J. W. Tappin, Reader in the Department of Physics as applied to Medicine and Dr R. L. Warren, Research Associate in the Courtauld Institute of Biochemistry and later the Institute of Nuclear Medicine, who developed with Dr Bosher techniques for the accurate measurement of the electrolyte concentrations of the minute quantities of endolymph available.

Since Dr Bosher's retirement in 1984 the Institute has extended its laryngeal research. Demonstration of laryngeal function by xeroradiography and by laryngography has been developed, which is leading to a new understanding of voice production in normal subjects and in those with functional and organic voice disorders.

The facilities of the Institute have been instrumental in the development of both undergraduate and postgraduate education and the specimens from the museum have been used for many years in the Final Fellowship examinations of the Royal College of Surgeons.

Rheumatology Research

In 1965, as a result of generous grants from the Arthritis and Rheumatism Council, the Nuffield Foundation and the University Grants

Committee, it was possible to build a Department of Rheumatology Research in the top floors of Arthur Stanley House. Further benefactions were received from Miss Elizabeth Kitson and the Wates Foundation and research projects were supported by the Medical Research Council, the Wellcome Trust and the Arthritis and Rheumatism Council.

The Department was opened in July 1965 with Professor Sir Charles Dodds as Honorary Director. Two senior members of the staff of the Courtauld Institute transferred to the new Department; Dr Ivan Roitt, who had just been appointed a Reader in Immunopathology, and Dr Deborah Doniach, who had been a Senior Lecturer since 1963. In addition there were three Lecturers, two Assistant Lecturers and two Research Assistants.

In 1968, on the retirement of Sir Charles Dodds, Professor C. A. Keele, Emeritus Professor of Pharmacology and Therapeutics, was appointed as Director for five years. On his retirement in 1973 he was replaced by Professor Roitt who, in 1968, had had the title of Professor of Immunology conferred on him and been appointed as Head of a new Department of Immunology.

RESEARCH

The possibility that rheumatoid arthritis might be caused by some micro-organism has often been proposed. In 1968 the alleged isolation of a type of mycoplasma from synovial fluid was thoroughly investigated, with negative results. Inflammatory exudates, such as synovial flud in rheumatoid arthritis, contain plasma kinins, peptides which can produce pain and vasodilatation. Their pathogenic role is even more probable in acute gouty arthritis since crystals of sodium urate promote kinin formation in synovial fluid in amounts capable of contributing greatly to the symptoms and signs. Identification of urate and other pathogenic crystals in synovial fluid has been developed in the Department by means of special microscopic techniques.

Research in the Department demonstrated the presence of rheumatoid factors (IgM and IgG antiglobulins) in virtually all patients with rheumatoid arthritis and analysis of the complexes present in the synovial fluids strongly suggested that IgG is the main, if not the only, autoantigen driving the pathogenic process in this common disabling disease. The very close proximity of the Department to that of Immunology and the Hospital Department of Rheumatology and the fact that there is now a single Head of both School Departments has promoted close collaboration in the research both in the laboratory and on patients. This is well illustrated by the combined studies identifying the prognostic features of disease in patients with early rheumatoid arthritis.

Immunology

The Department of Immunology was opened in 1968 in the upper floors of Arthur Stanley House and Professor I. M. Roitt has been Head of the Department since then. A Chair of Immunology was established in 1973 and Professor Roitt appointed to it. His academic career had started in Oxford, first in chemistry and then in physiology. He joined the staff of the Courtauld Institute of Biochemistry in 1953, working under Professor Frank Dickens at a time when concepts of immunology were being developed and very soon he was investigating these aspects. At that time research on thyroid disease was being carried out in the Hospital under Mr Rupert Vaughan Hudson by Dr Deborah Doniach, who had graduated at the Royal Free Hospital School of Medicine. After holding a variety of clinical appointments she had become a Trainee, and then a Junior Lecturer, in Clinical Chemistry in the Courtauld Institute followed by a registrar appointment at the West Middlesex Hospital before returning to The Middlesex in 1952 to carry out research in the Thyroid Clinic. She developed a particular interest in lymphadenoid goitre and this led to a most fruitful collaboration with Dr Roitt and Dr Peter Campbell, the present Director of the Courtauld Institute, who had come to the Institute in 1954 after working for five years at the National Institute for Medical Research where he had been investigating, among other things, the possibility that the mammary gland synthesized the antibodies present in milk and in colostrum.

In 1978 the title of Professor of Immunology was conferred on Dr J. H. L. Playfair. He had graduated in Medicine at Cambridge and King's College Hospital Medical School and after holding clinical posts spent four years in research at the Royal Marsden Hospital and two years in research in California before coming to The Middlesex Hospital Medical School as a Lecturer in 1965.

AUTOIMMUNITY

The collaboration of Drs Roitt, Doniach and Campbell and Mr Vaughan Hudson led to the publication in the *Lancet* in 1956 of a preliminary communication whose brevity (the length of a single column) was in inverse proportion to its far-reaching importance. The raised serum gamma globulin levels found in patients with lymph-adenoid goitre (Hashimoto's Disease) had recently been reported (1953), with the highest levels being found in untreated patients with large goitres. This finding, together with the infiltration of the thyroid gland with lymphocytes and plasma cells, strongly suggested to the authors that an immune response might be involved in the disease and that the raised gamma globulin in the serum of the patients represented anti-thyroglobulin. To test this hypothesis, precipitin reactions between the sera of patients with Hashimoto goitre gave precipitins, but normal subjects and patients with other thyroid diseases showed negative results.

The authors concluded that patients with lymphadenoid goitre are immunised against human thyroglobulin and suggested that destruction of the thyroid in the disease results from progressive interaction of thyroglobulin in the gland with the auto-antibody present in the patient's circulation. The authors also indicated that the precipitin reaction of serum with extract of human thyroid gland might prove a more specific diagnostic test for Hashimoto's Disease than estimation of serum gammaglobulin or liver-function tests.

The importance of this publication is well illustrated by the extent to which autoimmunity has been demonstrated in a wide range of other diseases and is being postulated in many more whose aetiology is still unknown. A vast literature has rapidly accumulated on the subject and yet, as Professor Campbell has since written 'Ivan prepared saline extracts of normal and thyrotoxic human thyroid glands and added these carefully to the serum. A precipitin ring soon formed at the interface. I still remember this experiment which Ivan demonstrated to us and in particular was struck that it required only the serum, the extract, a test tube and a pipette'.

TEACHING

The expansion of immunology, which is still continuing, has created an increasing demand for trained graduates and the Department has attracted a large number of PhD students and visiting workers from overseas. Teaching in the preclinical and clinical years has increased and full course units are available for the Intercalated BSc Honours Degree.

RESEARCH

The concept of autoimmunity put forward in 1956 has been expanded widely into other fields and international recognition of the Department has led to it being designated a reference laboratory for autoimmune serology by the World Health Organisation, with help being given to centres in other countries. The diagnostic value of autoantibody tests has been developed to cover a wide variety of different diseases and as a result there have been greatly increasing demands in respect of services for patients.

The research of Professors Roitt and Doniach and their colleagues has been strongly supported by substantial programme grants by the Medical Research Council for the study of immunopathological diseases. Autoimmunity affecting endocrine glands has been investigated intensely and has shed new light on the correlation of clinical and serological features of autoimmune thyroiditis and insulin-dependent diabetes. A strong parasitic immunology group, headed by Professor J. H. L. Playfair, has developed new strategies for the development of vaccines against malaria and other parasitic diseases. The extensive studies on allergy have indicated the importance of food allergy in a number of conditions.

The research of Professor Roitt led to him being elected a Fellow of the Royal Society in 1983 and he and Professor Doniach have received many other honours, including the prestigious Gairdner Foundation International Award in 1964.

Medicine

Professor Alan Kekwick was the first Professor of Medicine in the School, from 1946 until his retirement from the Chair in 1970. He was succeeded by Professor S. J. G. Semple who had been an undergraduate student at St Thomas's Hospital Medical School and after qualification held House Officer and Research Assistant posts in that hospital before serving in the Royal Army Medical Corps and subsequently working for two years in the Department of Pharmacology in the Medical School of the University of Pennsylvania, Philadelphia. Returning to St Thomas's he was appointed Lecturer, Senior Lecturer, Reader and, in 1969, Professor of Medicine before being appointed to the Chair at The Middlesex. His particular research interests lay in the field of respiratory medicine and physiology but, like Professor Kekwick before him, he had a broadly based experience. In 1983 the title of Professor of Metabolic Medicine was conferred on Dr J. L. H. O'Riordan and the title of Professor of Reproductive Endocrinology on Dr H. S. Jacobs. Dr O'Riordan had been appointed to the Medical Unit in 1966 as a Senior Lecturer and as Deputy Director of the Academic Department and had been appointed a Reader in 1978. Dr Jacobs had been a Reader in Gynaecological Endocrinology and Chemical Pathology at St Mary's Hospital Medical School before being appointed as a Reader at The Middlesex in 1981.

In addition to their responsibilities in the School and University, Professor Kekwick and Professor Semple have both held important offices in the Royal College of Physicians; Professor Kekwick was Censor and then Senior Censor and Professor Semple was Pro-Censor and then Second Censor of that College. Professor Semple was also Treasurer for five years of the Medical Research Society and a member of its executive committee. He also served on the Medical Research Council Committee as a member and then as chairman of one of its grants committees and as a member of the Systems Board. In 1983 he was elected to the committee of the Physiological Society.

ACCOMMODATION AND TEACHING

The Academic Departments of Medicine and of Surgery were both accommodated on the first floor of the Hospital; the laboratories and offices on the crosspiece, the medical wards on the east wing and the surgical wards on the west wing. When the Sir Jules Thorn Institute of Clinical Science was opened in 1974 it was possible to provide much greater additional space for both Departments in that building, as well as accommodation for other departments.

In addition to his responsibilities for a 'Firm' of students, as with all physicians on the staff, the Professor of Medicine became responsible for the organisation and coordination of the teaching of medicine in the School. Initially a Clinical Medicine Committee was established with one of the other physicians as Chairman, to review and advise on the teaching of clinical medicine but subsequently this became the Medical Teachers Committee and was chaired by the Professor of Medicine.

RESEARCH

From its beginning the Professorial Medical Unit has been closely involved in research and its extent has increased considerably over the years. Original work was done by Professor Kekwick on metabolic, hormonal and nutritional aspects of obesity and anorexia nervosa; studies in the latter group of patients being coordinated with research being undertaken by the Department of Psychiatry.

After his retirement, research on obesity continued under Professor Semple. It was found that the administration of ß-hydroxybutyrate to obese patients on a very low-calorie diet diminished the protein loss which usually occurs in the initial stages of dieting.

Professor Semple's main interest in research has been in the field of thoracic medicine and pulmonary physiology, most of the work being devoted to the chemical control of breathing in health and disease. The oscillations of carbon dioxide in arterial blood were shown to be an important controlling influence on breathing at rest and at the start of exercise. One of the most comprehensive mathematical models of the respiratory control system was developed by Dr K. B. Saunders while he was Senior Lecturer in the Department; he also carried out fundamental work on the effects of changes in gas density on respiratory function before being appointed to the Chair of Medicine at St George's Hospital Medical School.

For a number of years the endocrine control of mineral metabolism of bone has been studied extensively by Professor Jeffrey O'Riordan, working on parathyroid hormone, calcitonin and Vitamin D. The work on parathyroid hormone began by isolating the peptide and determining its amino acid sequence. This made possible the development of assays for parathyroid hormone which have helped in studies on secretion and have improved diagnosis in a number of fields such as the pre-operative localisation of parathyroid tumours. Work on Vitamin D has similarly improved diagnosis and has helped in the elucidation of problems of Vitamin D deficiency, hypersensitivity and resistance. As a result, The Middlesex has become a major referral centre for patients with disorders of calcium metabolism, including parathyroid disease and disorders of bone.

Surgical Studies

Professor P. B. Ascroft was appointed as the first Professor of Surgery in the School in 1947, for five years in the first instance, as was the practice at that time. In 1952 he indicated that for health reasons he did not wish to be reappointed and the School decided that the Chair should not be filled but that a post of Director of Surgical Studies should be created. Mr D. H. Patey was appointed to that post, with the same number of beds as had previously been allocated to the Professor. Up to that time the Department had been known, and listed in School and Hospital documents, as the 'Professorial Surgical Unit'. Without a professor such a title was no longer applicable, but in any case Mr Patey had opposed such a name because he considered that the connotations of the term 'Unit' were the exact opposite of those of the Latin '*Universitas Vestia*', from which the universities derived their name, and whose purpose was to emphasise the corporate character of the community. Accordingly, on Mr Patey's appointment the Department assumed the title of 'Department of Surgical Studies' and has retained that name since then.

In 1952, Mr L. P. Le Quesne, who until then had been Second Assistant in the Department, was appointed as First Assistant. In 1960 he was appointed a Consultant Surgeon on the staff of the Hospital and Assistant Director of the Department of Surgical Studies. In 1964, on Mr Patey's retirement, the School decided to fill the Chair, which had been in abeyance for twelve years, and Mr Le Quesne was appointed as the second Professor of Surgery in the School, a post which he held until 1984, although in 1983 he relinquished the Directorship of the Department to Professor M. Hobsley. In 1984 he retired from the Department and from the important posts which he had held in the University; Dean of the Faculty of Medicine and Deputy Vice-Chancellor since 1980, having been a member of the Senate since 1977 and Chairman of the Board of Studies in Surgery from 1974 to 1976. He had also been President of the Surgical Research Society and Chairman of the *British Journal of Surgery* and of the Federation of Associations of Clinical Professors.

Professor Hobsley joined the Department of Surgical Studies in 1964 as a Lecturer, becoming a Senior Lecturer in 1967 and a Reader in 1970. In 1975 the personal title of Professor of Surgical Science was conferred upon him and in 1983 he succeeded to the established Chair of Surgery in the School.

TEACHING

The teaching arrangements in respect of surgery were similar to those in medicine; after a temporary period with a Clinical Surgery Committee with one of the other surgeons as chairman, a Surgical

Education Committee was established with the Professor as chairman and he was responsible for the organisation and co-ordination of the teaching of surgery.

In his years as Director of the Department, Mr Patey made a major contribution to the development of the surgery of the parotid gland and, in association with Professor Thackray of the Bland-Sutton Institute, advanced our understanding of tumours of the gland. Work on the surgery of the salivary glands has been actively continued by Professor Hobsley.

Fluid and electrolyte disturbances in surgical patients have been a major field of research, particularly in relation to the changes in the renal handling of water and sodium in the postoperative period. In later years these studies have included measurement of the changes in aldosterone, cortisol and argenine vasopressin secretion following operation, and a study of the factors responsible for these changes. Another major area of research has been that of gastric physiology. Refined methods of measuring gastric secretion have been developed to study the acid secretion following vagotomy and the effects of that operation on gastric emptying, with particular reference to the aetiology of the dumping syndrome and of post-vagotomy diarrhoea.

In association with the Department of Nuclear Medicine the isotopic technique for the diagnosis of deep vein thrombosis was simplified and then used for studies of this important postoperative complication, including some of the first double-blind studies showing the efficacy of subcutaneous heparin and of graduated compression stockings in the prevention of this condition. In conjunction with the neighbouring Polytechnic of Central London, and with the Department of Physics as applied to Medicine, the mechanical forces acting on the normal foot and on that of patients with diabetic neuropathy have been measured. This has led to a clearer understanding of the aetiology of diabetic neuropathic ulceration of the foot.

In the field of operative surgery, in association with the Department of Radiology, and based on the detailed anatomical studies of Mr B. H. Hand, the staff of the Department made significant contributions to the development of operative cholangiography. Working together, Professor Le Quesne and the author (D.R.) developed the operation of laryngo-pharyngo-oesophagectomy with immediate pharyngo-gastric anastomosis in the treatment of pharyngo-oesophageal carcinoma, a technique which is now widely used in the treatment of this serious form of malignant disease. The operation has been adapted for use in other types of oesophageal carcinoma.

In 1954 Mr Patey formed the Surgical Research Society, of which he was the first Secretary and later President, a Society which has had a profound influence on surgery in the United Kingdom and which is one of the most active societies in the country.

Obstetrics and Gynaecology

Although the Medical Committee recommended in 1945 that Academic Departments should be established in Medicine, in Surgery and in Obstetrics and Gynaecology, no School Department in the last of these specialities came into being until 1969 and no Chair of Obstetrics and Gynaecology has been established at The Middlesex. The Department started in 1969 with Mr W. R. Winterton, Senior Obstetrician and Gynaecologist to the Hospital, as Director and with Mr S. J. Steele as Senior Lecturer. On the retirement of Mr Winterton in September 1970, Mr I. M. Jackson became Director of the Department until 1973 when the title of Reader was conferred on Mr Steele and he became Head.

At the time the Department was established, the future organisation of medical education and of the National Health Service was undergoing considerable change in an atmosphere of uncertainty and this hampered its further development. The restriction placed on staffing resulted in an increasing clinical responsibility being placed on the staff of the Academic Department at a time of the development of new techniques such as tubal microsurgery, colposcopy, laser surgery and paediatric gynaecological surgery.

TEACHING

Obstetrics and Gynaecology form one part of all qualifying examinations but the subjects are ones which present particular difficulties in clinical teaching, with large 'firms' being even more undesirable than in some other specialities. For experience in obstetrics, students, usually in pairs, have been taught not only at The Middlesex and Central Middlesex Hospitals but also at a number of other hospitals including the North Staffs (Stoke-on-Trent), Queen Elizabeth II (Welwyn), Orsett, Maidstone and West Wales (General) Hospital, Carmarthen. Some experience of gynaecology is also obtained during the stay at those hospitals but the main teaching in that subject has been provided at The Middlesex and the Hospital for Women.

In 1969 the Margaret Pyke Centre was opened by HRH Prince Philip, Duke of Edinburgh, in Mortimer Street as a centre of excellence in the whole field of family planning and in 1976 it became integrated into the National Health Service and is now located in Bateman's Buildings on the Hospital for Women site, Soho Square. The centre is now directed by a Senior Lecturer in Family Planning of the Department of Obstetrics and Gynaecology.

RESEARCH

Not surprisingly, a large proportion of the research of the Department has been concerned, on the one hand, with the promotion of pregnancy in infertile couples and, on the other hand, with the prevention of conception in those in whom it is not desired. Supported by the World Health Organisation, a study has been made of the detection of ovulation and a simple kit has been developed which women can use themselves at home. In 1973 the Department took over responsibility for karyotyping and cytogenetic services and semenology for the Hospital. In recent years an extensive research programme has been initiated at the Margaret Pyke Centre, where there are unique opportunities for research.

Psychiatry

Dr Noel Harris, Senior Physician in the Hospital Department of Psychological Medicine retired in 1959 and in June that year the Medical Committee of the Hospital and the Academic Board set up a Joint Sub-Committee to study a memorandum from the Dean, Professor B. W. Windeyer, advocating the establishment of a Chair of Psychiatry within the School. This was agreed in 1960, in addition to the replacement of Dr Noel Harris on the consultant staff of the Hospital. Dr J. D. N. Hill (Sir Denis Hill, 1966) was appointed Professor of Psychiatry from 1 March 1961. He had graduated at St Thomas's Hospital Medical School and had been Chief Assistant in the Department of Psychological Medicine at St Thomas's Hospital and later Senior Lecturer at the Institute of Psychiatry and Honorary

Physician to the Maudsley. He was one of the first Professors in Psychiatry to be appointed to a general medical school by the University of London, a Professor in the same subject being appointed at St Bartholomew's Hospital Medical School in the same year.

In 1966 Sir Denis Hill resigned to become Professor of Psychiatry in the Institute of Psychiatry and Professor J. M. Hinton was appointed to the Chair at The Middlesex. He was a graduate of King's College Hospital Medical School and, after holding House Officer and Casualty Officer posts in that hospital and serving in the Royal Army Medical Corps, he had held various appointments in general medicine, then at the National Hospital for Nervous Diseases and at the Maudsley Hospital before being appointed as First Assistant in the Academic Department of Psychiatry at The Middlesex in 1961. Professor Hinton continued as Professor of Psychiatry until his retirement in 1983.

ACCOMMODATION

Beds for the patients of the Academic Department of Psychiatry were provided within the Middlesex Hospital in Laffan Ward on the first floor of the Barnato-Joel Wing and also at St Luke's-Woodside Hospital. Initially the offices for the Professor and his staff were located in various rooms in the Old Medical School, but when the Department of Physiology moved into the new accommodation in the Windeyer Building, in 1963, the Department of Psychiatry transferred to the former Physiology and Anatomy Departments in the old School building in Riding House Street. Out-patients of the Academic Department were seen there, while the out-patients of the Hospital Consultants were seen in the Out-Patient Annexe in Cleveland Street. The opening of the Wolfson Building in 1979 not only provided new purpose-designed accommodation for the Academic Department but also provided space for the Hospital and University psychiatrists to work alongside each other on the same site.

TEACHING

The development of the Academic Department of Psychiatry was a recognition of the extent of psychiatric disorders and of the need for undergraduate education in the discipline. A full-time psychiatric clerkship was developed, involving not only The Middlesex and St Luke's–Woodside Hospitals but also the Central Middlesex, Horton,

Marlborough, Napsbury and Shenley Hospitals. When the Tottenham Mews Day Hospital was opened that was also used for teaching.

Part of the basic psychiatric education has been achieved by collaborative teaching by staff with special interests in organic, psychotherapeutic and social aspects. The Department also developed a co-ordinated behavioural sciences course which has gained a high reputation as a result of close collaboration between clinical psychologists, medical sociologists and clinicians.

RESEARCH

In spite of the heavy clinical responsibilities of the staff of the Academic Department research has been undertaken, usually in fields appropriate to a general teaching hospital. It has included the psychiatric aspects of epilepsy, some psychomotor disorders, the physiological and anatomical changes in the nervous system in dementia and a number of studies of anorexia nervosa and other disorders of eating. Rating scales of various psychological functions have been constructed, validated and subsequently used widely with some automated tests being devised. Psychologists and psychiatrists have collaborated to build up a Behaviour Therapy Unit which has improved the treatment of patients with obsessional disorder stammering and other problems. One continuing interest which would have appealed to Sir Joseph de Courcy Laffan, the benefactor of the Ward, which was originally devoted to cancer and which now provides beds for the Department of Psychiatry, has been research into the reactions of patients with cancer and terminal illnesses. From the foundation of the Department there has been continuing research into an assessment of interviewing techniques, analysed on video recordings. This method of research has also proved of great value in undergraduate and postgraduate education.

Reta Lila Weston Institute of Neurological Studies

The establishment of the Reta Lila Weston Institute of Neurological Studies and the subsequent appointment of the Francis and Renée Hock Director of the Institute resulted from generous benefactions inspired by Dr Michael Kremer. In 1969 a visitor staying in Britain had a stroke. Her husband had her rushed to hospital by ambulance but he was so alarmed at the apparent indifference of the hospital to which she had been taken that he insisted on her being transferred to

195

The Middlesex under the care of Dr Kremer. The husband was so impressed with the treatment accorded to his wife, even though she died, that on her death he made a most generous benefaction to found an Institute of Neurological Studies in her memory in order to foster research into neurological disorders in an institution which he considered had the requisite personnel but lacked the facilities to take full advantage of the expertise available. He insisted on anonymity and this was naturally respected. However, after his death in 1979, his daughters considered that it would then be appropriate to disclose that the generous benefactor was the late Mr Garfield Weston and that the trust fund endowing the Institute was named after his wife, Reta Lila Weston.

Dr Michael Kremer was appointed as the Director of the New Institute. He retired in 1974 and Dr C. J. Earl, who was then the Senior Neurologist on the consultant staff of the Hospital, was appointed to succeed him. Later another important step was taken, Dr Michael Kremer again being instrumental in the event. Mr and Mrs Hock expressed their desire to endow a Chair in Neurology within the Department. Unfortunately that did not prove possible but they kindly agreed to allow their generous benefaction to provide for the appointment of a whole-time Director of the Institute. Dr Earl offered to resign from the part-time directorship in order to make this possible and in 1979 Dr M. J. G. Harrison was appointed the Francis and Renée Hock Director.

RESEARCH

In the comparatively short time of its existence the Institute has already established a number of different research projects which have yielded results of significance. The Francis and Renée Hock Director, Dr Harrison, has carried out both experimental and clinical research on the pathogenesis of transient cerebral ischaemic attacks and carotid thromboembolism. The biology and pathology of myelinated nerve fibres have been studied with particular reference to the demyelinating diseases and, in studies on peripheral nerves, the distinctive pathophysiological characteristics of different toxic neuropathies have led to an increasing understanding of the basic biological processes of nerves. Electron microscopy has shed new light on the morphology of the regenerating node of Ranvier following nerve crush and has established that, contrary to earlier reports, nodes are present from the inception of remyelination. The Department is now engaged in developing techniques for the quantitative assessment of sensory loss in patients with peripheral neuropathy.

In conjunction with the Departments of Urology and Radiology of the Hospital there have been pioneering studies of bladder defects, both mechanical and neurogenic, and the procedures developed have been widely adopted as standard investigations. Further work is being undertaken jointly on sphincter control in a variety of conditions.

Radiotherapy and Oncology

As early as 1920, at the request of the School following a recommendation of the Medical Committee of the Hospital, the University established a Chair of Radiology tenable at The Middlesex Hospital Medical School. However the Board of Advisors decided that no candidate was available whom the University authorities considered suitable for professorial rank. In 1942 the University agreed to amend the title of the Chair to Radiology (Therapeutic) and to advertise the post. Mr B. W. Windeyer was appointed to become the first Professor at The Middlesex who was not laboratory based and one of the first Professors in the speciality in the country. When he retired in 1969, as Professor Sir Brian Windeyer, and became Vice-Chancellor of the University of London, the School and the University decided that the title of the Chair should become 'Radiotherapy', and Dr N. M. Bleehen was appointed Professor. He had been an Oxford and Middlesex undergraduate and after qualification he had, among other appointments, been both a Registrar and Senior Registrar in the Meyerstein Institute of Radiotherapy and had spent a year in the radiology department of the Stanford University Medical Center, California.

In 1975 Professor Bleehen was appointed to the Chair of Clinical Oncology in the University of Cambridge and the School once more decided on a change of name for the Department and Chair to that of 'Oncology'. In the following year Dr R. J. Berry was appointed Professor of Oncology. Born in the United States, he had graduated first in physics and biology at New York University and subsequently graduated in medicine from Duke University School of Medicine, North Carolina. Early in 1958 he spent some time in the Radiotherapy Department of the Churchill Hospital, Oxford and for a few years he was 'commuting' between England and the USA, and obtaining a number of qualifications in both countries, including a D Phil (Oxon), a Membership of the Royal College of Physicians (to be followed by a Fellowship a few years later), a Fellowship of the Royal College of Radiologists and an Honorary Fellowship of the American College of Radiology.

TEACHING

Postgraduate education has always played a prominent part in the activities of the Department and there are many consultants and professors throughout the world who received their postgraduate training at The Middlesex and at Mount Vernon Hospital, with which affiliations developed at a very early stage. Undergraduate teaching has also been undertaken throughout the Department's life but this increased considerably in 1974 when all students were attached to an oncology firm for a period during which they carried out the routine duties of a clinical clerkship and acquired further broadly-based medical experience as well as an overall experience of non-surgical cancer management in the wards and in the Out-Patient Department.

RESEARCH

From the outset there has been considerable collaboration with cancer research being undertaken in several different laboratories of the School, but in the early years the research undertaken in the Department was clinical and concerned with evaluating and improving existing methods of diagnosis and treatment at a time when many technological improvements were occurring in the field of radiation. The lectures delivered by Sir Brian Windeyer, the posts held by him and the honorary degrees conferred upon him are an indication of the contributions he made to the subject. To mention only a few appointments, he was Chairman of the Radioactive Substances Advisory Committee and National Radiation Protection Board, a member of the Grand Council and Executive Committee of the British Empire Cancer Campaign, Consultant Adviser in Radiotherapy to the Ministry of Health, and subsequently the Department of Health and Social Security, and President of the Faculty of Radiologists. In the field of education in general he was Dean of the Medical School from 1954–67, Dean of the Faculty of Medicine of the University of London and Chairman of its Academic Council before becoming Vice-Chancellor.

With the opening of the Sir Jules Thorn Institute of Clinical Science in 1974 the Department acquired laboratory facilities of its own and research has developed there, with grants from the Cancer Research Campaign, on the kinetics of cell proliferation and loss in human tumours and on aspects of tumour imaging. In addition, in conjunction with Professor R. M. Hicks of the Bland-Sutton Institute of Pathology, a contract was won from the US National Cancer Institute to develop human bladder organ culture systems and to study carcinogenesis in those cultures. For some years, in the Meyerstein Institute of Radiotherapy and Oncology, Dr A. M. Jelliffe has been Co-ordinator of the British National Lymphoma Investigation and the central secretariat of this multicentre prospective study has been incorporated into the Department of Oncology.

From the 1940s there has been close collaboration between the Radiotherapy Departments of The Middlesex and Mount Vernon Hospitals and in recent years Dr J. F. Fowler, Director of the Cancer Research Campaign Gray Laboratories at Mount Vernon Hospital, has been Visiting Professor at the Department of Oncology and Dr S. Dische, Consultant at Mount Vernon and a CRC Life Fellow has been appointed as a part-time Senior Lecturer in the Department. He was a Middlesex student and after qualification worked in the Radiotherapy and Pathology Departments.

Genito-Urinary Medicine

The Department of Genito-Urinary Medicine in the School is the only academic department in the country in that discipline and its creation was brought about by the imagination and perseverance of Dr R. D. Catterall who was appointed Consultant Venereologist to the Hospital in 1964 after being Physician-in-Charge of the Department of Venereology at The General Infirmary, Leeds. He became Consultant Adviser in the speciality to the Department of Health and Social Security and his work there and with the World Health Organisation led him to believe that it was desirable to establish university recognition and participitation in the subject if long-term advances were to be made in the control of what was already a major epidemic, with an estimated 200 million new cases of gonorrhoea and 40 million new cases of syphilis per year throughout the world, and with countless more not notified. Dr Catterall received considerable support and encouragement from his colleagues and successive Deans but resources had to be raised in order to create an academic Department. He turned for help to another Duncan, Mr Duncan Guthrie, whose war record in Special Operations had been followed by another remarkable postwar record in which he was closely involved in establishing no less than a dozen Chairs, in various subjects in different universities, as well as an Institute of Medical Genetics in Glasgow which had been named after him. The appeal which he launched, with Lord Cobbold as Chairman, was also successful in raising the resources necessary; one anonymous donor alone providing a benefaction of £200,000. As a result, the unique Duncan Guthrie Chair of Genito-Urinary Medicine was established in 1978 in the School and in October that year Dr M. W. Adler was appointed as the first Duncan Guthrie Professor. He was a Middlesex graduate whose postgraduate studies had been in general medicine, community medicine and sexually transmitted diseases and who, immediately before being appointed Professor, was Director of a Medical Research Council sexually transmitted disease project at The Middlesex.

TEACHING

In this subject the problems of teaching are largely related to the surfeit of patients and are just the reverse of those of some specialities where adequate experience can be obtained only by using a number of hospitals for teaching. The large numbers of out-patients attending James Pringle House (65,000 attendances per year) provide a wide variety of problems and as part of their attachment students attend clinics as well as lectures. The Department is also responsible for the teaching of postgraduate doctors and nurses. These attend as students on a British Postgraduate Medical Federation Course in Sexually Transmitted Diseases (STDs) and also Dermatology, a Joint Board of Clinical Nursing Studies Course in STDs and Courses in Family Planning. Finally, the Department offers clinical attachments for overseas graduates.

RESEARCH

The research activities of the Department cover three areas (1) Epidemiological, Statistical and Computing, (2) Clinical and Laboratory, (3) Behavioural and Educational. Given the complex factors associated with the spread of the STDs the Department is aiming to establish a multidisciplinary team of clinicians, laboratory workers, epidemiologists, statisticians and behavioural scientists working in close collaboration with other departments. Initially, the major research of the Department was in relation to the epidemiological aspects of STDs with particular reference to the facilities and and staff required for the control of STDs and the natural history of certain diseases such as pelvic inflammatory disease and genital herpes. Following this, more clinically and laboratory orientated studies have been established into the acquired immune deficiency syndrome (AIDS), hepatitis, genital herpes, gastrointestinal pathogens, cytomegalovirus and Epstein-Barr Virus.

Community Medicine

In the early sixties the Medical Unit considered the possibility of starting a Department of Preventive and Environmental Medicine and to that end appointed Dr Donald Hunter as (Honorary) Consultant in Occupational and Environmental Medicine. He had been Consultant at the London Hospital from 1927 to 1963 and, among other things, had been Director of the Medical Research Council Department for Research in Industrial Medicine and also a member of the World Health Organisation Expert Advisory Panel on Social and Occupational Health. Also, in May 1965, a vacant post in the Unit was filled by an Assistant who had experience in that field of study. This development led to the decision some years later to establish a separate Department of Community Medicine. The main accommodation for the Department was provided in Horace Joules Hall at the Central Middlesex Hospital but an office was also provided within the Bland Sutton Institute. Dr D. L. Miller was appointed to the Chair of Social and Preventive Medicine from 1 January 1972. After graduating at St Thomas's Hospital Medical School and holding House Officer posts he had, while serving in the Royal Air Force, been seconded to the Epidemiological Research Laboratory, subsequently held a Research Assistant appointment at the Royal Postgraduate Medical School and was then appointed an Epidemiologist in the Public Health Laboratory Service. Professor Miller resigned from the Chair at the end of 1982 to become Professor of Community Medicine at St Mary's Hospital Medical School.

TEACHING

The development of community medicine within the School coincided with an increased emphasis on social and preventive medicine in the Regulations of the University. As a result teaching in this subject became more formalised and concentrated. For practical purposes it was combined with the teaching of General Practice in the same section of the clinical timetable, as the two were regarded as complementary.

An early research project of the Department was the national childhood encephalopathy study which was set up in 1976 in response to public alarm that immunisation against whooping cough carried a risk of causing brain damage in a number of recipients. The prolonged and extensive investigation provided firm data which were not otherwise available. A multi-centre study was also undertaken on the value of laboratory microbiological investigations to assess the value of the tests performed in relation to patient care with a view to improving communication between clinicians and laboratory personnel which could lead to more effective use of microbiological laboratory resources.

Institute of Clinical Research and Experimental Medicine, Cobbold Laboratories

For many years, and certainly from the beginning of the century, the physicians and surgeons of the Hospital had realised the need for research facilities. The creation of the Bland-Sutton Institute had resulted from Sir John's appreciation of his lack of a laboratory in his early days and his expressed belief in the need for a more intimate association between the care of living patients and the study of disease. The Courtauld Institute of Biochemistry, the Courtauld Research Wards of the Hospital, the Ferens Institute of Otolaryngology and the Meyerstein Institute of Radiotherapy had followed, based on the same fundamental principle. In 1951 the Board of Governors of the Hospital considered that its endowment funds should provide an Institute of Clinical Research and Experimental Medicine in which the Hospital Consultants, their Registrars and Research Fellows could have access to first-class laboratories. A modern four-storey building close to the Hospital and Medical School was purchased, Latimer House in Hanson Street, and converted to provide these facilities. A Clinical Research Committee was established with two 'lay' members of the Board of Governors (one of whom would be Chairman), six members appointed by the Medical Committee and the Dean of the Medical School.

Professor Alan Kekwick, Professor of Medicine, was appointed as Director and the Institute was formally opened on 22 October 1953.

The new Institute soon demonstrated the part it could play in the work of The Middlesex. Within a few months three clinical research scholarships were made available by the Leverhulme Trustees and these provided, at a critical stage, not only resources for specific projects but also established a nucleus of senior whole-time research workers who exerted a stimulating influence on the whole Institute. Within the first year no less than twenty-four projects were started; the work being undertaken either by the Consultants of the Hospital themselves or by their Registrars or Research Assistants working under their direction. Over the years a remarkable variety of projects has been undertaken and during its thirty-two years to date nearly two hundred physicians and surgeons in training grades have worked in the Institute and a number are now Professors. Statistics relating to publications do not in themselves indicate the breadth or depth of the research projects but most of the Annual Reports list over thirty or forty publications based on work carried out in the Institute during the year. A number of them have been extensively cited subsequently in the world literature.

In 1971, Professor Kekwick retired from the directorship of the Institute and Dr J. D. N. Nabarro (Sir John Nabarro, 1982) was appointed to replace him. He had been appointed a Consultant Physician on the staff of the Hospital in 1954 and before and since then was heavily engaged in research as well as in clinical medicine. His research led to him being elected a Fellow of University College, London. When the Sir Jules Thorn Institute of Clinical Science was being planned, the Dean, Professor Walls, suggested the addition of an extra floor to enable the Institute of Clinical Research to move to the Island Site. When this occurred in 1974 the Institute was renamed the Cobbold Laboratories in recognition of the great contributions to the Hospital and School made by Lord Cobbold, who had just retired from the chairmanship of both. On the retirement of Dr Nabarro in 1981 it was decided that a new Clinical Research Committee should be established with equal representation from the District Hospital Medical Committee and from the Academic Board. It was also agreed that a Director should be appointed for the Cobbold Laboratories. Dr J. D. H. Slater was appointed Chairman of the Clinical Research Committee and Dr A. B. Kurtz was appointed Director of the Cobbold Laboratories.

Academic Departments

The development of new academic Departments in the School has led to the research of some specialties being undertaken in them rather than in the Institute as was necessary in the early days. A very close collaboration exists to obtain the maximum benefit of all the facilities available and the Cobbold Laboratories remain extremely active, particularly in the fields of endocrinology and metabolism in adults and in children.

—10—
Other Developments

Chairmen – Deans – Sub-Deans – Wardens of Astor
College – School Secretaries – Societies and Clubs –
Students Union

Many of the extensive developments which have occurred in the School
and Hospital since 1935 have been referred to already in different
chapters. There remains a need to bring together some of the accounts
in a composite manner and to mention other topics which have not yet
received attention. The aim of this chapter, therefore, is to correlate
some previous items, supplemented with further details where
necessary, and to refer to some other events, although only a few can
be included in the space available.

Chairmen

Few hospitals and medical schools, if any, can have been as fortunate
as The Middlesex in respect of those who have served as chairmen.
This has applied since those offices were first established but has been
particularly true during the last fifty years. In spite of being exceptionally
busy men with other important and heavy commitments the chairmen
have identified themselves with The Middlesex not only at meetings of
the Board or Council and on other formal occasions but also by making
informal visits and meeting patients and staff.

Reference has been made already to Mr S. A. Courtauld who was
Chairman of the Medical School from 1930 to 1946 and whose benefactions are commemorated by the Courtauld Institute of Biochemistry,

the Courtauld Lecture Theatre and the Courtauld Chairs of Anatomy and of Biochemistry.

Some mention has also been made of Lord Astor of Hever who was the first person to combine the two chairmanships – of the Board from 1938 and of the Council from 1946. His association with The Middlesex from 1920 up to his death in 1971 was a period of remarkable development in which the Hospital was almost entirely rebuilt and greatly enlarged and the Medical School was expanded to many times its 1935 size, by the construction of extensive new buildings. Lord Astor's services to the Hospital and School during that period were immense; his benefactions were incalculable and were made quietly and unostentatiously. Almost certainly his earliest support to the School came in 1920 with his endowment of the Chair of Physiology although it did not become public knowledge until many years later. The Dean, Mr Alfred Webb-Johnson, who, as Colonel Webb-Johnson, had amputated his leg at Wimereux during the First World War and thereby saved his life, went to see him in 1920 to talk about the School and of his hopes for fostering research and teaching by establishing Chairs in the medical sciences. Lord Astor (then Major, The Hon. J. J. Astor) showed a lively interest in the proposals and when he wrote to the Dean on 17 November 1920 he ended his letter by saying 'Anonymity would be the first condition of my support so I trust you will treat this confidentially'. That was to be the pattern of all his activities and he insisted on similar anonymity nine years later with what must be the largest single benefaction ever made to the Hospital or School, the provision of the outstanding nurses' home in Foley Street. It was only the introduction of the National Health Service in 1948 which persuaded him to agree to his name being attached to the building as it was then important to identify how so large a nurses' home could have been built to such a high standard.

In Dr Campbell Thomson's book published in 1935, Lord Astor was described then as 'one of the greatest benefactors of the Hospital and School' and that was before any of the great School developments mentioned in chapter 8. Lord Astor's retirement in 1962 and his move to the south of France did not end his abiding deep interest in The Middlesex and his continuing desire to help in every way possible. He continued to invite sisters, nurses and students to enjoy holidays on his estate at Pergomas and they have lasting memories of his generous and courteous hospitality.

Lord Cobbold, who succeeded Lord Astor in 1963, was also Chairman of both the Board of Governors and the School Council. He was Governor of the Bank of England from 1949 to 1961 and in 1963 became Lord Chamberlain; those being just two posts of exceptional responsibility among the many important offices which he held. Two years after he became Chairman, the Royal Commission on Medical Education was established and soon after that the Secretary of State for Social Services began planning the reorganisation of the National Health Service. So, although there continued to be considerable academic and structural developments taking place in the School and Hospital, many of the meetings of the Council and the Board of Governors had also to consider what evidence they should submit on university and health service matters and then subsequently decide on the actions to be taken in the light of reports and the decisions which were made. In all this, Lord Cobbold's great experience in wide issues of policy was of inestimable value. A number of people who had the opportunity of hearing or reading his speeches during the debates in the House of Lords on the Reorganisation Bill consider them to have been among the finest he has made and the most lucid and convincing in either House on that controversial subject.

Lord Cobbold's retirement in 1974 coincided with the reorganisation of the National Health Service and the abolition of the Boards of Governors. His successor as Chairman of the Council of the Medical School, Mr D. B. Money-Coutts, could not therefore also be Chairman of the Hospital but he became Chairman of the Special Trustees, responsible for the Hospital's endowment funds. He has also been closely involved in the Health Authorities which have since been responsible for the Hospital's management. He was a member, and then in 1978 Vice-Chairman, of the late Kensington and Chelsea and Westminster Area Health Authority (Teaching) and was elected Vice-Chairman of the Bloomsbury Health Authority soon after its formation in 1982, and Chairman of its Finance Committee.

Mr David Money-Coutts is Chairman of Coutts and Company, which he first joined in 1954, and is also a director of other companies. It is not surprising therefore that when he joined the Board of Governors in 1962 and School Council in 1963 he was in great demand to serve on the Finance Committees of both the Hospital and School. When he became Chairman of the Council of the School in 1974 the financial problems facing the universities were beginning to cause concern and his knowledge and experience proved invaluable.

The firm of Coutts was founded in 1692, in the reign of William and Mary, and is older than the Bank of England. The firm became bankers to the Hospital in 1761 but that arrangement, which worked so well for 213 years, was terminated in 1974 following the reorganisation of the National Health Service, although the Special Trustees still bank with Coutts. The 'Money' part of the family name is regarded as a pun by a number of people who do not know its origin. It is of interest that it originated from the marriage in 1850 of the Reverend James Drummond Money to Clara, grand-daughter of Thomas Coutts, banker to the Royal Family. *Punch* summed up the event neatly in a little ditty:

> Money takes the name of Coutts,
> Superfluous and funny
> For everyone considers Coutts
> Synonymous with money

Deans

Some reference has been made in previous chapters to Sir Harold Boldero, Sir Brian Windeyer and Professor Eldred Walls who were Deans from 1934 to 1974. Sir Harold was the nineteenth Dean in the School; the first was Dr Temple Frere who was appointed in 1856, twenty-one years after the School had been founded. Deans are elected annually, originally by the School Committee, and since 1948 by the Academic Board, with the concurrence of Council. There is no restriction on re-election and the term of office has varied considerably. Five Deans in the early period served for only one year and four for two years but Mr Andrew Clark was Dean from 1876 to 1886 and Dr H. Campbell Thomson from 1908 to 1919. Others served for four or six years and Mr Nunn for eight years.

Sir Harold Boldero was Dean for twenty years, from 1934 to 1954. After him Sir Brian Windeyer was Dean for thirteen years, from 1954 to 1967, and Professor Eldred Walls for seven years, from 1967 to 1974. He was succeeded by the author of this book who served for nine years, from 1974 to 1983, when Mr W. W. Slack was appointed.

Mr William Slack was an Oxford and Middlesex graduate who, among other things, was awarded an Oxford blue in football. After a number of posts as House Surgeon, Casualty Surgical Officer and Accident Officer at The Middlesex he was a Surgical Registrar at St Bartholomew's Hospital and later Resident Surgical Officer at St Mark's Hospital where his particular interest in coloproctology was fostered. He was Assistant Pathologist in the Bland-Sutton Institute, Senior Surgical Registrar at The Middlesex and Central Middlesex Hospitals and Instructor in Surgery at the University of Illinois before being appointed a Consultant General Surgeon and Senior Lecturer in Surgery at The Middlesex in 1962. In 1975 he was appointed Surgeon, and in 1983 Serjeant-Surgeon, to Her Majesty The Queen.

Sub-Deans

At the end of the last century an office of Sub-Dean was instituted and was held by the lecturers in anatomy or physiology but the post was abolished after the First World War. During the Second World War Professor John Kirk was appointed as Sub-Dean for the students at Bristol and then at Leeds. In 1962 the Dean, Sir Brian Windeyer, considered that the commissioning of the new School buildings and the establishment of new departments had increased the work to an extent which made it difficult for a part-time Dean to cover the commitments and the Academic Board and the Council agreed that a post of Sub-Dean should be established. Mr J. H. L. Ferguson, General Surgeon on the staff of the Hospital, was appointed. It was also decided to appoint a Sub-Dean at the Central Middlesex Hospital in view of the extent to which that hospital was participating in clinical teaching with a large number of students there throughout the year. Dr K. P. Ball, Physician to the Central Middlesex Hospital and a former Middlesex graduate, and Resident Medical Officer, was appointed.

In 1965 Mr Ferguson resigned as Sub-Dean and Professor E. W. Walls, S.A. Courtauld Professor of Anatomy, was appointed. When he became Dean in 1967, Mr W. W. Slack was appointed as Sub-Dean and served in that office until 1972 when Dr I. R. Verner, Anaesthetist on the staff of the Hospital, was appointed. In 1975 Professor J. B. Jepson, Professor of Biochemistry in the Courtauld Institute, was appointed. His death in 1976 was followed by the appointment of Professor P. H. S. Silver, S.A. Courtauld Professor of Anatomy, as Sub-Dean until 1982 when Mr R. P. Gould, Reader in Histology, was appointed. On his retirement in 1984, Dr A. L. Miller, Head of the Department of Chemical Pathology, was appointed.

At the Central Middlesex Hospital, Dr K. P. Ball was Sub-Dean from 1962 to 1972 and was followed by Mr J. F. Newcombe, General Surgeon. In 1978 Dr M. W. McNicol, General Physician, was appointed Sub-Dean at the Central Middlesex.

As will be described in the next chapter, at the end of 1981 the University of London decided on restructuring arrangements which meant that the Central Middlesex Hospital would cease to be associated with The Middlesex Hospital Medical School and that Middlesex students would be taught at the Whittington and Royal Northern Hospitals in Islington. Accordingly in 1982 it was decided that there should be a Sub-Dean in Islington and Mr J. P. S. Cochrane, General Surgeon, was appointed. He was a Middlesex graduate and was a Wellcome Research Fellow and then Lecturer in the Department of Surgical Studies at The Middlesex before being appointed a Consultant Surgeon in Islington.

POSTGRADUATE SUB-DEANS

In 1969 the School appointed also a Postgraduate Sub-Dean in response to its considerable commitments in the field of postgraduate education and the steadily increasing requirements for those wishing to enter any branch of practice. The first person to be appointed to the post was Dr P. A. J. Ball, General Physician on the staff of the Hospital. In 1971 Mr J. A. P. Marston, General Surgeon on the staff of the Hospital, was appointed and after four years, in 1975, he was succeeded by Dr K. B. Saunders, Senior Lecturer in the Department of Medicine and Honorary Consultant Physician to the Hospital. In 1979 Dr Saunders was appointed Professor of Medicine at St George's Hospital Medical School and Dr J. Tinker, Physician in Charge of the Intensive Therapy Unit of the Hospital, was appointed as Postgraduate Sub-Dean in the School.

In the late 1940s, higher degree courses were started as a vital feature of the Medical School. The teachers are actively engaged in research as well as in teaching and the various departments of the School are ideally equipped for conducting higher degree courses such as those for the MSc, in which the emphasis is on techniques, and for the M Phil and PhD, which are concerned with solving a problem by application of appropriate techniques. The first PhD students were associated with the Departments of Physiology, Anatomy and Biochemistry and the numbers were initially only one to three per department. In the 1970s the M Phil course was introduced and provides the equivalent of a 'probationary period'. All potential students are now registered for it in the first instance and satisfactory progress will lead, after twelve or eighteen months, to a change to a PhD registration. In 1983 there were fifty two postgraduate students in the School on the M Phil register and fifty on the PhD register, twelve students having been awarded a PhD degree during the year. At present the School provides, in collaboration with other schools of the University, MSc courses in clinical biochemistry, medical immunology, nuclear medicine, radiation biology and radiation physics. These courses last one year for full-time students and two years for part-time students. In 1983-84 there were five such full-time and sixteen part-time students on the register and ten had been awarded an MSc degree in the previous academic year.

In 1979 the School established a Higher Degrees Committee, with Professor F. Hobbiger, Professor of Pharmacology, as Chairman. In 1980 the University informed schools that it was prepared to delegate most of its powers concerning postgraduate degree courses, subject to decisions being taken by the Academic Board or an independent committee, and in 1982 the School established a post of Postgraduate Sub-Dean (Science). Professor F. Hobbiger was appointed.

Wardens of Astor College

When Astor College was opened in 1967 Dr P. A. J. Ball was appointed Warden and he continued in that office until 1974 when Mr R. P. Gould, Reader in Histology, was appointed. In 1978 he was succeeded by Dr W. F. Coulson, Senior Lecturer in the Courtauld Institute of Biochemistry.

School Secretaries

Reference was made in chapter 2 to Mr R. A. Foley who was Secretary of the School from 1921 to 1948 and to Miss Eileen Walton who came to the School in 1934 and, among other duties, assisted Dr Campbell Thompson with his book on the history of the first hundred years of the School. In 1949 she was appointed school Secretary in succession to Mr Foley and she held that post for sixteen years of extensive development in the school, including a considerable increase in student numbers and the construction of the Windeyer Building. On her retirement in 1965 Mr George Clark was appointed as Secretary. He was a graduate of the University of Liverpool and before coming to The Middlesex he had had wide experience of university administration, having been Assistant Secretary of University College London, Deputy Academic Registrar and Secretary of the Collegiate Council of the University of London and then Registrar of the University of Sheffield. In his earlier days, as a schoolmaster before the Second World War, one of his pupils had been the young Harold Wilson, now Lord Wilson of Rievaulx who became Prime Minister in 1964. While serving with the Royal Navy during the War George Clark had shared an office for a while with James Callaghan who became Prime Minister in 1976.

When George Clark retired in 1977, Mr Donald Eardley, Bursar at Aston University, was appointed and on his retirement in 1983 Dr Diana Sanders became Secretary of the School. She was born in New Zealand and graduated with a BA degree, followed by an MA at the University of Auckland. Later she came to England and was awarded a PhD by the University of London. Before coming to The Middlesex she was Assistant Secretary (Academic) of the London School of Economics.

Societies, Clubs and Other Events

Throughout the last fifty years there has been much activity in the School in addition to the teaching and research which are central to its existence. Some of the societies, and The Middlesex Hospital Club, have maintained a steady level of development as the number of students has increased, but not surprisingly there has been some fluctuation in the popularity, and in the competition successes, of individual sports clubs. Since 1947 a number of women's teams have been developed.

The Middlesex Hospital Medical Society reached the two-hundredth anniversary of its foundation in 1974 and has sustained throughout its history a high level of activity, with many visiting speakers addressing the society on a wide range of topics. In addition there is keen competition for the David Moore Prizes awarded for the best student papers presented to the society during the year.

The Middlesex Hospital Club celebrated its centenary in 1955. Its membership is open to all those who have qualified at The Middlesex and additionally to doctors who have worked for a year or more in the Hospital or the School; the number of its members has shown a considerable increase in recent years, most members joining soon after graduation. In 1967 the club established an annual bursary to help students meet the cost of travel during the elective period.

In 1980 the 100th **Annual Dinner** was held at the Savoy Hotel and to mark the occasion the Dean was invited to take the chair and propose the toast of The Middlesex Hospital and School instead of responding to that toast, along with the Senior Broderip Scholar, as has been the usual custom for many years. The first annual dinner was held in 1867 but there were no dinners during either of the two world wars nor in 1947 when one was arranged but had to be cancelled as a result of a restriction being placed on the numbers permitted to attend dinners in that year because of rationing.

The Middlesex Hospital Journal reached its fiftieth anniversary in 1947 and continued as a publication for several years after that in spite of the resurrection of the *Archives of The Middlesex Hospital* for a while in the 1950s. In 1970 a new publication run by the Students Union appeared, *Midthink.* It is not clear whether or not that was the only factor responsible but in 1971 the *Journal* ran into difficulties and the possibility arose of its ceasing to be published. It was saved by Professor Edward Williams who was willing to become editor for the 1972 edition and by Mr Patrick Moran, Finance Officer of the School, who became its business manager. In 1973, four students became assistant editors and in 1974 it again had a student editor. In 1980 more difficulties arose and there was no *Journal* after March of that year until the summer of 1984.

The history of the **Music Society** over the last fifty years reflects the interests of staff, students, nurses and physiotherapists. With the increase in the formation of national and regional youth orchestras and the increase in musical education nationally the quality of performance has improved, with performances in some years of great musical works to a high standard. In other years, dramatic talent has come to the fore and the Music Society has taken to the stage and produced musicals and light operas. Sometimes both talents have come together and there has been an outburst of music making. In 1935, after a few fallow years, the Musical Society was revived with a choir which sang carols in the Hospital chapel and an orchestra which was conducted by Jason

Kenkowich of the Royal College of Music, the first professional musician to train and conduct the orchestra. After the Second World War the Music Society became part of Marylebone's Stanhope Institute as an evening class and this enabled some payment to be made to the professional musician. In 1950 he was Colin Ratcliffe, who founded the United Hospitals Choir, with The Middlesex and St Mary's forming the nucleus of the new venture. The first performance, *Elijah*, was with the London Symphony Orchestra in the Royal Albert Hall on 30 May 1951, under Joseph Krips. Towards the end of the 1960s a madrigal group was organised and in 1970 funds were raised, following the initiative of Professor Peter Silver, which enabled a Steinway grand piano to be purchased for the new music room in Astor College.

In 1970 a young professional musician, Russell Gilbert, came from the Royal Academy to conduct the orchestra and Ronald Withers, on the staff of the Biology Department, conducted the Choral Society. They worked well together and two complete performances of the *Messiah* were given with Gilbert conducting one and Withers the other. There were about a hundred in the choir and over forty in the orchestra. Physiotherapists provided the inspiration for a theatre band which was formed in the early 1980s as an offshoot of the orchestra. In 1984 the choir toured Suffolk giving concerts and also sang evensong in Long Melford, Clare, Ely Cathedral and Brentwood.

The **Dramatic Society,** in keeping with some other societies and clubs, has had periods of continuing activity over a number of years interspersed with other occasions when it has not been strongly supported. From 1955 to 1965, shows for eleven years in succession were produced by Mrs Eileen Baker. These included *Lady Audley's Secret, Le Malade Imaginaire* and *The Long and the Short and the Tall.* The building of the Edward Lewis Theatre made a great difference to the scale and type of production possible but it is of interest that one large production in recent years was produced in the Vanbrugh Theatre of the Royal Academy of Dramatic Art.

The **Art Society** has held annual exhibitions for many years at which members of Council, staff of the School and students have exhibited and a high standard has been maintained. A notable prizewinner in 1953 was Colonel Astor with a fine oil painting. In 1955 the art exhibition formed part of the Hospital arts festival. The society has expanded its activities over the years and now includes photography and colour transparencies among its sections and these attract a number

214

of entries to the exhibitions. Some of these are of specific medical interest but many are general.

The tradition of the **Annual variety concert,** or 'Smoker', referred to in previous chapters, was a fine one and achieved much, inspiring generations of artistes, staff, students and public in supporting a worthy cause, the Cancer Charity. However, over the years its appeal waned with the changing pattern of entertainment and in 1964 the last of these concerts was held in the Scala Theatre. It was far from being a flop, and in many ways appeared to be as successful as its predecessors, but it was considered that it could not continue for much longer and that it was better to stop then rather than have it die of inertia within a few years.

The changing pattern of entertainment has had no effect on the popularity and success of the **Christmas concerts,** and the opportunities offered by the construction of the Edward Lewis Theatre in the Windeyer Building in 1959 are fully exploited by the many producers of the shows. The audiences pack the large theatre to capacity for each of the many performances each December. Over the years the artistic talents of the producers and cast, who came to be known as the 'Manic Depressives' in the late 1940s, have been supplemented by the ingenuity shown in devising titles for the various shows. Some of these have been based on other, well-known titles, cleverly modified to refer to some of the specialties or names of members of staff portrayed in the show. As a few examples, mention might be made of *Under Milk Drip, Lady Chatterley's Liver, Great Expectorations, Tabes in the Wood, Coldfinger, Oh What a Lovely Wart, Last Plaster in Paris, Kreme Crackers, Cilia and Cornea,* and *Beyond the Syringe.* Many a member of staff has emerged from the auditorium after one of the shows asking 'Do I really look like that?' or 'Do I have that habit?' On one occasion the title chosen for the show did not meet with the approval of the Matron who indicated that nurses would not be allowed to participate in a show with such a label. That presented no problem; within a very short time posters appeared everywhere announcing the forthcoming concert entitled *The Name's the Same.* Nobody could possibly have any objection to that and no further difficulties were encountered.

AMALGAMATED CLUBS

The various sports clubs of the School have been the scene of much activity over the years and they have given a great deal of enjoyment and exercise to a large number of students. Although competing in the events, rather than winning, is the essential feature it would be remiss to omit any reference to the successes of teams and individuals. The only reservation about recording those lies in the fact that the references must be incomplete and many worthy achievements are bound to be omitted.

The opening of the new sports grounds at Chislehurst in 1938, through the generosity of Sir Edward Meyerstein, provided excellent facilities and attracted large numbers to sports days and other events in the postwar period, and it is interesting to note that the 'Consultants' Walk' was often won by Professor Walls.

In athletics, the late war and immediate postwar years were successful ones for The Middlesex who were Inter-hospital champions in three successive years, and in 1959 and 1961 they won the University of London field events meeting, beating in the process teams from the very large colleges such as Imperial College and University College. On one memorable occasion in 1961 the United Hospitals six-man team competing against Oxford University and Trinity College Dublin at Oxford was composed entirely of athletes from The Middlesex.

At cricket The Middlesex won the Inter-Hospital Cup in 1953, for the first time since 1919, and repeated the success in 1955 and in 1970.

At rugby the Inter-Hospital Cup has not come to The Middlesex but in 1940-41, when there was only a seven-a-side competition, the School won the event without conceding a point to anyone and beat St Mary's 19-0 in the final.

On the water The Middlesex has had some notable successes. In 1945 and 1946 the eight won the United Hospitals Challenge Cup and in 1969 became only the second college to win the 'University Triple' – the Winter Regatta, the Head of the River and the Allom Cup. In 1970 both the eight and the four won the United Hospitals Regatta at Henley and the VIII won the Colleges' Regatta, open to colleges throughout the country, and this was the first time the event was won by a college of the University of London.

The Sailing Club won the Harvey Wright Gold Fruit Bowl (Inter-hospital) in 1949 and repeated the success in 1952 and again in 1977 when the Guinness Trophy also came to The Middlesex.

The Squash Club became United Hospitals champions in 1936 and holders of the First and Second Division cups. They won the Senior Cup again in 1939, in 1961 and in 1975.

A number of individuals have received national and even international recognition in particular sports. All of them deserve mention but only a few can be named. In the 1960 Olympic Games in Rome, the Middlesex student Elizabeth Ferris won a bronze medal in the high-board diving event, the first medal to be won by Britain in those games. She followed this with a silver medal in the British Empire and Commonwealth Games held in Perth, Western Australia, in 1962. At those same Commonwealth Games, Stuart Farquharson and David Lee-Nicholson, who did so much for Middlesex and University of London rowing, won a gold medal in the coxless pairs, breaking the previous record by over eight seconds. (David Lee-Nicholson was killed in a motorway accident in 1967, at the age of twenty-eight.) In 1984, Richard Budgett, who qualified in 1983, was in the coxed four which won a gold medal in the Los Angeles Olympic Games.

No reference has been made to the successes of a number of teams of nurses, physiotherapists and radiographers but mention should be made here of Jane Bullen (now Mrs T. Holderness-Roddam) who, while a Middlesex nurse, won a gold medal as a member of the three day event team in the 1968 Olympic Games in Mexico, riding Our Nobby. In 1976 she won the Burghley Horse Trials, in 1978 the Badminton Horse Trials and in 1977 was member of the team which won the European gold medal. In the 1956 Olympic Games in Melbourne the gold medal in fencing was won by Gillian Sheen who was working in the Department of Dental Surgery at the time.

STUDENTS UNION

In the summer of 1963 the Amalgamated Clubs and the Junior Common Room Society decided to dissolve their organisations and form The Middlesex Hospital Students Union; all existing clubs and societies becoming constituent clubs of the Union. Sir Eric Riches, who had been President of the Amalgamated Clubs was elected as Honorary President of the Union and Louis Herzberg President. The union has been responsible for the organisation of student affairs gener-ally and has elected representatives for meetings of the Academic Board and other committees in the School. Their input to discussions on teaching procedures has been considerable and a number of valuable surveys on various academic matters have produced information which would not otherwise have been available.

An important aspect of the union has been the close liaison which

rapidly developed with the other Middlesex students in nursing, physiotherapy and radiography. Appropriate constitutional arrangements were
made whereby there could be maximum collaboration between the
different groups even though the methods of funding were very different
for students of the University as compared with those students in
schools run by the National Health Service. As all those concerned are
involved in caring for patients it is widely agreed that the arrangements
which have been established have been of benefit.

CLUB 25

A recent development covering both the Hospital and School has been
the formation of a club for all those who have been members of staff
of either the Hospital or School, or both, for twenty-five years or more.
The idea for such a club was the brainchild of The Hon Mrs Hugh
Astor, Chairman of the League of Friends of The Middlesex Hospital,
and it was welcomed most enthusiastically. Under Mrs Astor's guidance
the new Club got off to an excellent start with an Inaugural Luncheon
in the School refectory in March 1983 and there was another luncheon
in 1984 in John Astor House. The concept of uniting all members of
staff of The Middlesex in this way typifies the spirit of the place and
the members of Club 25 have pleasure in wearing the club's crest on
brooches in the case of the ladies and ties for the men. Miss Marian
Frank, former Superintendent Radiographer, is Secretary of the Club.

—11—
University Restructuring

Inter-Departmental Committee – Introduction of the NHS – Royal Commission on Medical Education – Reorganisation of the NHS – Resource Allocation Working Party – London Health Planning Consortium – University Resource Allocations – Working Party on Medical and Dental Teaching Resources – Working Party on Medical Costs – Way Working Party – Final University Proposals on Restructuring – The Joint School – Prospective Single School

In December 1981 the Court and the Senate of the University of London adopted 'Final Proposals' for medical education in London. Those decisions followed prolonged discussions in a large number of committees during the previous four or five years but there was a background to the proposals which had extended over a much more prolonged period and which concerned National Health Service as well as University developments.

Inter-Departmental Committee, 1942–44

In 1942 the Minister of Health and the Secretary of State for Scotland established an Inter-Departmental Committee under the chairmanship of Sir William Goodenough to enquire into the organisation of medical schools, particularly in regard to facilities for clinical teaching and research. The Committee's report, published in 1944 began, after a preamble setting out its terms of reference and procedure, by stressing the dependence of any National Health Service on medical education in the following terms:

Properly planned and carefully conducted medical education is *the* essential foundation of a comprehensive health service. If such a service is to have continuing vitality it must be founded on highly developed and vigorous systems of general and professional education for members of the medical and allied professions, and it must evoke the enthusiastic and intelligent co-operation of the general public. The spirit of education must permeate the whole of the health service, and that service must be so designed and conducted that, among other things, it secures for medical education the necessary staff, accommodation, equipment and facilities. Medical education cannot be regarded as merely incidental to the hospital service.

A main recommendation of the report was the establishment of 'Medical Teaching Centres' based on university medical schools and groups of teaching hospitals ('parent' and 'associated') in as close proximity as possible to the medical school. It was also advocated that if a parent teaching hospital was to function efficiently as an institution for medical education in the interests of a National Health Service the governing body must be personal to the hospital.

In relation to specific arrangements for London, the Committee discussed the possibilities of Charing Cross Hospital, St George's Hospital and the Royal Free Hospital and their associated medical schools moving to sites in the outer parts of London or the County of Middlesex and also considered the possibilities of various amalgamations of medical schools, such as Charing Cross and/or St George's with the Westminster. As far as The Middlesex was concerned the report referred to the modern construction of the Hospital buildings and drew attention to the Bland-Sutton Institute of Pathology and the Courtauld Institute of Biochemistry. It suggested that a suitable 'Associated Hospital' would be one of the Highgate group of London County Council General Hospitals.

The National Health Service

When the National Health Service was introduced in 1948 the Government followed the recommendation of the Goodenough Committee that the governing body of a teaching hospital must be personal to the hospital and each had its own board of governors. This also served to stress the underlying principle enunciated by the Committee; the dependence of the Health Service on medical education. It meant that the Minister of Health had a direct responsibility for the teaching hospitals.

Royal Commission on Medical Education, 1965–68

In 1965 a Royal Commission was established to review the whole field of medical education and to make proposals in the light of national needs and resources. The Chairman was Lord Todd and Professor Sir Brian Windeyer, Dean of The Middlesex Hospital Medical School, was one of the twenty members. Its Report was published in 1968.

With its broad remit, the Commission made many recommendations on the curriculum, methods of teaching and student numbers as well as on the organisation of medical schools. It considered that medical schools should be large and based on the large hospitals which were then the policy of the government. In discussing the organisation of teaching hospitals the Commission took a view opposed to that of the Inter-Departmental Committee and recommended that the boards of governors of teaching hospitals in England and Wales should be abolished and that those hospitals should be brought within the framework of administration of the Regional Hospital Service generally. However this recommendation was coupled with the opinion that about one fifth of regional authority members should be university representatives and that the main hospitals associated with each medical school, and preferably any other hospitals in their immediate area, should be grouped under a single newly-constituted governing body with a small number of members, about half of whom should be nominated by the university concerned.

The Royal Commission proposed a series of mergers of the general medical schools of the University of London which would reduce their number from twelve to six and it was hoped that each new school would become an integral part of a multi-faculty University institution. It was also recommended that the special postgraduate teaching hospitals in London should be brought as soon as possible into physical proximity with the general teaching hospitals and that their associated postgraduate institutes be integrated with the appropriate general medical schools. It was acknowledged that the completion of the reorganisation proposed would take a long time and would not be realisable unless money was provided for the purpose. However no estimate was attempted of the resources which might be needed to implement the recommendations for London.

In respect of The Middlesex, the Royal Commission recommended that it should amalgamate with St Mary's and suggested that they

221

might well aim to become the Medical Faculty of Bedford College and incorporate also the Institutes of Dermatology and Orthopaedics.

Before the Royal Commission had been established and while its meetings had been taking place there had been discussions between members of staff of The Middlesex and University College Hospitals and Schools on the possibilities of collaboration, particularly in some specialised fields. The proximity of the two institutions made such an association not only attractive but very much easier to achieve than between any other general teaching hospitals or medical schools. Accordingly it came as a surprise when it was learned that more distant associations had been proposed for both The Middlesex and University College Hospital Medical Schools.

THE MIDDLESEX AND ST MARY'S

In accordance with the Report of the Royal Commission and the desire of the University to implement it as far as possible the talks between The Middlesex and University College were terminated and collaboration with St Mary's was explored in an extensive series of meetings, at least one of which was held in the Senate House with the Vice-Chancellor and Principal and also Senior Officers of the Department of Health and Social Security. A Joint Policy Committee was established, including representatives from Bedford College. A Clinical Services Committee was set up to examine the possible rationalisation of hospital services. Virtually every department of the medical schools and hospitals was reviewed in detail and in 1971 consideration was also given to the possibility of adopting a common curriculum. However that idea foundered because it was considered that the possible advantages of a common curriculum would not justify the disruption of the existing arrangements.

The Royal Commission had stipulated that the reorganisation proposed in London would not be realisable unless money was provided, and it wasn't. In its Statement of Quinquennial Policy for 1972–77 the School stated in its opening paragraph that 'It will be the policy of this School to co-operate with St Mary's Hospital Medical School in every possible way, but the view of The Middlesex, already stated to the University, that the complete amalgamation of the two Schools must be dependent on physical union on one site, is unchanged.' Resources for such a development were not forthcoming.

Reorganisation of The NHS, 1974

The reorganisation of the National Health Service in 1974 abolished the boards of governors of the general teaching hospitals, which then became the responsibility of Area Health Authorities (Teaching). The National Health Service Act specifies the duty of the Secretary of State for Social Services to make available such facilities as he considers are reasonably required by any university which has a medical or dental school, but the elimination of the boards of governors, directly responsible to the Secretary of State, resulted in his duty in respect of education and research becoming more remote than it had been previously. This change followed the recommendation of the Royal Commission on Medical Education but was not accompanied by the complementary proposals in respect of membership of health authorities and the governing bodies of the teaching hospitals.

Resource Allocation Working Party (RAWP)

In May 1975 the Secretary of State for Social Services appointed a Working Party under the chairmanship of Mr J. C. C. Smith, Under Secretary, DHSS, to review arrangements for distributing NHS capital and revenue to Health Authorities and to Districts. In August that year it issued an Interim Report and in September 1976 presented its definitive Report. The Working Party advocated that the calculation of revenue targets for Regions, Areas and Districts should be determined essentially on the basis of populations weighted in respect of age, sex and other factors. There was also a Service Increment for Teaching based on student numbers. The Report accepted that not enough is known about the determinants of health needs and the Working Party also saw a clear and pressing need for improvement in the data routinely collected and for achieving, through research, a better appreciation and understanding of the factors on which future resource allocation decisions need to be based. Nevertheless the Report then went on to state that it was unlikely that such improvements would call into question any of the principles involved.

When the Report was published there was criticism of the validity of the many weighting factors used in the complex calculations and some members of the Working Party themselves expressed serious doubts about the application of the formulae to the small populations of Areas

223

and Districts. It was also pointed out that cuts in revenue allocations could destroy health services far faster than they could be created elsewhere from redistribution of capital allocations.

The formulae which were used were claimed to make appropriate allowance for the large numbers of commuters and visitors using the health services of the inner cities but the use of a population base, coupled with the declining populations in the cities, resulted in teaching areas being calculated as 'over-target' even though for some Teaching Areas it was shown that the percentage of the regional revenue allocation to the Area was slightly less than the percentage of the Region's clinical services provided by the Area. But whether the formulae were valid or not, their use resulted in reduced allocations of resources to teaching districts with inevitable effects on medical and dental education.

London Health Planning Consortium, 1977–81

After the reorganisation of the National Health Service in 1974 there were, in the four Thames Regions, twenty-three Area Health Authorities and sixty-five Districts. The Regional Health Authorities were responsible for co-ordinating the activities of their own Areas and Districts but there was a need for some form of planning for London as a whole. Following discussions between the Department of Health and Social Security, the University Grants Committee, the University of London and the four Thames Regional Health Authorities a London Health Planning Consortium was established in 1977

> To identify planning issues relating to health services and clinical teaching in London as a whole; to decide how, by whom and with what priority they should be studied; to evaluate planning options and make recommendations to other bodies as appropriate; and to recommend means of co-ordinating planning by health and academic authorities in London.

The Chairman of the Committee was Mr J. C. C. Smith, Under Secretary, DHSS, and there were five other DHSS members, eight officers of the Thames Regional Health Authorities, two members from the University Grants Committee, five from the University of London (including the author of this book, Dean of the School) and two from the postgraduate teaching hospitals and institutes. After considering the population and social characteristics of London and the pattern and ˙

use of London's hospitals the Consortium produced, in 1979, a 'Profile of Acute Hospital Services in London'. After considering comments on that document, the Consortium produced, in February 1980, a Discussion Document, 'Towards a Balance', which set out a framework for future acute hospital services by reconciling service with teaching needs. The Consortium also established study groups to examine and report on the particular specialities cardiology and cardiothoracic surgery (which reported in October 1979), Radiotherapy and Oncology (November 1979), Neurology and neurosurgery (February 1980), ENT services (February 1980), ophthalmology services (March 1980), primary health care in Inner London (May 1981).

These general and specialist documents took into account the declining population of Inner London, with a further fall of about twelve per cent predicted in the next ten years, although the rate of decline appeared to be slowing down. The Consortium predicted a fall in the need for acute hospital beds in the Thames Regions as a whole, particularly in Inner London, but it was notable that a small increase was indicated for acute beds in the District with The Middlesex Hospital. In the other Teaching Districts of the Thames Regions reductions varying from fourteen per cent to twenty six per cent were predicted. The increase for The Middlesex included beds for regional specialities, particularly cardiothoracic surgery and radiotherapy and oncology. Although there were a large number of Regional Board officers on the Consortium, the plans which were later produced by the Thames Regional Health Authorities proposed much greater reductions in Teaching Districts than had been agreed as appropriate in 'Towards a Balance'.

University Resource Allocations

For many years revenue allocations to the universities from the University Grants Committee and to its schools, colleges and institutes from the University of London were determined on a quinquennial system. Submissions were made in the usual way for the 1972–77 quinquennium and in January 1973 the University Grants Committee announced its 'Final Quinquennial Grants' for the five year period. However, that was to be the last such statement because the system then had to be abandoned as a result of the reduction of government finance for the universities and the difficulty of planning even one year ahead.

225

This deterioration promoted consideration of ways in which adjustments could best be made. All the activities of the University of London were reviewed but it is not surprising that with its very large Faculty of Medicine particular attention was directed at an early stage to an examination of ways in which academic standards could be maintained in medicine and dentistry in spite of the decline in resources. In response to a request from the University the Conference of Metropolitan Deans established an Adjustment Working Group in Medicine which noted the greatly increased costs of maintaining the new medical schools and of financing the development of departments to teach new subjects in the curriculum. It advised the University that if economies had to be made there was a need for a special comprehensive enquiry.

Working Party on Medical and Dental Teaching Resources

In February 1979 the University established a Working Party under the chairmanship of Lord Flowers, Rector of Imperial College, to recommend what redevelopment of resources available for medicine and dentistry should be adopted to maintain the present standards of medical and dental education and research in London. The Working Party was asked to assume that the agreed target of undergraduate and postgraduate students would be maintained; that the total funding of medical and dental education in the University would not be reduced as a direct consequence of any recommendations of the Working Party; and to take into account the possible effects of demographic trends and DHSS resource allocations in London.

The Working Party sought the written opinions of the various medical and dental schools, colleges and institutes of the University on various general issues and then made a number of visits. On 10 September 1979 the Chairman and other members of the Working Party came to The Middlesex Hospital Medical School for preliminary informal discussions with the Dean and a few members of staff. After a number of general issues had been raised enquiries were made about the liaison with St Mary's Hospital Medical School consequent upon the Royal Commission's recommendations. The School was then asked to consider the possibility of establishing a link with the School of Medicine of University College and two or more postgraduate institutes. A complementary proposition had been put to the Provost and Deans of

226

the Medical and Clinical Faculties of University College earlier in the day and it was made clear that such an arrangement would replace any link with St Mary's and would not be additional to it. The Middlesex and University College were asked to meet forthwith and prepare a joint response by 31 October, based on a combined undergraduate clinical intake of 240 medical students and fifty to seventy dental students. Meetings were arranged quickly and on 30 October a joint reply was delivered to the Working Party supporting its proposal to build on the acknowledged strengths of the two institutions and welcoming the opportunity of close co-operation, not only with each other but also with postgraduate institutes. It was pointed out that there were complementary strengths in a number of academic fields and that the close proximity of The Middlesex to University College would allow useful collaboration and rationalisation which had not proved workable in the more distant links which had been proposed by the Royal Commission.

The response also considered the type of association which the Working Party might be contemplating recommending to the University. It was pointed out that there was a danger that any attempt, *ab initio*, to impose rigid constitutional arrangements would impede progress towards real collaboration by raising understandable anxieties and by provoking unnecessary legal arguments about details at that critical stage of the relationship. After frank and friendly discussions it had been considered that the most fruitful policy to pursue at that stage would be one which promoted every opportunity to collaborate closely together but which did not start by trying to define a specific type of governance which had to be achieved. It was admitted in the joint response that the experiences of the University in relation to the recommendations of the Royal Commission might not have encouraged the belief that much would be achieved simply by collaboration and that therefore the Working Party might be tempted to recommend coercion. However, it was pointed out that the atmosphere in 1979 was very different from that in 1968. Then, each medical school in London had firmly believed that it was capable of an independent existence with adequate academic strengths over a wide range of subjects. By 1979 it was recognised that such an ideal was no longer attainable and also that the Health Service would not provide in every teaching hospital all the facilities required for a comprehensive medical education. In other words, the essential need for co-operation and for an element of

227

rationalisation had become clear and the geographical proximity of The Middlesex and University College, coupled with their complementary strengths in a number of academic disciplines, offered unique opportunities for collaboration which were not available elsewhere.

The Report of the Flowers Working Party was published in February 1980 and proposed that the existing thirty-four separate establishments should be grouped into six Schools of Medicine and Dentistry. The rebuilding of the greatly expanded Charing Cross Hospital and Medical School at Fulham and the St George's Hospital and Medical School at Wandsworth, which was still under construction, had resulted in an excess of preclinical facilities and to meet this situation the Working Party recommended that the preclinical course for medical and dental students at King's College should be phased out. It also proposed that the Westminster Medical School, most of whose students received their preclinical education at King's College, should be closed.

It was proposed that The Middlesex Hospital Medical School should form part of a 'University College School of Medicine and Dentistry' along with the Royal Free Hospital School of Medicine, the Institute of Orthopaedics, the Institute of Laryngology and Otology, the Institute of Neurology, the Institute of Child Health and the London School of Hygiene and Tropical Medicine. The Preclinical Departments of the Royal Free Hospital School of Medicine in Hunter Street would be closed and preclinical teaching in the new School confined to The Middlesex and University College sites, with a preclinical intake of 240 medical students per annum and an additional clinical intake of thirty students from Oxford and Cambridge. It was further proposed that the links of The Middlesex with the Central Middlesex Hospital should cease and that, in addition to the general and postgraduate teaching hospitals, students of the new School should also be taught at the Whittington Hospital. It was proposed that the Central Middlesex Hospital should become associated with the 'St Mary's and Royal Postgraduate School of Medicine and Dentistry'.

As would be expected, the Report was the subject of prolonged and detailed discussion in individual schools and in the committees and councils of the University. The Middlesex response welcomed the opportunity of a special relationship with University College and some of the postgraduate institutes but urged the University not to adopt the proposals of the Working Party to alter so radically the size and administrative structure of the existing institutions. The School also advised that its forty-year links with the Central Middlesex Hospital should not be broken.

UNIVERSITY REACTIONS TO THE REPORT OF THE FLOWERS WORKING PARTY

The Joint Medical Advisory Committee of the University (JMAC) considered that the changes proposed by the Flowers Working Party were too drastic; that the speed of the proposed implementation was too fast; that more reliance should be placed on evolving new relationships other than the Report envisaged; and that the size of some of the conglomerates proposed would produce unwieldy administrative units. The JMAC did endorse the proposal that joint schools should be established; that some activities would have to be concentrated; and that progress in re-allocating resources should be monitored.

Proposals based on the opinions of the JMAC were formulated by the Joint Planning Committee and submitted to the Senate in October 1980. The Joint Planning Committee had proposed that its Report should be adopted as the policy of the University but an amendment to that proposal was narrowly carried, by 27 votes to 25, which had the effect of deleting that recommendation but did encourage those medical schools which had expressed their willingness to become joint schools to move as rapidly as possible towards that end. A further amendment, carried on a show of hands, requested the Joint Planning Committee, in consultation with the Joint Medical Advisory Committee, to re-examine arrangements for reducing the over-provision of preclinical teaching capacity within the University and to report back to the Senate not later than 18 February 1981. This tight timetable had been dictated by a further deterioration in the financial position; just before the Report of the Flowers Working Party had been published the government had announced its policy to increase substantially the fees charged to overseas students and to reduce the grant to universities by £100 million within three years.

In order to be in a position to reach reasoned decisions on reducing the over-provision of preclinical facilities the Joint Planning Committee established a Working Party on Medical Costs with the Deputy Vice-Chancellor, Professor L. P. Le Quesne, as Chairman. There were nine other members initially, including one from the London School of Economics and one from the London Business School.

In order to meet the timetable imposed upon it the Working Party on Medical Costs met nearly every week from November 1980 to February 1981 and a team of management consultants was employed to make financial enquiries and calculations. While the remit of the Working Party had been determined by considerations of the excess preclinical provision resulting from the development of the new enlarged medical schools it soon became clear that reductions in preclinical facilities could not be considered in isolation from the clinical activities. As a result, the terms of reference were extended and a further two members appointed to the Working Party.

The two-volume report of the Working Party was published on schedule in February 1981 containing comprehensive tables which provided a wide range of academic as well as other data. There was a detailed analysis of the breakdown of costs associated with seventeen different ways in which undergraduate medical teaching could be arranged for the planned intake. Some of the options costed involved the phasing out of preclinical or clinical studies from individual schools or, in some cases, the closure of whole schools.

The data illustrated the extent to which costs were dominated by salaries and wages and, therefore, that the most effective way of cutting expenditure was by reducing staff. Accordingly the tables showed potential costs at different staff/student ratios from current levels to 1:10 preclinical and 1:7 clinical. The costings also demonstrated the extent to which medical schools in new buildings were significantly more expensive to run than those in older buildings.

The analysis showed that an overall reduction to an academic staff/student ratio of 1:10 preclinical and 1:7 clinical, with a proportionate reduction of other staff, would achieve savings in the University of £2.2 million. Closure of a complete school might produce further savings, in some cases of nearly £1 million, but closure of preclinical or clinical teaching alone would not be nearly so effective in reducing costs. The statistics showed that, allowing for a few minor capital works in some schools, if St George's Hospital Medical School was completed as planned there would be capacity in the University for a preclinical intake of 1480 medical students, compared with the target figure of 1200.

The tables in the Report indicated that in relation to cost per student

The Middlesex was fifth in rank order in the University, about 12 per cent above the average. The preclinical unit costs were high as a result of having the unique Departments of Biology as applied to Medicine and Physics as applied to Medicine with consequent high staff/student ratios. On the other hand the School's clinical costs were below the University average.

The Report showed that in many of the assessments of academic achievement The Middlesex Hospital Medical School was at, or somewhat above, the average for the University but the research grants attracted to the School were well above the University average in relation to the numbers of academic staff; in the clinical field 73 per cent higher. The tables also revealed that in the eleven years from 1970 to 1980 no less than seventy-three Distinctions had been awarded to Middlesex students in the Final MB BS examinations of the University of London whereas no more than fifty-seven had been awarded to the students of any other school, and that was a somewhat larger school than The Middlesex as assessed by the number of students taking those examinations.

Revised University Proposals: March 1981

The Le Quesne Working Party had assembled and tabulated expeditiously a large amount of information which had not been available previously but its Report did not delineate any single option which would obviously commend itself. At its meeting on 10 March 1981 the Joint Medical Advisory Committee discussed whether it should recommend that work on rebuilding St George's Hospital Medical School should be discontinued so as not to expand the capacity as fully as planned but it was considered that construction should not be halted at that stage. Additionally, the JMAC considered that the medical student entry to King's College should not be phased out. It was also decided to recommend to the Joint Planning Committee that the London and St Bartholomew's Hospital Medical Colleges should form a joint school on a site or sites to be determined; that Charing Cross Hospital Medical School and the Westminster Medical School should merge; and that the Royal Free Hospital School of Medicine should consolidate in Hampstead. Then an entirely new option was raised in respect of The Middlesex, St Mary's and University College. It was proposed that a joint school should be formed of all three (and incorpo-

231

rating two or more postgraduate institutes) with the object of achieving significant cost savings by the closure of one preclinical and one clinical school. Although there were obvious major disadvantages in the proposal the JMAC decided to accept it so that the proposition could be thoroughly investigated and costed.

The recommendations of the JMAC were adopted by the Joint Planning Committee and incorporated into a Report, 'Revised Proposals: March 1981', for submission to the Court and Senate. The Middlesex Hospital Medical School considered the position and set out its views in a letter which was sent to the Senate. The School indicated the warm welcome which it had given to the initial proposal to form a joint school with University College and two postgraduate institutes on a compact site but considered that there were compelling reasons for opposing any recommendation which might result in closing its preclinical facilities, which were ideally sited in substantial modern purpose-built accommodation which formed part of a building which also provided study-bedrooms for 236 students. St Mary's and University College also submitted letters to the Senate indicating their objections to the newly proposed scheme. At its meeting on 25 March the Senate took note of the letters but accepted that the proposed investigation should proceed.

THE WAY WORKING PARTY

Following the decision of the Senate, with which the Court concurred, a Working Party was established, with Sir Richard Way as Chairman, to investigate the proposal concerning The Middlesex, St Mary's and University College. In addition to the Chairman there were two other independent members and four representatives of each of the schools involved. It soon became clear to the Working Party that the scheme was academically unsound. It was also not practical; it would concentrate job losses in the University on one or two schools and compulsory redundancies would be inevitable.

Having agreed unanimously that the scheme it had been set up to consider was unacceptable the Way Working Party addressed itself to the problem of adjusting medical student intakes to the various schools of the University which would take account of the decisions already reached by Senate and would also prove a practical way forward. This option was then incorporated into the Working Party's Report.

Final University Proposals: November 1981

The Report of the Way Working Party was considered by the JMAC. The reasoning, set out at length in the Report, was accepted and the Working Party's proposal was approved, although the precise figures suggested for student intakes were adjusted slightly after further consideration by a small sub-committee, which also devised a programme of interim adjustments to numbers for the years before the definitive intakes would be reached in 1985. The recommendations of the JMAC, based on the report of the Way Working Party, were accepted by the Joint Planning Committee and incorporated into a Report, 'Medical Education in London: Final Proposals: November 1981', which was adopted by both the Court and the Senate in December 1981 as the policy of the University on the future of medical education in the University; the Vice-Chancellor to take steps to implement the various proposals.

The final decisions of the Court and Senate meant that within the University of London there would be four combined schools and four which would remain as single schools, although a collaboration was envisaged between St Mary's Hospital Medical School and the Royal Postgraduate Medical School at Hammersmith. The arrangements, with the definitive preclinical and clinical medical student intake numbers (omitting dental students) would be:

The Middlesex HMS/University College	195/215
Guy's HMS/St Thomas's HMS	195/225
London HMC/St Bartholomew's HMC	200/250
Charing Cross HMS/Westminster MS	155/175
St George's HMS	150/160
St Mary's HMS	100/110
Royal Free HMS	100/100
King's College and Kings College HMS	105/115
Total	1200/1350

Decisions were also taken in respect of the postgraduate institutes during the various deliberations within the University. After considerable discussion it was agreed that the Cardiothoracic Institute and the Institutes of Cancer Research, Child Health, Neurology, Ophthalmology and Psychiatry should continue as separate institutes; that the

233

Institutes of Laryngology and Otology, of Orthopaedics and of Urology should become part of the Joint School with The Middlesex and University College; that the Institute of Dermatology should be associated with the Joint School of Guy's and St Thomas's; that the Institute of Obstetrics and Gynaecology should be affiliated with the Royal Postgraduate Medical School at Hammersmith; and that the Institute of Basic Medical Sciences at the Royal College of Surgeons should cease to be an institute of the University. The London School of Hygiene and Tropical Medicine would continue as a separate school of the University.

The decisions of the University on the postgraduate institutes were being made at about the same time as the Secretary of State for Social Services was considering the arrangements which he would make in his 1982 NHS restructuring. In general, the postgraduate hospitals associated with institutes which were to remain as separate entities were placed under the control of special health authorities, as occurred also with the Hammersmith Hospital, whereas the hospitals associated with those institutes entering joint schools became part of the District Health Authority responsible for their general teaching hospitals.

The Joint School

From the time of the visit of the Flowers Working Party in September 1979 the general proposals put forward at that meeting were widely accepted at both The Middlesex and University College although there was considerable uncertainty on the type of association which should, or could, develop. It was for that reason that the University was urged to allow the linkage to evolve and not be forced into any preconceived mould. Many informal discussions took place while the deliberations in the University were being pursued and in January 1982, within a month of the Court and the Senate agreeing their final proposals, steps were taken to establish a formal Joint School Co-ordinating Committee of The Middlesex Hospital Medical School, University College and the Institutes of Laryngology and Otology, of Orthopaedics and of Urology. Each institution would retain its existing form of governance but the Committee would consider ways in which their activities 'might be co-ordinated in order to promote the maximum academic strength in medicine and dentistry which can be achieved within the resources available; and more generally to consider suggestions for future develop-

234

ments in the Joint School'. The Committee would report to the Academic Board of each institution and through the Boards to the Councils or Committees of Management. The first meeting of the Committee was held on 26 April 1982. Sir James Lighthill, Provost of University College, was elected Chairman and Sir Douglas Ranger, Dean of The Middlesex, Vice Chairman.

It was not envisaged that the formation of the Joint School Co-ordinating Committee should curtail the informal discussions which were taking place and it served to encourage a number which would probably not have occurred otherwise. It was considered that the remit of the Committee would be primarily academic and that the members should be nominated by their Academic Boards but as there were bound to be financial implications to many academic developments it was agreed that the Finance Officers of The Middlesex and University College should be in attendance.

Two particular developments have followed discussions in the Joint School Co-ordinating Committee; the adoption of a common clinical curriculum and the establishment of a number of joint departments.

COMMON CLINICAL CURRICULUM

An early review of teaching practices indicated that there were good reasons for not making any fundamental changes to the preclinical teaching arrangements, although greater collaboration would be encouraged. There was, however, an urgent need to co-ordinate clinical teaching. The recommendation of the Flowers Working Party in respect of the Central Middlesex Hospital had been incorporated into the decisions of the University and the School's long association with that hospital would terminate in most subjects in September 1983. For some years the Whittington Hospital had been teaching University College students and The Middlesex was delighted when they expressed a willingness to take an increased number of students from the Joint School. The staff of the Royal Northern Hospital, closely associated with the Whittington as one of the Islington Group of Hospitals, were also willing to join in the teaching programme and additional help was forthcoming from the staff of the Edgware General Hospital. There was therefore considerable clinical teaching capacity available but it needed to be closely co-ordinated so that students could obtain the maximum benefit from the facilities available on different sites. This required all the clinical students to be grouped together, irrespective of where they had obtained their preclinical education. After extensive discussions a common curriculum was agreed and in the first clinical year all students now spend about one third of their time in The Middlesex Hospital, about one third in University College Hospital and about one third in the Islington Group of Hospitals.

JOINT DEPARTMENTS

One of the fundamental concepts in relation to the Joint School was that of promoting greater academic strength in combination than could be achieved separately. From this it followed that in a number of subjects there would be advantages in combining departments functionally and, where it seemed appropriate, on a single site. There was certainly no wish to disturb arrangements which were already functioning well and where there was adequate academic strength. Accordingly, it was agreed to review departments routinely when a Head left. That practice has been followed and a number of Joint Departments have been established. The person appointed as Head of the Joint Department has normally been accorded that title for five years in the first instance.

The first Joint Department to be established was in histopathology; Professor Neville Woolf, Bland-Sutton Professor of Histopathology being appointed as Head. New appointments were made to vacant chairs in Medical Microbiology, Professor J. R. Pattison; Psychiatry, Professor Rachel Rosser; Community Medicine, Professor M. G. Marmot. When Professor Neil retired from the John Astor Chair of Physiology in September 1984 it was decided to create a Joint Department, with Professor T. J. Biscoe, Jodrell Professor of Physiology at University College as Head; Professor J. R. Stephens was appointed to the John Astor Chair. University College has had an academic Department of Geriatric Medicine for some time and on the retirement of Professor A. N. Exton-Smith, it was decided that it should become a Joint Department and Professor M. Hodkinson became Barlow Professor on 1 January 1985. Professor R. H. T. Edwards resigned from the Chair of Medicine in University College in 1984 and from 1 January 1985, Professor S. J. G. Semple, Professor of Medicine at The Middlesex, became Head of the Joint Department.

Prospective Single School

In 1983 it was considered that the increasing academic collaboration had determined a need for associated administrative collaboration. By then the Joint School had experienced the progressive reduction of the Recurrent Court Grant and had assessed the implications of reduced staff/student ratios. Accordingly it was felt that it was time to start discussions on the possibility of converting the Joint School into a single school. By the summer of 1984 the concept of setting up a single school of medicine within University College had been approved in principle in all the relevant committees and councils and a Unification Sub-Committee has now been established. This is meeting at frequent intervals to consider the detail of such a school with a view to its formation on 1 August 1987.

Bibliography

The Story of The Middlesex Hospital Medical School, H. Campbell Thomson, John Murray, London, 1935.

The Middlesex Hospital. The names of the wards and the story they tell. C. D. Shaw and W. R. Winterton, Stephen Austin and Sons, Hertford, 1983.

The Middlesex Hospital Journal, Volumes 1–84.

The Middlesex Hospital 1745–1948, Hilary St George Saunders, Max Parrish, London, 1949.

The Story of St Luke's Hospital, Brigadier C. N. French, William Heineman Medical Books, London, 1951.

The Central Middlesex Hospital, The first sixty years 1903–63. J. D. Allan Gray, Pitman Medical Publishing Co, 1963.

Sir Charles Bell, Sir Gordon Gordon-Taylor and E. W. Walls, E. & S. Livingstone, Edinburgh and London, 1958.

Safer than a Known Way, Philip Newman, William Kimber, London, 1983.

APPENDIX 1

Chronological Summary

1745 The Middlesex Infirmary established in two small terraced houses in Windmill Street, leased from Mr Goodge

1746 Infirmary renamed The Middlesex Hospital. First Hospital pupils enrolled

1747 Maternity beds opened – the first in a general hospital

1755 Foundation Stone of new Hospital on present site laid by the Earl of Northumberland (Duke of Northumberland, 1766), President of Hospital

1757 New Hospital opened

1774 The Middlesex Hospital Medical Society founded

1792 The Middlesex Hospital Cancer Charity founded

1835 The Middlesex Hospital Medical School founded, built and opened

1855 The Middlesex Hospital Club founded

1856 First Dean appointed – Dr Temple Frere

1897 First issue of The Middlesex Hospital Journal

1914 Bland-Sutton Institute of Pathology opened

1920 Major, The Hon. J. J. Astor elected to the Board of Management
Joel Chair of Physics endowed and filled
Chair of Pathology established and filled (Bland-Sutton Chair, 1945)
Chair of Physiology endowed anonymously and filled (John Astor Chair, 1932)
Chair of Radiology established, advertised, but not filled

1921 Major, The Hon. J. J. Astor elected to School Council
Chair of Chemistry established and filled

239

1924   S. A. Courtauld Chair of Anatomy endowed and filled

1925   Chair of Biochemistry established and filled (Courtauld Chair, 1928)

1927   Ferens Institute of Otolaryngology opened, 8 February

1928   Courtauld Institute of Biochemistry opened by HRH Prince Arthur of Connaught, 14 June

1929   Foundation Stone of the new (present) Hospital laid by HRH The Duke of York

1930   Mr S. A. Courtauld elected Chairman of School Council

1931   New Nurses' Home (John Astor House, 1948) opened by Princess Alice

1934   Dr H. E. A. Boldero appointed Dean

1935   **Centenary of The Middlesex Hospital Medical School**
Rebuilt, enlarged Hospital opened by HRH The Duke of York, 29 May

1938   Major, The Hon. J. J. Astor elected Chairman of the Board of Management
Meyerstein Institute of Radiotherapy opened
Department of Pharmacology and Therapeutics established

1939   The Second World War, 3 September
Preclinical students evacuated to Bristol for Christmas Term
Clinical students in hospitals throughout Sector V

1940   Preclinical students return to The Middlesex for Spring and Summer Terms
Heavy bombing of London
Preclinical students evacuated to Leeds for two years
Clinical students concentrated at The Middlesex, Central Middlesex, Mount Vernon and Tindal House Hospitals

1942   Chair of Radiology (Therapeutic) established and filled
Preclinical students return to The Middlesex from October

1945   End of the War in Europe, 8 May
End of the Second World War, 14 August
Bicentenary of the Hospital (celebrations deferred)

1946   Retirement of Mr S. A. Courtauld
Chair of Medicine established and filled
Major, The Hon. J. J. Astor elected Chairman of School

Council
Philip Hill Chair of Experimental Biochemistry endowed and filled
Hospital Bicentenary celebrations
Department of Chemistry assimilated into Courtauld Institute of Biochemistry

1947   Chair of Surgery established and filled
        Women undergraduate students admitted to the School

1948   National Health Service established, 5 July
        The Middlesex Hospital Medical School established as a 'Body Corporate'
        Board of Management disbanded
        Board of Governors of The Middlesex Hospital established, embracing The Middlesex Hospital Teaching Group

1951   Latimer House purchased to create an Institute of Clinical Research and Experimental Medicine

1952   Chair of Surgery vacated. Director of Surgical Studies appointed

1953   Institute of Clinical Research and Experimental Medicine opened, 22 October

1954   Professor B. W. Windeyer appointed Dean *vice* Sir Harold Boldero

1956   Colonel, The Hon. J. J. Astor created Baron Astor of Hever

1957   Building work on Windeyer Building commenced

1959   Phase I of Windeyer Building opened by Lord Astor of Hever, 16 December

1960   Chair of Biology as Applied to Medicine established and filled
        Chair of Psychiatry established, filled 1961

1961   Institute of Nuclear Medicine established, Director appointed

1962   Lord Astor of Hever retires from chairmanship of Board of Governors and School Council

1963   Lord Cobbold appointed Chairman of Board of Governors and School Council
        Students Union formed from Amalgamated Clubs and Junior Common Room Society

1964   Chair of Surgery filled

1965 Academic Department of Rheumatology Research established

1966 Chair of Pharmacology established and filled

1967 Astor College opened by Her Majesty Queen Elizabeth The
Queen Mother, 31 May
Professor E. W. Walls appointed Dean *vice* Professor Sir Brian
Windeyer

1968 Institute of Nuclear Medicine building opened
Horace Joules Hall at Central Middlesex Hospital opened by
Professor Sir Owen Saunders
Department of Immunology established

1969 Academic Department of Obstetrics and Gynaecology
established, Director appointed
Institute of Neurological Studies endowed (anonymously until
1979) by Mr Garfield Weston in memory of his wife Reta
Lila Weston

1971 Death of Lord Astor of Hever, 19 July
School of Pathology opened by HRH Prince Philip Duke of
Edinburgh, 17 December
Chair of Social and Preventive Medicine established, filled 1972

1973 Chair of Immunology established and filled
Examination Hall/Gymnasium built alongside Astor College

1974 Sir Jules Thorn Institute of Clinical Science opened by Her
Majesty Queen Elizabeth The Queen Mother, 30 May
Reorganisation of The National Health Service
Board of Governors of the Hospital abolished
Responsibility for The Middlesex Hospital transferred to the
Kensington and Chelsea and Westminster Area Health
Authority (Teaching)
Lord Cobbold retires from the Chairmanship of the School
Council
Mr D. B. Money-Coutts appointed Chairman of the School
Council and of the Special Trustees of the Hospital
Mr D. Ranger appointed Dean *vice* Professor E. W. Walls

1975 Post of Director of The Bland-Sutton Institute of Pathology
discontinued
Separate Academic Departments of Haematology,
Histopathology and Microbiology established

1978   Astor College Extension opened to provide a total of 236
study-bedrooms in the building
Duncan Guthrie Chair of Genito-Urinary Medicine endowed
and filled
School establishes Planning and Resources Committee

1979   Wolfson Building opened by Sir Leonard Wolfson, 3 July
Francis and Renée Hock Directorship of Reta Lila Weston
Institute of Neurological Studies endowed and filled
University Working Party on Medical and Dental Teaching
Resources established

1981   University adopts 'Final Proposals' on Medical Education in
London, December

1982   Joint School formed of The Middlesex Hospital Medical
School, The School of Medicine, University College
London, and the Institutes of Laryngology and Otology, of
Orthopaedics and of Urology
School Departmental structure adjustments
Restructuring of the National Health Service
The Middlesex Hospital, University College Hospital, Royal
National Orthopaedic Hospital, Royal National Throat, Nose
and Ear Hospital, St Peter's Group of Hospitals become the
responsibility of the Bloomsbury Health Authority within the
North East Thames Regional Health Authority
Joint Department of Histopathology formed in Joint School

1983   Mr W. W. Slack appointed Dean *vice* Sir Douglas Ranger
Joint Department within the Joint School established in
Medical Microbiology
Common clinical curriculum introduced for all students of the
Joint School

1984   Joint Departments within the Joint School established in
Physiology and Psychiatry

1985   **School sesquicentenary**
Joint Departments within the Joint School established in
Medicine, Geriatric Medicine and Community Medicine

APPENDIX 2
Chairmen of the Board of Management,* 1935–48

1924 – 38   HRH Prince Arthur of Connaught
1938 – 48   Colonel, The Hon. J. J. Astor

* The Board of Management of the Hospital and the School was disbanded in 1948 as a consequence of the introduction of the National Health Service and the establishment of the Medical School as a separate body corporate

APPENDIX 3
Chairmen of the Board of Governors,* 1948–74

1948 – 62   Colonel, The Hon. J. J. Astor
            (Lord Astor of Hever, 1956)
1963 – 74   Lord Cobbold

* The Board of Governors was established in 1948 on the introduction of the NHS and abolished in 1974 on the reorganisation of the NHS

APPENDIX 4
Chairmen of the Council since 1935

1930 – 46   Mr S. A. Courtauld
1946 – 62   Colonel, The Hon. J. J. Astor
            (Lord Astor of Hever, 1956)
1963 – 74   Lord Cobbold
1974 –   Mr. D. B. Money-Coutts

APPENDIX 5
Chairmen of the Building Committee since 1936

1936 – 54*   Dr H. E. A. Boldero
             (Sir Harold Boldero, 1950)
1955 – 62   Colonel, The Hon. J. J. Astor
             (Lord Astor of Hever, 1956)
1963 – 79** The Hon. John Astor

* The 'Accommodation Sub-Committee'
** The Building Committee was disbanded in 1979 on the completion of the Wolfson Building

APPENDIX 6
Chairmen of the Finance Committee since 1935

1921 – 48   Mr R. C. Davis
1948 – 65   Mr. F. H. Doran
1965   Mr. J. H. Hambro*
1966 – 71   Lord Latymer
1971 – 78   Mr. W. P. Courtauld
1978 – 83   Mr A. J. Macdonald-Buchanan
1983 –   Mr D. H. Clarke

* Died 4 December 1965

APPENDIX 7
Deans since 1935

1934 – 54   Dr H. E. A. Boldero
            (Sir Harold Boldero, 1950)
1954 – 67   Prof. B. W. Windeyer
            (Sir Brian Windeyer, 1961)
1967 – 74   Prof. E. W. Walls
1974 – 83   Mr D. Ranger
            (Sir Douglas Ranger, 1978)
1983 –   Mr W. W. Slack

APPENDIX 8
Sub Deans since 1935

1939   Prof. J. Kirk (at Bristol)
1940 – 42   Prof. J. Kirk (at Leeds)
1965 – 67   Prof. E. W. Walls
1967 – 72   Mr W. W. Slack
1972 – 75   Dr I. R. Verner
1975 – 76   Prof. J. B. Jepson*
1976 – 82   Prof. P. H. S. Silver
1982 – 84   Mr R. P. Gould
1984 –   Dr A. L. Miller

* Died 7 May 1976

Postgraduate Sub-Deans

1969 – 71   Dr P. A. J. Ball
1971 – 75   Mr J. A. P. Marston
1975 – 79   Dr K. B. Saunders
1979 –   Dr J. Tinker

Postgraduate Sub-Deans (Science)

1982 –   Prof. F. Hobbiger

Sub-Deans at the Central Middlesex Hospital

1967 – 72   Dr K. P. Ball
1972 – 78   Mr J. F. Newcombe
1978 – 82   Dr M. W. McNicol

Sub-Dean at Islington

1982 –   Mr J. P. S. Cochrane

APPENDIX 9
School Secretaries since 1935

1921 – 48   Mr R. A. Foley
1949 – 65   Miss Eileen M. Walton
1965 – 77   Mr G. Clark
1977 – 83   Mr D. E. Eardley
1983 –   Dr Diana F. Sanders

APPENDIX 10
Chairmen of the School Committee, 1935–48

1930 – 44   Dr E. A. Cockayne
1944 – 45   Prof. J. McIntosh
1945 – 46   Prof. S. Russ
1946 – 47   Dr D. McAlpine
1947 – 48   Prof. E. C. Dodds
              (Sir Charles Dodds, 1954
              Sir Charles Dodds, Bart., 1964)

1. The Chairmen were elected annually. Until 1944 all the Chairmen were clinicians and it was the custom to re-elect for several years. In 1944 the decision was taken to make a break with both those customs.
2. In 1948 the School Committee was replaced by the Academic Board

APPENDIX 11
Chairmen of the Academic Board since 1948

1948 – 49   Dr G. E. Beaumont
1949 – 50   Prof. Samson Wright
1950 – 51   Mr M. H. Whiting
1951 – 52   Prof. R. W. Scarff
1952 – 53   Dr G. E. S. Ward
1953 – 54   Prof. F. Dickens
1954 – 55   Mr H. W. Breese

1955 – 56   Mr C. P. Wilson
1956 – 57   Dr B. R. M. Johnson
1957 – 58   Prof. J. E. Roberts
1958 – 59   Dr A. Willcox
1959 – 60   Prof. E. W. Walls
1960 – 61   Mr P. H. Newman
1961 – 62   Prof. A. Kekwick
1962 – 63   Dr F. Campbell Golding
1963 – 64   Mr D. H. Patey
1964 – 65   Mr A. J. B. Goldsmith
            (Sir Allen Goldsmith, KCVO, 1970)
1965 – 66   Prof. C. A. Keele
1966 – 67   Dr F. R. Bettley
1967 – 68   Prof. E. Neil
1968 – 69   Mr W. R. Winterton
1969 – 70   Prof. L. P. Le Quesne
1970 – 72   Mr D. Ranger
            (Sir Douglas Ranger, 1978)
1972 – 74   Prof. R. H. S. Thompson
1974 – 76   Dr A. C. Boyle
1976 – 78   Prof. L. P. Le Quesne
1978 – 80   Dr J. D. N. Nabarro
            (Sir John Nabarro, 1982)
1980 – 82   Prof. L. Wolpert
1982 – 84   Prof. S. J. G. Semple
1984 –   Prof. I. M. Roitt

Chairmen of the Academic Board are elected annually. Until 1970 it was the custom to elect for only one year. At the beginning of the 1970–71 session it was decided that re-election for a second year should become the usual practice

Heads of Academic Departments, 1935–85

Department	Dates	Head
Chemistry	1920–46	Dr W. B. Tuck (Professor, 1921)
Physics	1920–46	Prof. S. Russ
Physics as Applied to Medicine	1946–70	Prof. J. E. Roberts
	1970–82	Prof. J. F. Tait
Medical Physics and the Institute of Nuclear Medicine	1982–	Prof. E. S. Williams
Biology	1922–59	Dr J. H. Woodger (Professor, 1948)
Biology as Applied to Medicine	1960–65	Prof. D. R. Newth
	1966–82	Prof. L. Wolpert
Anatomy and Biology as Applied to Medicine	1982–	Prof. L. Wolpert
Anatomy	1920–37	Prof. T. Yeates
	1937–49	Prof. J. Kirk
	1949–74	Prof. E. W. Walls
	1974–82	Prof. P. H. S. Silver
Anatomy and Biology as Applied to Medicine	1982–	Prof. L. Wolpert
(S. A. Courtauld Professor of Anatomy	1982–	Prof. B. A. Wood)
Physiology	1930–56	Prof. S. Wright
	1956–84	Prof. E. Neil
	1984–	Prof. T. J. Biscoe*
(John Astor Professor of Physiology	1984–	Prof. J. A. Stephens)

* Jodrell Professor of Physiology, University College London, and Head of the Joint School Department of Physiology

Appendix 12

Department	Dates	Head
Pharmacology and Therapeutics	1938–68	Dr C. A. Keele (Professor, 1952)
	1968–	Prof. F. Hobbiger
Bland-Sutton Institute of Pathology	1920–48	Prof. J. McIntosh
	1948–65	Prof. R. W. Scarff
	1966–73	Prof. G. W. A. Dick
	1973–74	Prof. A. C. Thackray (Acting Head)
Histopathology	1975–	Prof. N. Woolf (Head of Joint School Department, 1982)
Microbiology	1975–81	Dr R. E. M. Thomson
	1981–84	Dr J. L. Stanford (Acting Head)
Medical Microbiology	1984–	Prof. J. R. Pattison (Head of Joint School Department)
Haematology	1975–84	Prof. J. W. Stewart
Biochemistry	1925–28	Prof. E. C. Dodds
Courtauld Institute of Biochemistry	1928–65	Prof. E. C. Dodds (Sir Charles Dodds, 1954; Sir Charles Dodds, Bart., 1964)
	1965–75	Prof. R. H. S. Thompson
	1976–	Prof. P. N. Campbell
Chemical Pathology	1984–	Dr A. L. Miller (Head of Sub-Department of Chemical Pathology from 1957)
Ferens Institute of Otolaryngology	1927–37	Mr F. J. Cleminson
	1937–45	Mr S. Hastings
	1945–62	Mr C. P. Wilson
	1962–64	Mr J. P. Monkhouse
	1965–83	Mr D. Ranger (Sir Douglas Ranger, 1978)
	1983–	Mr R. A. Williams
Rheumatology Research	1965–68	Prof. Sir Charles Dodds, Bart.
	1968–73	Prof. C. A. Keele
	1973–	Prof. I. M. Roitt
Immunology	1968–	Prof. I. M. Roitt
Institute of Nuclear Medicine	1961–64	Prof. J. E. Roberts
	1964–82	Prof. E. S. Williams

Department	Dates	Head
Medical Physics and Institute of Nuclear Medicine	1982–	Prof. E. S. Williams
Department of Molecular Endocrinology	1982–	Prof. R. P. Ekins
Medicine	1946–70	Prof. A. Kekwick
	1970–	Prof. S. J. G. Semple (Head of Joint School Department, 1985)
Surgery	1947–52	Prof. P. B. Ascroft
Surgical Studies	1952–64	Mr D. H. Patey
	1964–83	Prof. L. P. Le Quesne
	1983–	Prof. M. Hobsley
Obstetrics and Gynaecology	1969–70	Mr W. R. Winterton
	1970–73	Mr I. M. Jackson
	1973–	Mr S. J. Steele
Psychiatry	1961–66	Prof. J. D. N. Hill (Sir Denis Hill, 1966)
	1966–83	Prof. J. M. Hinton
	1984–	Prof. R. M. Rosser (Head of Joint School Department, 1984)
Institute of Neurological Studies*	1969–74	Dr M. Kremer
	1974–79	Dr C. J. Earl
Reta Lila Weston Institute of Neurological Studies	1979–	Dr M. J. G. Harrison (Francis and Renée Hock Director

* Endowed anonymously by Mr Garfield Weston in memory of his wife

Department	Dates	Head
Radiotherapy	1942–69	Prof. B. W. Windeyer (Sir Brian Windeyer, 1961)
	1969–75	Prof. N. M. Bleehen
Oncology	1976–	Prof. R. J. Berry
Genito-Urinary Medicine	1978–	Prof. N. M. Adler
Community Medicine	1972–82	Prof. D. L. Miller
	1982–85	Dr. J. H. Fuller (Acting Head of Department
	1985–	Prof. M. G. Marmot (Head of Joint School Department)

Department	Dates	Head
Geriatric Medicine	1985–	Prof. M. Hodkinson (Head of Joint School Department)
Clinical Research and Experimental Medicine	1953–71	Prof. A. Kekwick
	1971–81	Dr J. D. N. Nabarro (Sir John Nabarro, 1982)
Cobbold Laboratories	1981–	Dr A. B. Kurtz

(Chairman Clinical Research Committee 1981 – Dr J. D. H. Slater)

APPENDIX 13
The Middlesex Hospital Medical School

Numbers of new undergraduate students entering the School

Year	1st MB BS			2nd MB BS			Clinical		
	Men	Women	Total	Men	Women	Total	Men	Women	Total
1935–36	30	–	30	17	–	17	21	–	21
1945–46	35	–	35	23	–	23	24	–	24
1955–56	27	6	33	24	6	30	22	4	26
1965–66	24	2	26	46	13	59	17	3	20
				Basic Medical Sciences			Clinical		
1975/76				58	33	91	18	2	20
1982/83				50	40	90	16	10	26

After the 1982–83 entry the numbers were no longer comparable because of the restructuring within the University and the formation of the Joint School of Medicine described in chapter 11.

APPENDIX 14

The Middlesex Hospital
Honorary and Consultant Staff from 1935

1. The titles 'Honorary' and 'Consultant' are explained on pages 19 and 120, where the changes resulting from the introduction of the National Health Service in 1948 are described.

2. The dates indicate the total period as an Honorary or as a Consultant or as an Honorary Consultant, irrespective of the nature of the contract. In the case of the Honorary Consultants the year given as the starting date does not necessarily coincide with that of appointment or promotion within the Medical School or University. Before 1948 The Middlesex Hospital and Medical School was a single institution. Honorary Consultant contracts with the Hospital for staff of the School were introduced in 1950 and that is given as the starting date for a number of senior staff of the School even though they had held their same University appointments for several years before that.

3. After 1948 the list includes all the institutions forming The Middlesex Hospital Teaching Group. The staff of The Hospital for Women, St Luke's-Woodside Hospital and the Arthur Stanley Institute who were not also on the staff of The Middlesex Hospital at that time are shown as having been appointed in 1948.

4. The list does not include Consultants appointed in a *locum tenens* capacity nor those appointed for limited periods in connection with research projects or for other special purposes.

5. An asterisk indicates the date of death of those who died prior to retirement.

Name	Dates	Speciality
Dr R. A. Young (Sir Robert Young, 1947)	1902–36	General Medicine
Mr W. Sampson Handley	1905–37	General Surgery
Mr G. Gordon-Taylor (Sir Gordon Gordon-Taylor, 1946)	1907–46	General Surgery

Mr W. F. Victor Bonney	1908–37	Obstetrics and Gynaecology
Mr Somerville Hastings	1910–45	Otolaryngology
Mr A. E. Webb-Johnson	1911–46	General Surgery/Urology
(Lord Webb-Johnson, 1948 Sir Alfred Webb-Johnson, 1936)		
Dr H. MacCormack	1912–46	Dermatology
Dr C. E. Lakin	1912–46	General Medicine
Dr E. A. Cockayne	1913–45	General Medicine
Mr W. Warwick James	1913–39	Dental Surgery
Mr R. Affleck Greeves	1914–46	Ophthalmology
Dr G. E. S. Ward	1918–53	General Medicine/Cardiology
Mr A. S. Blundell Bankart	1920–46	Orthopaedic Surgery
Mr E. L. Pearce Gould	1920–40*	General Surgery
Dr G. E. Beaumont	1920–53	General Medicine
Dr T. Izod Bennett	1920–46*	General Medicine
Dr R. E. Apperly	1919–44	Anaesthetics
Dr J. H. Douglas Webster	1921–47	Physical Medicine and Radiotherapy
Mr F. J. Cleminson	1922–37	Otolaryngology
Mr M. H. Whiting	1922–50	Ophthalmology
Dr H. P. Crampton	1922–45	Anaesthetics
Mr A. T. Pitts	1922–39*	Dental Surgery
Mr W. Turner Warwick	1923–49*	General Surgery
Dr Douglas McAlpine	1924–55	Neurology
Dr H. E. A. Boldero	1925–54	General Medicine
(Sir Harold Boldero, 1940)		
Dr D. E. Bedford	1926–63	General Medicine/Cardiology
Mr R. Vaughan Hudson	1928–59	General Surgery
Mr E. W. Riches	1930–62	General Surgery/Urology
(Sir Eric Riches, 1958)		
Mr D. H. Patey	1930–64	General Surgery
Mr A. L. Packham	1930–56	Dental Surgery
Mr C. P. Wilson	1930–62	Otolaryngology
Mr H. W. Breese	1930–59	Dental Surgery
Mr L. C. Rivett	1930–47*	Obstetrics and Gynaecology
Mr F. W. Roques	1930–63	Obstetrics and Gynaecology
Dr A. E. W. Idris	1931–54	Anaesthetics
Dr H. K. Graham Hodgson	1933–55	Radiology
(Sir Harold Graham Hodgson, KCVO, 1950)		
Dr A. A. Moncrieff	1934–46	Paediatrics
(Sir Alan Moncrieff, 1964)		
Mr P. Wiles	1935–59	Orthopaedic Surgery
Dr B. R. M. Johnson	1936–59*	Anaesthetics
Dr H. L. Marriott	1936–66	General Medicine

Dr F. D. Howitt	1937–54*	Physical Medicine
Mr P. B. Ascroft (Professor, 1947)	1937–52	General Surgery
Mr W. R. Winterton	1938–70	Obstetrics and Gynaecology
Mr J. P. Monkhouse	1938–64	Otolaryngology
Dr N. G. Harris	1938–59	Psychiatry
Dr F. W. Roberts	1939–49	Anaesthetics
Mr J. W. Schofield	1939–63	Dental Surgery
Mr D. Greer Walker	1939–76	Dental Surgery
Mr Rainsford Mowlem	1940–63	Plastic Surgery
Prof. B. W. Windeyer (Sir Brian Windeyer, 1961)	1942–69	Radiotherapy
Dr F. C. Golding	1944–66	Radiology
Dr Eric Samuel	1944–46	Radiology
Dr F. R. Bettley	1946–74	Dermatology
Mr A. J. B. Goldsmith (Sir Allen Goldsmith, KCVO, 1970)	1946–73	Ophthalmology
Mr R. S. Handley	1946–74	General Surgery
Dr A. Willcox	1946–63*	General Medicine
Mr C. J. B. Murray	1946–75	General Surgery
Mr P. H. Newman	1946–76	Orthopaedic Surgery
Dr O. P. Dinnick	1946–82	Anaesthetics
Dr M. Kremer	1946–73	Neurology
Dr B. A. Sellick	1946–78	Anaesthetics
Prof. A. Kekwick	1946–72	General Medicine
Dr G. D. Hadley	1946–73	General Medicine
Dr E. W. Hart	1947–73	Paediatrics
Mr T. Holmes Sellors (Sir Thomas Holmes Sellors, 1963)	1947–67	Cardiothoracic Surgery
Miss D. J. K. Beck	1947–56*	Neurosurgery
Mr I. M. Jackson	1948–79	Obstetrics and Gynaecology
Dr A. J. H. Hewer	1948–82	Anaesthetics/Clinical Measurement
Dr J. A. Hobson	1948–75	Psychiatry
Mr L. G. Phillips	1948–55	Obstetrics and Gynaecology
Mr F. Neon Reynolds	1948–52*	Obstetrics and Gynaecology
Mr T. Ivor Hughes	1948–67	Obstetrics and Gynaecology
Mr H. M. Fouracre Barns	1948–59*	Obstetrics and Gynaecology
Mr J. R. Dickinson	1948–74	Obstetrics and Gynaecology
Dr Donald Blatchley	1948–61	Anaesthetics
Dr Tamsin M. Wynter	1948–69	Anaesthetics
Dr Helen M. B. Alcock	1948–60	Anaesthetics
Dr Angus J. Smith	1948–69	Anaesthetics
Dr G. F. Panton	1948–73	Anaesthetics

Dr Frances V. Gardner (Dame Frances Gardner, 1975)	1948–78	General Medicine
Mr R. M. Handfield Jones	1948–57	General Surgery
Dr W. S. C. Copeman	1948–65	Rheumatology
Dr H. F. Turney	1948–65	Rheumatology
Dr G. K. Stone	1948–60	Rheumatology
Dr W. S. Tegner	1948–68	Rheumatology
Dr E. T. D. Fletcher	1948–55	Rheumatology
Dr Doris M. Baker	1948–60	Rheumatology
Dr O. A. Savage	1948–68	Rheumatology
Mr S. L. Higgs	1948–58	Orthopaedic Surgery
Mr W. D. Coltart	1948–62	Orthopaedic Surgery
Dr F. Gwynn Nicholas	1948–62	Radiology
Mr O. V. Lloyd-Davies	1949–70	General Surgery
Miss Margaret D. Snelling	1949–79	Radiotherapy and Oncology
Dr A. C. Boyle	1949–83	Rheumatology
Prof. E. C. Dodds (Sir Charles Dodds, 1954)	1950–65	Chemical Pathology
Prof. R. W. Scarff	1950–65	Pathology
Prof. F. R. Selbie	1950–54*	Medical Microbiology
Dr A. C. Thackray (Professor, 1966)	1950–74	Histopathology
Dr C. A. Keele (Professor, 1952)	1950–68	Pharmacology & Therapeutics
Mr D Ranger (Sir Douglas Ranger, 1978)	1950–82	Otolaryngology
Mr D. Ainslie	1950–70	Ophthalmology
Mr J. H. L. Ferguson	1952–77*	General Surgery
Dr R. Semple	1952–54	General Medicine
Mr L. P. Le Quesne (Professor, 1964)	1952–84	General Surgery
Dr F. H. Scadding	1953–79	General Medicine
Dr W. Somerville	1954–79	Cardiology
Dr J. D. N. Nabarro (Sir John Nabarro, 1982)	1954–81	General Medicine
Dr D. H. P. Cope	1954–82	Anaesthetics
Dr T. M. Chalmers	1954–63	General Medicine
Mr J. R. Belcher	1955–82	Cardiothoracic Surgery
Dr R. H. Meara	1955–83	Dermatology
Dr R. W. Gilliatt (Professor, Institute of Neurology, 1962)	1955–83	Neurology
Dr J. N. Pattinson	1956–80	Radiology
Dr C. G. Whiteside	1956–81	Radiology
Dr A. M. Jelliffe	1956	Radiotherapy and Oncology

Mr V. Logue	1956–68	Neurosurgery
Dr S. Mattingly	1957–81	Rheumatology
Dr J. W. Stewart (Professor, 1969)	1959–84	Haematology
Dr R. E. M. Thompson	1959–81*	Microbiology
Dr W. K. Pallister	1960	Anaesthetics
Mr H. P. Cook	1960	Oral Surgery
Mr D. R. Sweetnam	1960	Orthopaedics
Dr E. J. M. Campbell	1960–62	General Medicine
Mr R. T. Turner-Warwick	1960	General Surgery/Urology
Prof. J. D. N. Hill (Sir Denis Hill, 1966)	1961–66	Psychiatry
Dr A. W. Beard	1961	Psychiatry
Mr R. L. Lloyd-Jones	1961	Obstetrics & Gynaecology
Dr E. R. Lester	1961–63	Anaesthetics
Mr R. A. Williams	1962	Otolaryngology
Mr W. W. Slack	1962	General Surgery
Dr J. M. Hinton (Professor, 1966)	1962–83	Psychiatry
Mr Noel Thompson	1963–77	Plastic Surgery
Mr Ian Ranger	1963–64	General Surgery
Dr R. W. Emanuel	1963	Cardiology
Mr Donald Winstock	1963	Oral Surgery
Mr I. H. Griffiths	1963–74	Urology
Dr D. J. Watterson	1963–64	Psychotherapy
Dr R. J. K. Brown	1964–84	Paediatrics
Dr I. R. Verner	1964	Anaesthetics
Dr B. E. Kendall	1964	Radiology
Dr R. D. Catterall	1964–83	Genito-Urinary Medicine
Dr P. A. J. Ball	1964–85	General Medicine
Dr Anne Bolton	1964–83	Child Psychiatry
Dr J. D. H. Slater	1964	General Medicine
Dr E. S. Williams (Professor, 1971)	1964	Nuclear Medicine
Mr W. S. Lund	1965–68	Otolaryngology
Dr Alexander Shapiro	1965–80	Mental Subnormality
Dr Pamela M. Fullerton (Dr Pamela M. Le Quesne, 1969)	1965	Neurology
Prof. R. H. S. Thompson	1965–75	Biochemistry
Mr J. A. P. Marston	1965	General Surgery
Mr John Andrew	1965–84	Neurosurgery
Dr J. V. T. Gostling	1965–65	Virology
Dr E. Wolf	1965–78	Psychotherapy
Dr H. H. O. Wolff	1965–1967	Psychotherapy
Dr Malcolm Chapman	1966	Radiology
Professor G. W. A. Dick	1966–73	Pathology

Dr A. L. Miller	1966	Chemical Pathology
Dr D. M. S. Dane	1966–82	Virology
Dr Deborah Doniach (Professor, 1974)	1966–77	Immunopathology
Dr M. A. Epstein	1966–68	Experimental Virology
Dr J. O. W. Beilby	1966–84	Cytology and Gynaecological Histopathology
Dr A. H. Crisp	1966–67	Psychiatry
Dr J. R. Seale	1966–76	Genito-Urinary Medicine
Mr M. F. Sturridge	1967	Cardiothoracic Surgery
Dr J. L. H. O'Riordan (Professor, 1983)	1967	General Medicine
Dr G. Kazantzis	1967	Community Medicine
Dr W. G. Joffe	1967–74*	Psychotherapy
Dr R. Levy	1967–71	Psychiatry
Dr O. W. Hill	1968	Psychiatry
Mr Michael Hobsley (Professor, 1975)	1968	General Surgery
Dr P. J. Crosland-Taylor	1968–80	Haematology
Dr Helen C. Grant	1968–82	Neuropathology
Dr J. F. Arthur	1968–69	Histopathology
Dr Mary Corbett	1969	Rheumatology
Dr John Wedgwood	1969–80	Geriatrics
Dr D. Garfield Davies	1969	Otolaryngology
Mr S. J. Steele	1969	Obstetrics and Gynaecology
Prof. N. M. Bleehen	1969–75	Radiotherapy
Dr P. J. Bennett	1969	Anaesthetics
Dr D. St. J. Brew	1969	Histopathology
Dr G. Farrer-Brown	1969–76	Histopathology
Mr P. A. MacFaul	1970–83	Ophthalmology
Prof. S. J. G. Semple	1970	General Medicine
Dr S. K. Bosher	1970–84	Otology
Dr J. L. Stanford	1970	Medical Microbiology
Mr A. Cameron	1970–74	General Surgery
Dr C. J. Earl	1971	Neurology
Mr G. D. Pinker	1971–81	Obstetrics and Gynaecology
Mr M. F. Stranc	1971–76	Plastic Surgery
Dr Margaret F. Spittle	1971	Radiotherapy and Oncology
Dr P. P. Anthony	1971–77	Histopathology
Mr R. D. Illingworth	1972–74	Neurosurgery
Dr W. J. O'Brien	1972	Anaesthetics
Dr K. B. Saunders	1972–80	General Medicine
Dr E. S. Chesser	1972	Psychiatry
Prof. D. L. Miller	1972–82	Community Medicine
Dr D. J. Williams	1973–84	Accident and Emergency
Dr M. J. G. Harrison	1973	Neurology

Dr K. E. Britton	1973–76	Nuclear Medicine
Dr G. Laszlo	1973–74	General Medicine
Dr P. B. Cotton	1973	General Medicine
Mr M. A. Edgar	1974	Orthopaedic Surgery
Mr A. M. Hamilton	1974	Ophthalmology
Dr C. G. D. Brook	1974	Paediatrics
Dr G. M. Levene	1974	Dermatology
Dr Jack Tinker	1974	Intensive Therapy
Mr E. J. G. Milroy	1974	Urology
Dr E. M. Ross	1974–84	Paediatrics
Dr T. C. B. Stamp	1974	General Medicine
Mr R. C. G. Russell	1975	General Surgery
Mr D. N. L. Ralphs	1975–84	General Surgery
Dr P. R. Boyd	1975–83	Psychiatry
Dr H. W. D. Davies	1975	Psychiatry
Dr A. J. E. Duddington	1975	Psychiatry
Dr K. J. T. Wright	1975–79	Psychotherapy
Dr A. C. Macfie	1975–77	Psychiatry
Mr M. A. Pugh	1975	Obstetrics and Gynaecology
Mr D. W. T. Roberts	1975	Obstetrics and Gynaecology
Dr M. W. Adler (Professor 1978)	1975	Genito-Urinary Medicine
Prof. N. Woolf	1975	Histopathology
Prof. I. M. Roitt	1975	Immunopathology
Dr J. Brostoff	1975	Clinical Immunology
Dr A. W. Peck	1976	Clinical Pharmacology
Prof. R. J. Berry	1976	Oncology
Dr P. L. Lantos	1976–80	Neuropathology
Dr P. J. Ell	1976	Nuclear Medicine
Prof. F. Hobbiger	1976	Pharmacology
Dr J. S. Bingham	1977	Genito-Urinary Medicine
Dr Judith A. Hulf	1977	Anaesthetics
Mr R. L. Liversedge	1977	Oral Surgery
Dr M. J. Raphael	1977	Radiology
Mr J. Guillebaud	1978	Family Planning
Mr D. N. Ross	1978	Cardiothoracic Surgery
Dr M. D. Buckley-Sharp	1978	Chemical Pathology
Dr G. P. J. Beynon	1978	Geriatrics
Dr B. A. Snowdon	1978	Psychiatry
Dr J. Newman	1978–81	Histopathology
Dr D. MacDiarmid	1978	Psychotherapy
Dr J. H. Lacey	1978–79	Psychiatry
Dr R. M. Bowen-Wright	1979	Anaesthetics
Dr Carmel A. E. Coulter	1979	Radiotherapy and Oncology
Dr A. B. Kurtz	1979	General Medicine
Dr R. H. Swanton	1979	Cardiology

Dr J. H. Fuller	1979	Community Medicine
Mr J. L. Osborne	1979	Obstetrics and Gynaecology
Mr Roy Sanders	1979	Plastic Surgery
Dr Monica H. Greenwood	1979	Psychiatry
Dr S. J. Machin	1980	Haematology
Dr G. A. W. Rook	1980	Medical Microbiology
Dr G. F. Bottazzo	1980	Clinical Immunology
Dr R. J. Jacoby	1980–83	Psychiatry
Dr B. Felicity Dirmeik	1980	Psychotherapy
Dr R. R. Mason	1981	Radiology
Dr Jean H. Pitfield	1981–83	Radiology
Dr H. S. Jacobs (Professor, 1983)	1981	Endocrinology
Dr R. S. Tedder	1981	Virology
Dr N. McI. Johnson	1981	General Medicine
Dr J. R. Croker	1981	Geriatrics
Dr J. S. H. Cohen	1982	General Practice
Dr W. R. Lees	1982	Radiology
Mr T. Treasure	1982	Cardiothoracic Surgery
Dr J. M. Holton	1982	Medical Microbiology
Dr J. W. Rode	1982	Histopathology
Dr D. R. Katz	1982	Histopathology
Dr M. E. Shipley	1982	Rheumatology
Dr W. Aveling	1982	Anaesthetics
Dr Catherine Bullen	1983	Anaesthetics
Dr A. Mindel	1983	Genito-Urinary Medicine
Prof. J. R. Pattison	1984	Medical Microbiology
Mr J. H. Scurr	1984	General Surgery
Prof. Rachel M. Rosser	1984	Psychiatry
Dr Anne M. Kilby	1984	Paediatrics
Dr Pauline M. Dowd	1984	Dermatology
Dr D. C. Linch	1984	Haematology
Dr D. Rickards	1984	Radiology
Prof. M. G. Marmot	1984	Community Medicine
Dr H. M. Wieselberg	1984	Child Psychiatry
Prof. H. M. Hodkinson	1985	Geriatrics

INDEX

*Chairs, Departments, Institutes and Schools are lised under subject, e.g. Anatomy, Department of.
Appendices are not included as they in essence form their own index.*

Index

Index

Index

London County Council, 19, 48, 91, 117, 133
London County Council General Hospitals, 220
London Health Planning Consortium, 224–5
London Hospital, 28, 101, 104, 113
London Hospital Medical School, 104, 233
London School of Hygiene and Tropical Medicine, 228, 234
London School of Medicine for Women, 104, 108, 114
London Symphony Orchestra, 214
London University, 36, 43, 57, 90–1, 108–9, 114, 136, 154–5; athletics, 216; Board of Advanced Medical Studies, 67; diplomas, 47; Faculty of Medicine, 20, 158; final proposals (1981), 233–6; joint school proposals, 231–3; London Health Planning Consortium, 224; and the NHS, 114, 115–16; postgraduate institutes, 130–1; resource allocations, 225–6; restructuring, 210, 219; Royal Commission on Medical Education proposals, 221; single school proposals (1983), 237; Working Party on Medical and Dental Teaching Resources, 226–9; Working Party on Medical Costs, 229, 230–1
London Working Group, 127
London Zoological Society, 55
Lord's cricket ground, 51
Ludgrove Preparatory School, 69
Lyell Gold Medal, 102

McAlpine, Dr Douglas, 46, 69, 86, 97, 102
MacCormac, Dr Henry, 46, 100, 101, 102
Macdonald-Buchanan, Mr A. J., 128
Macdonald-Buchanan, Lady, 136
Macdonald-Buchanan, Sir Reginald, 136
Macdonald-Buchanan School of Nursing, 136
McIntosh, Professor James, 30, 31–2, 34, 87, 99, 173–4, 177
Mackenzie-Mackinnon Scholarship, 35
McLean, Professor Patricia, 179–80
McNicol, Dr M. W., 210
Magee, Professor P. N., 179, 181
Maidstone Hospital, 192
Margaret Pyke Centre, 193
Marlborough Court, 134
Marlborough Hospital, 194
Marmot, Professor M. G., 236
Marriott, Dr Hugh L., 21, 39, 41, 42, 50, 76, 86, 96

Marriott, Miss Marjorie, 106
Marston, Mr J. A. P., 210
Mary, Queen, 159
Mason, Dr W. H., 60
Maternity Ward, 79
Matrons, 106
Matthew, Sir Theobald, 95
May, Edna, 51
May and Baker Laboratories, 65
Mayneard, Professor, 59
Medical Act (1950), 47
Medical Committee, 95, 96, 97, 104–5, 108, 116–17, 119, 121, 123, 130, 192, 193, 197, 202
medical firms, 38, 39–42
Medical Microbiology, Department of, 151
Medical Physics, Department of, 153
Medical Physics and Institute of Nuclear Medicine, 164
Medical Register, 108
Medical Research Council, 35, 156, 160, 163, 183–4, 187, 188, 200, 201; Unit of Bacterial Chemistry, 35, 66, 99, 176
Medical Research Society, 188
Medical School Accommodation Sub-Committee, 61
Medical Society, 49, 53–4, 55, 70, 121, 212
Medical Society of London, 53
Medical Teachers Committee, 188
Medical Unit, 187–9, 201
Medicine, Chair of, 96–7, 187
Medicine, Department of, 97, 97–8, 147, 153, 158, 187–9
Melhado Memorial Biology Laboratories, 29
Mellanby, Sir Edward, 77, 107
Metabolic Medicine, Professor of, 187–8
Meyerstein, Sir Edward, 27–8, 48, 58, 67–9, 91, 216
Meyerstein, Lady, 91
Meyerstein, Miss Phyllis, 28
Meyerstein Institute of Radiotherapy, 27, 28, 59, 88, 141–2, 162, 197, 199, 202
Meyerstein Scholarship, 67–8
Meyerstein Ward, 79
Microbiology, Department of, 173–4
microwaves, 98–9
Middlesex Hospital, admissions, 22; bed occupancy, 21–2; bicentenary, 106–7; district responsibility, 121–2; expenditure, 22; income, 22; medical developments, 139–44; new buildings, 132–3, 132–9; new departments, 142–4; and the NHS, 117–21; and NHS reorganisation (1974), 126–7, 133; and the NHS

restructuring (1982), 133; pre-NHS organization, 20–3; private patients, 23; in Second World War, 74–9; shared staff with School, 140; surgical firms, 42–5; see also individual wards and departments
Middlesex Hospital Club, 54–5, 212–13
Middlesex Hospital Journal, 15–16, 29, 50, 55, 60, 69, 90, 213
Middlesex Hospital Medical School, Academic Departments, 158–204; buildings, 28–30; clinical education, 38–9, 84–5, 107; curriculum, 36–9, 235–6; final University proposals, 233–6; and the Flowers Working Party, 226–9; Joint Departments, 236; Joint School proposals, 231–7; medical firms, 38, 39–42; new buildings, 132–4, 145–57; and the NHS, 114–17; and the NHS reorganisation (1974), 154–5; and the NHS restructuring (1982), 130–1; postgraduate education, 46–7, 210–11; preclinical education, 37–8, 80–3; professorial staff, 30–3; rebuilding (1930s), 61–2; rebuilding (1950s and 60s), 58, 145–57; research, 62–7; Royal Commission on Medical Education proposals, 221–2; in Second World War, 80–5; shared staff with Hospital, 140; single school proposals, 237; staff, 30–6; students, 48–53; surgical firms, 38; teaching arrangements, 36–48; women students, 23, 108–10; Working Party on Medical Costs, 231
Middlesex Hospital Teaching Group, 120, 139, 175, 180
Midthink, 213
midwifery, 45
Miller, Dr A. L., 180, 210
Miller, Prof D. L., 201
Milroy, Mr Euan J. G., 142
Ministry of Health, 57, 92–3, 113, 114, 117–19, 123, 133–6, 143, 146, 198, 219–20
molecular biophysics, 163–4
Molecular Endocrinology, Department of, 164–5
Moncrieff, Sir Alan, 46, 76, 86, 90, 100–1, 103
Money-Coutts, Mr David B., 124, 128, 131, 207–8
Money-Coutts, The Hon. Thomas B. (Lord Latymer), 95–6, 116
Monkhouse, Mr J. P., 61, 86, 182
Monro, Mr R. S., 97
Moran, Lord, 66

Index

Index